Wrestling Tough

Mike Chapman

Human Kinetics

Library of Congress Cataloging-in-Publication Data

Chapman, Mike, 1943-
  Wrestling tough / Mike Chapman.
    p. cm.
  Includes bibliographical references and index.
  ISBN 0-7360-5637-8 (soft cover)
  1. Wrestling. I. Title.
  GV1195.C47 2005
  796.812–dc22

                                        2005001904

ISBN-10: 0-7360-5637-8
ISBN-13: 978-0-7360-5637-3

Developmental Editor: Leigh Keylock; **Copyeditor:** Robert Replinger; **Proofreader:** Sue Fetters; **Indexer:** Betty Frizzéll; **Permission Manager:** Carly Breeding; **Graphic Designer:** Nancy Rasmus; **Graphic Artist:** Sandra Meier; **Photo Manager:** Dan Wendt; **Cover Designer:** Keith Blomberg; **Photographer (cover):** © Donald Miralle/Getty Images; **Printer:** Versa Press

On the cover: Wrestler Dennis Hall displays the effort and intensity that helped him become a Greco-Roman world champion and Olympic silver medalist.

Human Kinetics books are available at special discounts for bulk purchase. Special editions or book excerpts can also be created to specification. For details, contact the Special Sales Manager at Human Kinetics.

Printed in the United States of America

10   9   8   7   6   5   4   3   2

Human Kinetics
Web site: www.HumanKinetics.com

United States: Human Kinetics
P.O. Box 5076
Champaign, IL 61825-5076
800-747-4457
e-mail: humank@hkusa.com

Canada: Human Kinetics
475 Devonshire Road Unit 100
Windsor, ON N8Y 2L5
800-465-7301 (in Canada only)
e-mail: orders@hkcanada.com

Europe: Human Kinetics
107 Bradford Road
Stanningley
Leeds LS28 6AT, United Kingdom
+44 (0) 113 255 5665
e-mail: hk@hkeurope.com

Australia: Human Kinetics
57A Price Avenue
Lower Mitcham, South Australia 5062
08 8277 1555
e-mail: liaw@hkaustralia.com

New Zealand: Human Kinetics
Division of Sports Distributors NZ Ltd.
P.O. Box 300 226 Albany
North Shore City
Auckland
0064 9 448 1207
e-mail: info@humankinetics.co.nz

Wrestling Tough

CONTENTS

Part II   The Essence of Wrestling Tough

FOREWORD

From the minute I started reading *Wrestling Tough*, I thought, "You'd better be ready to pack your gear and get to the gym." It is a very motivational book. It gets the fire burning! It puts history right in front of you. When you read about John Smith, Arnold Schwarzenegger, and Dan Gable, it makes you want to do what they did. The stories about sport stars are very motivating and they relate well to wrestling, which relates well to life.

Young athletes who read this book will have a better chance to make the best situation out of their opportunities. They can act on it and seize the moment. Then there's no regret because this is a blueprint, right in front of them. Regret is when something passes you by. The book makes me want to do it again, to train and compete. There's really no better life than when you are training, competing, and winning at the highest level.

Wrestling Tough is not only informative and motivational, but it's entertaining, as well. I highly recommend it to anyone.

Tom Brands
Olympic champion
World champion
Three-time NCAA champion
Head wrestling coach, Virginia Tech University

INTRODUCTION

Over 4,000 years ago, in the stronghold city known as Uruk, a warrior-king named Gilgamesh ruled over his people with an iron hand. He was strong and cunning, and it was said that no man could match Gilgamesh in any type of activity. Then one day a stranger from the forest, a wild man named Enkidu, challenged Gilgamesh to a contest. The two great warriors were determined to see who was superior by engaging in the purest form of contest available. That style of engagement is still in use today all around the world. We call it wrestling.

Their titanic struggle is recorded in *The Epic of Gilgamesh*, the oldest piece of literature in existence. Uruk was located in the land known as Sumer. According to some historians, Sumer is also the site of the Garden of Eden, the legendary spot from which God sent Adam and Eve into exile for disobeying his orders. The Tigris and Euphrates rivers still run through the land once ruled by Gilgamesh. That territory is now known as Iraq.

The sport of wrestling that we participate in today is at least as old as the most ancient written stories. Wrestling is older than most of the nations on earth. It is almost as old as humankind itself.

Although their objectives are basically the same, more than 50 different versions of wrestling are practiced around the world, in at least 150 nations. Wrestling contests are common in the highlands of Sweden and in the frozen wastelands of Siberia. Matches occur in the deserts of Africa, in the hills of Australia, and between tiny huts on the endless plains of Mongolia, all with different rules and attire. Men—and, recently, women—wrestle in great cities like New York and Moscow, in tiny farm hamlets from Maine to California, and in countless villages overseas.

Wrestling is the universal sport of the civilized world, talked about in the Bible and praised in the halls of Congress. People of great prestige and influence today hold the sport and its heroes in esteem, just as people of great power revered them thousands of years ago.

Although over 40 centuries of history hold the sport together, it is also united by the demands that it imposes on those who pursue it at the highest levels. It is certainly humankind's oldest sport, but it may also be its most demanding sport. The characteristics that wrestling requires of its followers are twofold: first, steadfast physical preparation, and second, a mental resolve that may be beyond the capability of the athletes of most other sports.

"Wrestling is not for everyone," candidly admits Dan Gable, America's most famous product of the sport. "But it should be."

Wrestling should be for everyone, in Gable's estimation, because it provides preparation for the battles of life itself. Perhaps more than anyone who has ever been rolled through the grass or been pushed across a mat on his face in pursuit of wrestling honors, Gable understands what the sport is all about. He understands its demands and what it offers in return to those who meet the demands and excel at the highest levels. As the winner of 181 consecutive matches in high school and collegiate competition over seven years, and the winner of an Olympic gold medal in 1972, Gable dedicated his existence to wrestling on two levels. He excelled first as a competitor and later as a coach, directing others to the same Olympian heights that he himself ascended.

What Gable stresses about success is what you need to understand if you are to rise above the crowd. "It doesn't come overnight," says Gable. "If you want to accomplish anything that's worthwhile, you've got to be associated with a great system year around, for many years."

The key to overwhelming success, says Gable, is to focus at all times on what it takes to win consistently, at every level. That focus comes only through association with a system and a philosophy that have demonstrated that they can and will work.

The goals of *Wrestling Tough* are many. As someone who has been around the sport of wrestling for over 40 years, I believe that to appreciate it fully, one needs a general understanding of where the sport came from and how it evolved to become what it is today. The essence of studying history is to grasp the basic elements of the subject and to apply its meaning to life in general.

In the pages of this book, we will study the key moments in the careers of many great champions of wrestling and other sports. We will assess the training methods that they used to break through barriers and climb the highest mountains. Among the athletes whom we will briefly meet in these pages are such enduring legends as Rocky Marciano, Muhammad Ali, Michael Jordan, Arnold Schwarzenegger, and Lance Armstrong. We will discuss coaches like John Wooden and Vince Lombardi, as well as many of the best-known wrestlers of all time.

We will look at how the top wrestlers developed mental toughness and a sense of confidence. We will explore the attacking mindset and the importance of psyching up for competition. Through these pages, we will begin to comprehend how champions confront and overcome overwhelming odds and how they develop the dedication and commitment essential to success. We will come to understand the link between physical and mental toughness and how athletes develop the will to win.

"Many coaches believe that an athlete's success depends on four factors: (1) physical ability, (2) physical training, (3) mental training, and (4) desire or drive. The percentages of these four factors may vary from athlete to athlete and even with the same athlete from game to game" (Clarkson 1999, 69).

Tom Brands, 1993 world champion and 1996 Olympic gold medalist, believes that wrestling has two basic keys: "Of course, the physical preparation is absolutely essential. But then the mental part kicks in. The mental preparation is what takes you to the next level." To understand what the highest levels of competition are all about, you have to have understand "the zone" and the mental side of competition.

One of the most respected high school wrestling coaches of all time was Howard E. Ferguson, who built an amazing program and record during his years at St. Edward High School in Lakewood, Ohio, a suburb of Cleveland. In his 15-year career there, his teams won 82 tournament championships in a row, including seven Ohio state championships.

"Life is easy when the going is good," wrote Ferguson in his popular book, *The Edge*. "Mental toughness comes into play when the going gets bad. Mental toughness is also the ability to keep working towards a long-term goal, while going full throttle to win a short-term battle, even in the face of adversity.

"You see, for us [his coaching staff at St. Edward's] it's more than just conditioning. It's showing a group of young men that they can do something they never thought they could. It's tradition. It's pride. It's mental toughness" (Ferguson 1990, 6-13).

For 35 years I was a newspaper journalist, working mostly as a sports editor and managing editor of daily newspapers. During that time I was fortunate to observe many of America's finest wrestlers in action, having attended 35 NCAA championships, two Olympic Games, and two world championships. As editor of several papers, I covered the University of Iowa wrestling team during the 20 years when it dominated the sport, rolling off nine consecutive NCAA team titles and drawing huge crowds to its arena.

Boxing is another sport that I have a fondness for, and I had the pleasure of covering five world championship boxing matches, including Muhammad Ali's last title fight against Larry Holmes in 1980. I have spent time with Ali on two other occasions.

My wrestling background includes creating *W.I.N. Magazine*, the Dan Hodge Trophy (which goes each year to the top collegiate wrestler in the United States), and the International Wrestling Institute and Museum in Newton, Iowa. My work on wrestling has caused me to be featured in the A&E Network documentary *The Unreal Story of Pro Wrestling*, and on the *ESPN Sports Century* special on Dan Gable. In addition, I have been featured in numerous regional TV and radio shows and in numerous magazine articles, speaking about the sport of wrestling.

I have had the privilege of rubbing shoulders with most of America's greatest amateur and professional wrestlers of the last half century. I say all of this not to boast of my good fortune but to let the reader know that I have spent considerable time in conversation with many of the top athletes, coaches, and historians in wrestling. Although I came to the sport late in life as a competitor, I wrestled for several years in the United States Navy and one year in college. I also competed in judo, sombo, and weightlifting events.

In short, wrestling has played a key role in my career and my life. And I have observed many remarkable moments in the wrestling world—moments that I am eager to share with you.

Through the pages of this book, you will encounter dramatic stories of fortitude, determination, dedication, sacrifice, goal setting, and pain tolerance. Along the way, you will come to understand the value of wrestling in many ways, both by studying its path through history and by listening as men of towering success reveal its influence on their lives and careers. Those examples will help guide your preparation for both physical and mental training.

Through the words and experiences of great champions like Bill Koll, Dan Hodge, Wayne Baughman, Dan Gable, John Smith, Tom Brands, Kurt Angle, and many more, we will mold a composite image of the ultimate mental wrestler. Finally, this book will provide an understanding of what wrestling was, what it is, and what it can be to you. I hope that *Wrestling Tough* will help you succeed in the sport of Gilgamesh—and in life as well.

PART I

Fundamental Steps to Wrestling Tough

1

Choosing to Wrestle

Most social historians agree that sport plays a valuable role in world society in general, and in American society in particular. At the very start of the Olympics, in 776 B.C., the Games were so important that warring Greek city-states suspended all hostilities so that they could partake in the Games under peaceful conditions.

Throughout the civilized world, and even in less civilized areas, sport has taken on an important meaning. It teaches individuals and groups how to set priorities, work within the structure of rules, dedicate oneself (or an entire group) to a predetermined task, accept stringent training rules, and, ultimately, come together in pursuit of a common goal. At times, sport has allowed people to cut through cultural and racial barriers. Sport has on occasion reduced tension between potential enemy nations. In the latter regard, sport has served as a substitute for aggressive behavior between both individuals and countries, probably averting wars in many instances through the centuries.

"Games are a sublimation of combat between individuals or between cities, regions or countries," wrote Thomas Tutko in his book *Sports Psyching*. "As great warriors have always been great heroes, the warriors of our times, the professional athletes, now often receive the social benefits of generals. The process starts in the schoolyard" (Tutko and Tosi 1976, 42).

The process does indeed start in the schoolyard; many wrestlers of today are well into the sport by age six or seven, with hundreds of matches to their credit. That is a startling change from two or three decades ago, when a wrestler could go through an entire career with no more than 200 matches. But our sport culture has changed dramatically, and so have most individual sports, wrestling included. Sport has become omnipresent and ubiquitous; in short, sport is everywhere, all the time!

Sport is the perfect way for youngsters to show who they are and how they perform under varying degrees of pressure. It offers equal opportunity for all boys and girls to show what they can do in a contest, no matter what shape the contest takes—from baseball to volleyball, from sprints on land to sprints in water, from golf to tennis. Nowhere is that test more evident than when young men and women begin to wrestle.

As already noted, wrestling is a universal sport that stretches back into the predawn of history. The ancient Greeks loved combative sports like wrestling, boxing, and pancratium most of all. "These grueling sports reveal much about the aspirations and values of ancient Greece, about what was deemed honorable, fair and beautiful, both in the eyes of those who competed and those who traveled to Olympia to watch," wrote Michael B. Poliakoff in an article entitled "Ancient Combat Sports" (2004).

Today, wrestling is practiced all around the world, in many different styles. It has been a staple of the American sports experience since the first Europeans arrived in the 1500s. The two most imposing figures in all of American history, George Washington and Abraham Lincoln, were wrestlers of some reputation and skill.

Although amateur wrestling receives far less media attention and publicity than many other sports do, there are nearly one million practitioners and former practitioners in America. According to the National High School Federation, some 10,000 high schools and junior high schools in the United States offer wrestling, with an estimated 245,000 participants. Nearly 280 colleges offer programs, a figure that includes programs in all three NCAA divisions, the NAIA, junior colleges, and club programs.

USA Wrestling, the national governing body of the sport, has 130,000 dues-paying members, and the AAU has nearly 50,000 registered wrestlers. The latter figure places wrestling third in size among the list of 26 sports sanctioned by the AAU.

College wrestling draws huge crowds in some sections of the country. The University of Minnesota holds the all-time dual meet record of 15,646 for a 2002 clash with the University of Iowa, and the Division I NCAA tournament is often sold out. For the last five years

© Human Kinetics

Two wrestlers battle on the mat for position. An estimated 10,000 high schools and junior high schools in America have scholastic wrestling programs.

in a row, over 85,000 fans have attended the three-day NCAA Division I championships. Wrestling is one of just four sports that make money at the tournament level for the NCAA championships.

Many educators promote sport as an ideal way of teaching the values and disciplines that help people succeed in life. Wrestling certainly has its proponents. Dennis Hastert rose from being a successful high school wrestling coach in Yorkville, Illinois, to being Speaker of the House of Representatives, third in line to the presidency. He attends several wrestling events each year and has become one of the leading advocates of the sport.

"The sport of wrestling is a tremendous builder of the values and characteristics which are needed to succeed in any walk of life," Speaker Hastert said in 2000. "Much of what I have managed to achieve in life I owe directly to the years I spent in the wrestling room, as an athlete and a coach. Wrestling is a great educational tool."

THE DEMANDS OF WRESTLING

Wrestling has a wondrous heritage and powerful support system. It also demands certain attributes from those who hope to excel.

"Anybody who has ever wrestled knows that no other sport tests your will to win quite the same way," writes Kurt Angle, who won two NCAA titles and was a world and Olympic champion, as well. "Five minutes on the mat in a tough match can seem like an hour of hell. I played other sports growing up and nothing pushed me to the limits of my endurance and conditioning like wrestling" (Angle 2001, 79).

Wrestling demands so much that a person with the necessary athletic skills to perform at a high level may be unable to do so because he or she lacks the required mental and emotional makeup. Each athlete must make that discovery for himself or herself. No sport can be the sport for everyone.

"Certain people belong in certain sports," said tennis legend Billie Jean King. "It depends on the person, their body type, their capacities, their mentalities. Certain sports are made for certain people—every athlete must find the sport for which he or she is best suited."

Peggy Fleming, who won an Olympic gold medal in figure skating as well as numerous national titles, offered some tremendous advice for a young person contemplating a future in any sport: "The most important thing is to love your sport. Never do it to please someone else, it has to be yours. That is all that will justify the hard work needed to achieve success."

The greatest figure in baseball history agreed with Fleming: "The most important thing that a young athlete must do is to pick the right sport," said Babe Ruth. "Not one that they like just a little bit but one that they love. Because if they don't really love their sport, they won't work as hard as they should."

Wrestling is unique among scholastic sports in that a strict diet is essential for success. Tremendous discipline is required with regard to eating habits. Athletes in such sports as basketball, baseball, hockey, and golf don't have to weigh themselves on a regular basis to compete, but wrestlers do just that. Wrestlers must be under the class limit for the weight classification that they have selected. For example, if a wrestler wants to compete in the 155-pound class and he normally weighs 162 or 163 pounds, he will need to trim 7 or 8 pounds to do so. He shouldn't take off the extra weight quickly; rather, he should gradually work off the excess poundage over a week or 10 days.

Most young wrestlers find that they can compete more effectively without excess poundage. Although many football players are determined to put on extra muscle in the off-season and increase their body weight, wrestlers need to monitor their weight on a consistent basis, paying particular attention to the types of food that they eat. They live by the scales during the season. In that regard, other family members—especially mothers—often become deeply involved in the sport, at the preparation level, trying to fix meals that will provide the proper nutrition and giving emotional support to the wrestler in the struggle to curb the somewhat natural tendency to eat more than is necessary.

For decades, weight cutting in high school was regarded as a necessary evil of the sport, and in the 1950s through the 1980s, many young wrestlers cut more weight than was appropriate or healthy. But in the last 10 to 15 years or so, wrestling administrators, coaches, and parents have learned that athletes should never cut large amounts of weight. Most high school associations have weight limits that restrict how much weight an athlete can trim. In addition, many coaches now frown upon an athlete trying to trim off too much weight, and they may even forbid it.

Still, no scholastic sport requires as much diet control as wrestling. It's simply a fact of life for those youngsters who choose wrestling as their sport.

On the other side of the coin, many young athletes feel a certain pride as they see their bodies tighten and their resolve grow stronger. Watching one's diet enforces the need for discipline in the sport, and that self-discipline can carry over into other aspects of life. Many young wrestlers who have learned how to control their food intake also know how to discipline themselves in the classroom.

Numerous businesspersons give considerable credit to wrestling for helping them learn how to cope with the demands of life. The wrestling room has proved to be a great educational tool, in many ways.

"Each sport . . . makes different demands on aspects of the athlete's personality and his ability to emotionally adapt himself to the requirements of the game," wrote Tutko. "Even if you are well suited for a position physically, you also need to be suited for it psychologically" (Tutko and Tosi 1976, 28). He makes the point that linemen in football need to have different psychological traits, depending on whether they are on the offensive or defensive side of the ball.

But every rule has expectations. As we will see in the following pages, a person of any physical type—even a young man with no legs beneath the knees—can be a resounding success in wrestling, and an athlete of any personality type can win an Olympic title. Of course, the athlete must train extremely hard and must climb to new heights mentally and physically to prepare for such competition, but it can be done!

THE WRESTLING TEST

Coaches of other sports have always respected wrestling as one of the best tests of an athlete's mettle and mental toughness. Paul "Bear" Bryant became a legend at the University of Alabama in the 1950s and 1960s, winning six national titles and making the Crimson Tide the most feared football team in the nation. When he retired in 1982, he had the most victories (323) of any football coach in collegiate history. He earned the nickname "Bear" when he accepted a challenge to wrestle a bear at a circus when he was a teenager.

Bryant held wrestling in such high esteem as a developer of athletes, physically and mentally, that he made the Alabama football team work out in the wrestling room in spring practice, shooting takedowns and engaging in live scrimmages. No one was exempt, not even superstar quarterbacks like Joe Namath and Ken Stabler.

"Everyone was expected to wrestle," said Tom Drake, who served as Bryant's line coach as well as the head wrestling coach. "He just knew that wrestling would make his players tougher both mentally and physically. Coach Bryant really respected wrestling and believed in it."

Wrestling also has a side benefit that most other sports do not offer: Wrestling can serve as an effective means of self-defense. Although many of its practitioners have always known that wrestling was at least as effective for self-defense as the more highly hyped Oriental martial arts like karate and tae kwon do, it took the advent of mixed martial arts events like the Ultimate Fighting Championships in the mid-1990s to convince the rest of the sports world. Men with tremendous wrestling backgrounds, like Dan Severn and Randy Couture, achieved stunning success at the highest level, and suddenly the martial arts world embraced wrestling.

Like other combative disciplines, wrestling exists on two levels: It is both a sport and a martial art. The world has long accepted other forms of stylized combat such as kung fu, karate, and judo as martial arts. Wrestling should be viewed in the same way. As with karate and kung fu, basic elements of training and preparation are essential to achieving success, at any level. The traditional martial arts have long understood the connection between mental and physical preparation, but wrestling has only recently come to appreciate this link. Many books discuss the physical aspect of wrestling preparation, but few delve deeply into the mental and the emotional side.

If you have decided that the sport of wrestling is for you, then you have already taken the huge first step on the journey to self-fulfillment. As you will discover in the following pages, you can prepare yourself for greater successes in many ways. One of them is to read about the obstacles that other great champions have met and overcome on their paths to success.

But the most important ingredients in the journey will be found deep inside you. When it comes to wrestling success, no factors weigh as heavily as your commitment, your desire, and your mental toughness.

SUMMARY

Wrestling is a universal sport that traces its history back over 5,000 years. It is highly popular in schools and clubs around the nation and has gained respect in the past decade as a means of self-defense similar to that offered by the Oriental martial arts. But wrestling also demands tremendous drive and determination from those who choose it. The path to success is not easy. The journey requires unwavering commitment and a mountain of hard work, but the destination is well worth the effort if you decide that wrestling is a sport that suits your mental and physical makeup.

2

Understanding Toughness

Few competitors understand mental toughness to as high a degree as Steve Fraser does. A wrestler of somewhat limited athletic skills, he willed himself to make the 1984 Olympic team in the punishing Greco-Roman style of wrestling. With a relentless, pounding style of wrestling, he made the team by defeating two formidable foes, two of the best Greco-Roman wrestlers his weight class had ever seen, 1980 Olympian Mark Johnson and Mike Houck, who in 1985 would become a world champion himself.

After making the Olympic team, Fraser won five straight matches in Los Angeles to become the first American ever to win an Olympic medal in Greco-Roman wrestling. The key match in his march to the gold medal came in the quarterfinal round when he defeated two-time world champion Frank Andersson of Sweden. Fraser simply pummeled Andersson into submission, winning 4-1.

In 1997, while serving as Greco-Roman coach for USA Wrestling, the sport's national governing body, Fraser wrote a column in which he explained his viewpoint on what it takes to be a great performer, assessing the variables of talent, skill, and toughness.

> When talking about talent we must realize that every wrestler has talent; some have it big and some not so big. This is the great gift given to you by Mother Nature. Theoretically, talent defines the potential of your athletic achievement. The idea is that if you are gifted, or a real "natural," you can be great. If you are not gifted then nothing special can happen athletically.

> I do not believe this theory. We've all seen wrestlers with limited talent become great performers. I consider myself

one of those wrestlers that lack natural talent. We've also seen wrestlers with great talent never truly reaching their full potential. Why?

Next, we look at the nature of skill. Whereas talent is a gift, skills are learned. The mechanics of running, jumping, shooting, hitting and kicking are skills. They are acquired through hard work, repetition and practice. Theoretically, skills affect achievement in wrestling in much the same way as talent does. If your skills are strong, you can be great! If your skills are weak, your potential is limited. Again, I think we've all seen some successful wrestlers with skills that were marginal to good at best. So how do wrestlers with no special talent and average-to-good mechanics become the best?

Talent and skill are important contributors to achievement in sport, but I don't think they are the most important factors. So many highly successful athletes exist today who are not gifted or have not achieved mechanical perfection. They are everywhere in every sport—golf, tennis, baseball, basketball, football, boxing, skating, hockey, soccer and wrestling. So what is the critical factor in wrestling achievement? It's called toughness!

What is toughness? Toughness is the ability to consistently perform at a high level no matter what the competitive circumstances are. In other words—no matter what happens, no matter what is thrown at you, no matter what adversity you are faced with—you will still be able to bring all your talent and skills to life on demand.

Toughness is being able to perform at your ideal competitive state of mind and body. It is simply the optimal state of physiological and psychological arousal for performing at your peak. You are most likely to perform at your peak when you feel

confident,
relaxed and calm,
energized with positive emotion,
challenged,
focused and alert,
automatic and instinctive, and
ready for fun and enjoyment.

Toughness is learned. Make no mistake about it. Toughness has nothing to do with genetics. It is acquired the same way skills are. If you don't have it, it just means you haven't learned it yet. Anyone can learn it at any stage in his or her life.

Toughness is mental, physical and ultimately emotional. What you think and visualize, how you act, when and what you eat, the quantity and quality of your sleep and rest, and especially your physical conditioning level, can all have a great effect on your emotional state. Tough thinking, tough acting, fitness, proper rest and diet are prerequisites for feeling tough.

Your emotions control your ideal competitive state of being. Some emotions are empowering—freeing your talent and skill. Other emotions are disempowering and lock your potential out. Empowering emotions are those associated with challenge, drive, confidence, determination, positive fight, energy, spirit, persistence and fun. Disempowering emotions are those associated with feelings of fatigue, helplessness, insecurity, low energy, weakness, fear and confusion.

Learning to access empowering emotions during competition, especially in difficult situations, is the basis for learning to be a great fighter. That's what toughness is all about.

Reprinted with permission of Steve Fraser.

MOVING PAST SETBACKS

An essential form of mental toughness is the ability to deal with setbacks, which will occur in the career of any world-class athlete. A popular saying in the wrestling world goes like this:

Never been a horse can't be rode,

Never been a cowboy can't be throwed.

In other words, everyone is going to experience setbacks in his or her career. It's simply unavoidable. And the manner in which one deals with setbacks is critical. Some call it attitude.

"Attitude is the glue that brings all of the physical and mental training together. We live or die by attitude," said powerlifting champion Steve Knight.

Attitude can also be defined by one's mental state of recovery after a bad experience. That, too, is an essential part of being able to perform well. Few wrestlers have understood the power of attitude as well as Wade Schalles did, a man who experimented in all forms of wrestling and won major titles in collegiate, freestyle, and Greco-Roman wrestling, as well as in judo and sombo.

"Being a student of the game of wrestling is terribly important," said Schalles, "and the ability to retain the experience is critical. However, the most important quality is this: How fast can you forget a negative experience? In golf, if you have a bad shot you can be all screwed up for the next hour, replaying it over and over.

"If you get pinned in wrestling, the question is, Can you forget that experience and move ahead, putting it out of your mind? If you can't, then you can no longer play the game the way it should be played, you won't take the risks you need to take to score and win, because you can't forget the negative experience and freeze up.

Steve Fraser (left) battles a foe during the 1984 Olympics in Los Angeles. Fraser won this match and went on to win the gold medal in the 198-pound class.

"If you are in the swimming pool, you have to let go of the gutter to be able to swim to the other side. You can't start saying, 'What if I drown?' You have to wipe that out of your mind.

"As a junior in high school, I was going to face a wrestler who was a state runner-up the year before and had already beaten me, and I was very apprehensive. It was working on me, and my coach knew it. We were riding in a car, and he got tired of my whining. He grabbed the rear view mirror and pulled it right off the window and threw it in the back seat. My eyes were as big as saucers.

"He shouted at me, 'Why did I do that? To show you that the rearview mirror only shows what is behind you, in the past. It's not near as big as the windshield, which you need to see where you are going. That's much more important than where you've been. Forget about that loss. It's in the past. You're going to beat him this time.

"And guess what? I did beat that kid. In fact, I pinned him.

"The point my coach was making is that you have to forget the negative experiences. That's one of the keys to mental toughness."

Ed Banach had to draw on his mental toughness and make an attitude adjustment to win his third NCAA championship in 1983. He had won NCAA crowns as a freshman and sophomore at 177 pounds but lost in the finals his junior year to Mark Schultz of Oklahoma. Tired of cutting tremendous amounts of weight, he moved up to 190 pounds for his senior season and lost three times to Mike Mann, a talented and tough senior from Iowa State.

Dan Gable, Banach's coach, formulated a plan for Ed to improve his mental toughness (see chapter 9, "Paying the Price"), and Ed had the mental strength to accept it. But he also had to learn how to forget past negatives.

"I used too much energy thinking about the last dual meet that I lost to Mann," said Banach. "I finally learned the lesson of not thinking about the loss too much. I tried to forget that and to model myself after Gable and Bruce Kinseth (the 150-pounder who pinned his way through the Big Ten tournament and the NCAA tournament in 1979 to win the outstanding wrestler award at both meets). Bruce was phenomenal in his training, both mentally and physically. No one trained as hard, and Bruce was able to block out all his negative thoughts."

What is the main difference, then, between those who reach the highest plateau and those who come close but don't quite make it? The power to overcome problems like negative thinking rests in the mind, but it may also be pure old grit, better known as perseverance.

"Most people give up too soon," said sports psychologist Thomas Tutko. "They are unprepared for the plateaus and the emotional problems they meet there" (Tutko and Tosi 1976, 14).

THE INTIMIDATION FACTOR

Some athletes give up too soon if the foe is able to intimidate them and make them surrender mentally. This circumstance happens most often in the early stages of a career, when an athlete judges a foe mostly on appearance, but it can even happen to seasoned competitors. Early in his career, Mike Tyson presented such a menacing appearance that other boxers were actually afraid to get in the ring with him. In the first decade of his career Alexander Karelin terrified many opponents with his physique and his scowling.

Intimidation by appearance is an approach that has its roots in the dawn of sports competition, dating back many centuries.

Tiberius Claudius Marcianus was a renowned wrestler in the ancient Olympics, living around 300 years before Christ. We don't know what he looked like, because no artwork survives and, of course, we have no photographs. But we do have an indication that he must have been an extremely impressive and intimidating fighter for a foe to see standing across from him, as was Karelin in the years 1990 through 2000.

In one competition in which Marcianus participated, it is reported that "when he undressed, all his opponents begged to be dismissed from the contest" (Poliakoff 2004, 44).

Judging a book by its cover is easy, and that was certainly how opponents sized up Tiberius Claudius Marcianus. But appearances can also be misleading and downright dangerous. Some of the greatest wrestlers were not the most intimidating in physical appearance, including great pinners like Wade Schalles and Randy Lewis.

On the other hand, some of the most impressive physical specimens lack that certain something that it takes to be a good athlete, let alone a great one. A young wrestler in the navy learned that lesson many years ago. After a wrestling workout, he wandered into the boxing area and observed over a dozen pugilists going through a session. One boxer in particular, named Frank, caught his attention.

"He was an unbelievable physical specimen," said the wrestler much later. "He moved like a cat and every muscle was pronounced. He was ripped. I watched him on the speed bag and was amazed at his skills and quickness. He was tremendous with the skip rope and he made the heavy bag snap to attention every time he hit it.

"I was friends with the boxing coach—in fact, he was always trying to get me to give up wrestling and try boxing—and so I asked about the big fight program coming up. He ran down the list of who he thought would win. I was shocked when he didn't mention Frank. When I asked why, the coach just shrugged and said, 'Come to the show and see for yourself.'"

The wrestler went to the boxing show that weekend and watched as Frank came down the aisle in his long robe and leaped into the ring. He threw lightning punches and skipped around the ring in a style that would have impressed Muhammad Ali. He threw punches in stunning combinations while the boxers were being introduced. The other fighter merely glowered at him; he appeared slow and pudgy by comparison. It looked like it would be an easy night for Frank.

When the fight started, Frank began bobbing, weaving, and flicking out jabs like a well-oiled machine. He was winning the first round easily when suddenly his opponent caught him with a right hand on the chin. It was a light punch, but Frank was clearly hurt. Sensing his opportunity, the other fighter tore into him and Frank fell seconds later like a sack of hammers. He was out cold!

"It looked like the other guy barely hit him!" the wrestler mumbled to the boxing coach the next day.

The coach, a wise old veteran of the ring wars, shook his head sadly. "Yeah, Frank's got all the tools to be a champion," said the coach, "but he also has a glass jaw. He simply can't take a punch of any kind. The truth is, he looks like a world-beater but he can't fight like one. Because of one fatal flaw, he'll never amount to anything in this sport!"

The lesson was clear: Never judge a book by its cover.

In wrestling, the case is much the same. One major flaw—an Achilles heel—can be the downfall of an athlete who otherwise seems to have it all. In wrestling, the Achilles heel is most often a lack of discipline or desire to do what it takes to be a winner. We've all known athletes who have the physical tools to be outstanding wrestlers but lack the inner drive and discipline required to be successful.

Appearances can be impressive, but they can also be deceiving. More than anything else, in sport it's the size of the heart and innate physical ability, both physical and mental, to withstand the opponent's best shots that will determine victory.

"The various pressures you have in sports don't just act by themselves; they mix," wrote Tutko and Tosi. "They come at you from different directions and you are caught in the middle. One pressure makes you act and feel one way, while another says to act in the opposite way. Your personal needs, which already have an element of conflict in them, now run up against the societal pressures, for you are culturally conditioned to be a strong competitor and to go for the big one whenever you can" (Tutko and Tosi 1976, 29).

Appearances don't make a great athlete, and it is important for wrestlers, especially young ones, not to judge a book by its cover. Sometimes outward appearances only mask a fatal flaw in the opponent. Much of sports competition is physical, of course, but much is also mental. Don't allow yourself to lose the mental battle before the physical battle even gets under way.

SUMMARY

"What is toughness?" asks 1984 Olympic champion Steve Fraser. He says that toughness is the ability to perform consistently at a high level no matter what the competitive circumstances are. In other words—no matter what happens, no matter what is thrown at you, no matter what adversity you face—you will still be able to bring all your talent and skills to life on demand. This concise definition works well in all circumstances.

Toughness also demands that you be able to deal with the forces of intimidation. In wrestling it is never wise to judge a book by its cover, one way or the other. Some of the best wrestlers in history did not have the appearance of being outstanding; others may look like Hercules but bring little to the table other than their appearance. Anyone who wants to compete at the highest level needs to understand the essence of toughness and to understand that appearance isn't what makes a person a great wrestler. Wrestlers also need to understand that physical and mental toughness are linked together. One of the first orders of business will be to build a strong base of confidence, in both your decision to wrestle and in yourself.

3

Building Confidence

Confidence is essential for anyone in any sport, from tennis to baseball to wrestling. An athlete needs confidence to feel that he or she can participate effectively. Confidence may be faint at the outset and slow in coming, but it is an essential element for successful participation. A person is unlikely to attain any goal without having at least some degree of confidence that he or she can reach it.

Those who choose to participate in wrestling soon confront one undeniable and overwhelming truth about humankind's oldest sport: Few activities are as demanding and require as much confidence to be successful.

In wrestling, more than in any other sport, the adage that follows, which remains anonymous, holds true:

If you think you are beaten, you are;

If you think that you dare not, you don't;

If you'd like to win but you think you can't,

It's almost certain you won't.

If you think you'll lose, you've lost;

For out in the world you'll find

Success begins with a fellow's will.

It's all in the state of mind.

If you think you are outclassed, you are;

You've got to think high to rise;

You've got to be sure of yourself before

You can ever win a prize.

Life's battles don't always go

To the stronger or faster man;

But sooner or later the man who wins

Is the man who thinks he can!

Confidence is one element that is required. Those who would seek to acquire a basic skill in wrestling and then to achieve high levels of success will discover that the demands are as high as the rewards of which they dream. Becoming a state high school champion, a national collegiate champion, or a national freestyle or Greco-Roman champion will require thousands of hours per year, for many years, of training, both on and off the mat. Those who strive to be champions will perform countless drilling sessions, sparring sessions, weight-training sessions, and long, lonely runs, at all hours of the day and night. Highly successful wrestlers will learn to control their diets almost year around and to deny themselves the common pleasures that most of their friends and companions take for granted.

If you dream of becoming an Olympian—and why shouldn't you dare to fashion such lofty dreams?—the demands are 10 times greater.

The successful wrestler needs a wide arsenal of skills and equipment if he or she desires to become one of the best in the nation and the world. For certain, the wrestler needs the physical makeup and framework. But he or she also must have an abundance of the mental equipment. Although physical training is the basic building block for success, it is in the mind where truly great wrestlers are born and their dreams cultivated.

No less an authority that John Smith, six-time world and Olympic champion, makes that clear at the outset.

"The attitude, and the mind, is where it all starts," said Smith, who left competition to become a highly successful coach at Oklahoma State University.

FROM FOUNDATION TO FIRM BELIEF

The first great mental attribute that any wrestler needs is confidence. The athlete needs to believe that he or she has a true chance of winning every match, from the first kids' bout to the last international showdown. The wrestler needs to have total confidence that success will come each time that he or she steps onto a mat, or at least that the opportunity to win will be present, no matter who the foe.

Nothing gives a wrestler as much confidence as the knowledge that he or she can wrestle the entire length of the match at the highest level without the fear of becoming tired.

Think how confident you would feel if every time you took the mat you knew that you would be able to perform at 100 percent the entire way! You could shoot and shoot and shoot, throw moves and struggle, all without the nagging thought lingering in the back of your consciousness that you might tire or burn yourself out. Confidence is the key to such performance. But where does such confidence come from?

"Confidence is only born out of one thing—demonstrated ability," claims Bill Parcells, one of the most successful coaches in NFL history. "It is not born of anything else. You cannot dream up confidence. You cannot fabricate it. You cannot wish it. You have to accomplish it."

None of us is born with confidence, of course. Confidence grows with the body, through an ongoing series of positive and reinforcing events. It can be nurtured and developed with the passing years, or it can be severely damaged at an early age. Even Michael Jordan, considered by some the greatest athlete of the 20th century, had to work extremely hard to restore his confidence after it was kicked across the basketball court when he was still in his formative years.

Jordan's confidence suffered a devastating blow when he was cut from the junior high basketball team back home in Wilmington, North Carolina. Being cut was an extremely painful experience for him, and he was determined not to let it happen again. He started working with a new focus and commitment to improve his basketball skills.

He began by setting small goals. "As I reached those goals," he says, "they built on one another. I gained a little confidence every time I came through. Take those small steps. Otherwise, you're opening yourself up to all kinds of frustration."

Confidence is the bedrock on which Dan Gable constructed his entire career, first as an athlete and then as a coach. Ever since the day he entered West Waterloo (Iowa) High School in the fall of 1964, Gable was determined that no one would ever be able to fatigue him on a wrestling mat. He trained with that thought uppermost in mind at every practice, on every run, in every weight-training session. That commitment was the driving force behind his 181 consecutive victories in high school and college matches, a streak that endured for seven years. It was also the driving force behind his back-to-back world and Olympic triumphs in 1971 and 1972.

Confidence was the trademark of the great wrestling dynasty that Gable constructed at the University of Iowa. During his 21 seasons as head coach in the 1980s and 1990s, the Hawkeyes became the most successful collegiate sports program in the entire nation. To a man, Hawkeye wrestlers were confident that they had outworked every foe they would encounter. That confidence was born through the incredible workout sessions that Gable and his assistant coaches forced them through, day after day, month after month.

Gable's obsession with training when he was an athlete enabled him to build a reputation that demoralized nearly every foe he faced in his postcollege career. In a tournament in Russia, a great Soviet Union wrestler quit in the middle of a match with Gable, waving him off. The Soviet wrestler was done, finished, because Gable had broken his spirit with his high-level pressured attack, and because the Soviet wrestler knew that Gable would only grow stronger during the match while he, the Soviet, grew weaker.

Gable's incredible training pushed his confidence to the highest level imaginable and caught the imagination of athletes and coaches the world over. As his hand was being raised over his last victim in the 1972 Olympics, famed sportscaster Frank Gifford had this to say to a worldwide television audience watching in unabashed admiration: "Dan Gable has won the gold medal at 149.5 pounds . . . and in my book he may be the most dedicated athlete I have ever known."

The statement was a stunning compliment from Gifford, who was an All-American football player at the University of Southern California and an All-Pro in the National Football League. During his long athletic and broadcasting career, he rubbed shoulders

Mike Chapman Collection

Dan Gable works over a foe during his great college career at Iowa State University. Gable was 64-0 in high school and 118-1 in college for a combined scholastic record of 182-1. He also set the NCAA record with 25 consecutive pins in 1969-70.

with most of the world's finest athletes, from Muhammad Ali and Arnold Palmer to Mickey Mantle and Joe Namath. Yet he was proclaiming for all to hear that an amateur wrestler was perhaps the most dedicated athlete in the world!

Before the Olympics, the Soviet Union's wrestling leaders were so determined to stop Gable that their coaching staff said its no. 1 goal in 1972 was to find a wrestler who could defeat him. Several years later, in a book titled *Wrestling Is a Man's Game*, Soviet authorities expressed their high regard for Gable's unique approach to the sport.

"We were quite surprised to see the famous American matman Dan Gable train. . . . Gable was able to carry phenomenal running loads. We chanced to watch him in Sofia (Bulgaria) in 1971. The championships at which he became world champion ended the day before but on the next day he ran around the stadium circle after circle. He didn't spare himself during training sessions, working for hours without rest. Although one cannot agree with everything in his training methods, the tremendous industriousness of the American matman tells.

"Gable astounded us with his inexhaustible energy and at the same time with his perfect technique. We were used to recognizing a great master by his filigree technique, precision and expediency of action. Gable refuted all these notions.

"Out on the mat, he cascaded on his opponent, a mass of pushes and pulls. Beginning one element, he would drop it unfinished and launch into another one, then a third one and so on. . . . Then tiredness would envelop his opponent as if a shroud. That's when Gable would get up steam" (Preobrazhensky 1981, 64).

Let's reread the phrases the generally bland Soviet writer used to describe Gable and his training methods:

a. Phenomenal running load
b. Tremendous industriousness
c. Astounded us
d. Inexhaustible energy

Gable had trained himself to the point that he knew in the deep recesses of his mind that he was the best-conditioned wrestler in the entire world. He was completely confident in his training methods and in his commitment to those principles. Gable was 100 percent confident in his ability to wrestle all out every second but, just as important, so were his foes. The Soviets were stunned by what they saw, and so were the coaches from other nations. In the words of the Soviet writer, Gable's (a) phenomenal running load, (b) tremendous industriousness, and (d) inexhaustible energy served to (c) astound them and to intimidate the wrestlers who had to face him on the mat and deal with those qualities.

At this point in his career, Gable enjoyed a tremendous psychological edge over every other 149.5-pound wrestler in the world. All had heard of his incredible work ethic and conditioning, and all must have questioned deep down inside whether they could pay the price that Gable would make them pay.

"Once you reach a certain point, wrestling becomes mental," Gable said repeatedly in the following decades. "To be at the very highest level takes an incredible mental commitment."

Anyone who followed Gable's career should have known that he would take this philosophy into the coaching ranks. The big question was whether Gable could find enough high school wrestlers who would pay the price to wrestle his way—an extremely demanding style that requires tremendous mental commitment to all-out physical excellence. The answer to that question was not long in coming.

Before Gable's arrival at the University of Iowa in the fall of 1972 as assistant coach to Gary Kurdelmeier, the Hawkeye program had never won an NCAA team title. The closest the Hawks had come was third place in 1962. Just two years before the Kurdelmeier-Gable coaching team took over, Iowa had placed 30th at the NCAA tournament, tied with Idaho State and Utah.

The transformation of the Iowa program was amazing and immediate. Iowa was seventh in the first year of Gable's assistantship, and then moved up to fifth. In just the third year, 1975, the Hawkeyes won their first NCAA team title ever! Gable took over as head coach for the 1977 season. By the time Gable retired, in 1997, Iowa had dominated the collegiate wrestling scene as no program ever had. Iowa won 21 consecutive Big Ten championships under Gable, and 15 NCAA team titles. That record was an amazing testimony to the wrestling philosophy of Dan Gable.

He did it by instilling in his wrestlers a commitment that bordered on the fanatical, and by forcing his wrestlers to reach a confidence level that no opponent could match. The young wrestlers who came to Iowa and survived the rigors of the program became new men, new athletes. Those who wore the Hawkeye colors onto the mat were athletes who had discovered the true meaning of the words *commitment* and *confidence*.

Dan Gable built his entire philosophy on the commitment to developing total confidence in one's ability to outperform all others, through preparation. It was the cornerstone to the astonishing success of the University of Iowa's program during the Gable era.

"When I observe wrestlers walking onto the mat, I know who's going to win—the one who's confident," said Gable. "There is only one legitimate way to have a lot of confidence—to be mentally tough, be prepared technically and be in superior condition."

"The Iowa wrestling room is not for everyone," said Randy Lewis, a two-time NCAA champion and four-time All-American there. "I have seen two- and three-time state champions come in and buckle under the mental and physical strain. When you first come into the room, you get your butt kicked, no matter who you are and how good a high school wrestler you were. That's just the nature of things in that room. You have to accept that and be willing to work though it. It takes a certain type of person to survive the system."

Even stars like Ed and Lou Banach and Tom and Terry Brands had to pay this price as pure freshmen, taking their licks from the upperclassmen. All four of them would eventually become multiple NCAA champions and world or Olympic champions, but during the first year they would experience long dry spells without scoring more than a few points during an entire practice.

The process can take a long time. In fact, few wrestlers can make the adjustment quickly.

"It isn't done overnight," Gable told a writer. "If you want to accomplish anything that's worthwhile, you've got to be associated with a great system year around. When we started to build the wrestling program at the University of Iowa, we had to create something to believe in" (Arangio 2002, 28).

THE POWER OF PHYSICAL PREPARATION

Nothing can match the confidence that comes from knowing that you are in superb shape. That was a lesson Kurt Angle learned while competing for the gold medal in the 1996 Olympics in Atlanta. He had battled his way to the finals in the 220-pound class against a great Iranian wrestler named Abbas Jadidi, who had gained the finals with an 8-1 victory over Russia's six-time world champion.

Angle and Jadidi fought to a 1-1 tie in regulation time and then battled through a scoreless three-minute overtime. The decision was now in the hands of three judges. Over 7,000 fans and the two contestants waited breathlessly for the decision to be announced. Angle felt that he had won because the Iranian had been exhausted in the overtime, stalling for extra time while the American ran back to the center of the mat after each time-out, showing the judges that he was ready to keep wrestling.

"Actually, I was exhausted too," said Angle later, "but I had spent two solid years training eight hours a day, going to extremes like running 200-yard sprints up the hills of Pittsburgh, carrying a training partner on my back so that I would never give in to fatigue. I loved being pushed to the limit like this because I knew that I was the best-conditioned wrestler in the world. If it had been up to me, we would have kept wrestling to settle it ourselves because I knew Jadidi was completely out of gas" (Angle 2001, 14).

There it was, in black and white—total confidence in one's ability to wrestle all out, the entire way. Kurt Angle was the picture of supreme and hard-earned confidence. In the end, it paid off. The referee came to the center of the mat, stood next to the two warriors as the packed house held its collective breath, and then lifted Angle's hand high in the air as the victor. Kurt Angle's two years of incredible workouts had paid off in the ultimate fashion: He was awarded the gold medal and became an Olympic champion for all time.

The underlying principle was believing in one's ability to go all out, all the time. The goal for athletes like Gable and Angle was to be able to set a pace that foes simply could not match because they didn't have the training and, subsequently, the confidence to perform at that accelerated pace. Angle had paid the price and knew his own ability.

Ironically, another legendary coach in a far different sport half a continent away employed much the same philosophy.

Kurt Angle (top) controls Mark Kerr in a battle of national champions during the USA Wrestling National Freestyle Championships in Las Vegas in 1995. After a scoreless match, Angle was awarded the victory on a referee's decision. Kerr went on to become a champion in mixed martial arts contests while Angle won gold medals at the 1995 world championships and the 1996 Olympics.

Basketball and wrestling are dissimilar, in nearly all ways. Wrestling dates back 5,000 years, whereas basketball dates back about 150 years. Whereas wrestling is considered a combative sport, basketball is considered a skill sport. Wrestling matches, like basketball games, are determined by the total points of the team, but in wrestling each person must be selfish when his or her time to perform comes. Whereas basketball coaches stress teamwork during the actual flow of competition, wrestling coaches tell their athletes to focus on their individual matches and to let the team score take care of itself.

But at UCLA in the 1960s, John Wooden developed a style of play that, like Gable's, revolved around his athletes' ability to build confidence in their training sessions. Like Iowa wrestling sessions, UCLA basketball training sessions focused on conditioning, because Wooden knew that confidence comes from conditioning and that conditioning is how an athlete can break the spirit of an opponent.

"I was disinclined to play so-called mind games with opponents," said Wooden many years after coaching his last game. "However, there was one idea I used that was aimed directly at the opponents' physiology as well as their psychology.

"Never did I want to call the first time-out during a game. Never. It was almost a fetish with me because I stressed conditioning to such a degree. I wanted UCLA to come out and run our opponents so hard that they would be forced to call the first time-out just to catch their breath. I wanted them to have to stop the running before we did.

"At that first time-out the opponents would know, and we would know that they knew, who was in better condition. This has a psychological impact" (Wooden 1997, 122).

John Havlicek was an All-American basketball player at Ohio State and went on to a terrific professional career with the Boston Celtics. He was best known for his nonstop hustle and an indefatigable approach to the game. Lean and hard, he seemed never to tire even in the final stages of the game when fatigue became a factor for all players.

"Over the years, I have pushed myself mentally and I have pushed myself physically," he explained. "A lot of people say, 'John Havlicek never gets tired.' Well, I get tired. It's just a matter of pushing myself. I say to myself, 'He's as tired as I am; who's going to win this mental battle?' It's just a matter of mental toughness."

John Wooden believed in building confidence through conditioning, just as Gable did a decade later. Employing that philosophy, Wooden fashioned the most impressive record in the annals of college basketball. When he retired in 1975, his UCLA teams had won 10 NCAA titles, including a streak of 7 in a row! At one point, the Bruins won 88 consecutive games. With power players like Kareem Abdul-Jabbar and Bill Walton setting the pace, Wooden's UCLA squads became the most respected—and feared—team of all time in college basketball.

Confidence, says Wooden, was a key element in that success.

"Perhaps we gained an advantage by having so much confidence in our own ability to play near our potential (because of our detailed and disciplined preparation) that it kept us from becoming fearful of another team," said Wooden. "It goes back to focusing on what you can control. We did have . . . total control over preparing to execute our game" (Wooden 1997, 121).

Take away the basketball, and it could be Gable talking. Iowa practices were incredibly intense and focused on the Iowa style of wrestling, which was full steam ahead and endurance oriented. Hawkeye wrestlers didn't care what your style was because they were determined to make you wrestle their style—Gable's style. Iowa practice sessions were focused on their style and what they did best, just as UCLA basketball practices were focused on John Wooden's style and what UCLA did best as a team.

Make the other fellow play your game and the chances are high that you will succeed in winning the contest, because you will have the confidence that comes from total preparation. Both Dan Gable and John Wooden understood that philosophy and worked it into their coaching scheme from day one.

SUMMARY

Confidence in your training system and belief in the program you are invested in are key elements to success. Athletes must know that they are doing every day in practice what it takes to win at the highest level. Having total faith in your ability to wrestle all out for the duration of the match brings a sense of confidence that nothing else can match. Even if you make mistakes early on, you will have the confidence of knowing that you can make up for them by wrestling harder in the second half of the match than your foe can, tiring out your opponent so that he or she will make mistakes down the homestretch.

Dan Gable epitomized this philosophy during his scholastic career, when he compiled a record of 182-1 at West Waterloo High School in Iowa and at Iowa State University. He also became one of the greatest pinners in wrestling history because he was in superb condition physically. Pinning is an aggressive form of wrestling that can tire the athlete out both physically and mentally. But Gable's confidence in his training regime gave him the mental edge to go all out with his pinning efforts, knowing that the other man would tire and break before he did.

Confidence was the cornerstone of the great UCLA basketball teams during the era of Coach John Wooden and of the University of Iowa wrestling program during Gable's coaching career. During his 21 years as head coach of the Hawkeyes, his teams won 15 NCAA team championships, earned 21 consecutive Big Ten titles, and crowned 106 Big Ten individual champions—more than the other 10 schools in the conference combined. His athletes fed off the knowledge that they were better trained than any athlete they would go against, and they knew that they could sustain their efforts at a higher pace than their foes could. The result was a record string of achievements at every level, including at the Olympic Games. Nine of Gable's athletes made Olympic teams and won medals, four of them gold.

After building confidence, the next step is to come to grips with two terms that will determine the height of your success—dedication and commitment.

4

Dedicating and Committing to Goals

Whenever fans and experts discuss the best of the best—men like Rocky Marciano in boxing, Arnold Schwarzenegger in body-building, Michael Jordan in basketball, and Alexander Karelin and John Smith in wrestling—they use terms like *fanatic* and *obsessive* to describe the athletes' training sessions. All of those athletes have been labeled extreme in their dedication to their sport and their commitment to excellence.

Although most boxers of his era would take five to six weeks to prepare for a title fight, Marciano would move into an austere training camp in the mountains as much as three months before a bout for the heavyweight championship. He simply loved being off by himself with just his trainers and sparring partners, where he could box, run, and train like no other fighter on the planet. His total commitment to conditioning gave Marciano the edge in many of his fights.

When he retired as the undefeated heavyweight boxing champion of the world in 1956, Marciano had a record of 49-0, with 43 knockouts. Most experts maintained that Rocky's unmatched emphasis on conditioning, often considered extreme, was the key to his success.

"Even in the months when he had no fight in sight, Rocky would train in the Catskills, jogging, hiking, sparring, punching the bag, skipping rope, doing calisthenics," wrote Red Smith, one the finest sports columnists ever. "Rocky Marciano couldn't box like Tunney and probably couldn't hit like Louis, but in one respect he had no challenger: he was the toughest, most completely dedicated fighter who ever wore gloves."

"Marciano's preoccupation with physical conditioning cannot be overstressed," wrote Everett Skehan (1977). Marciano understood the power of dedication and commitment, and how total it had to be, especially for a person in the combative sports.

"There is no doubt that man is a competitive animal," said Marciano, "and there is no place where this fact is more obvious than in the ring. There is no second place. Either you win or you lose. When they call you a champion, it's because you don't lose. To win takes a complete commitment of mind and body."

Working extremely hard in practice, all the time, is the hallmark of dedication and one of the greatest tests of commitment. It's true in any sport, in any endeavor, whether in the classroom or in the workplace. It's a test that Michael Jordan passed with flying colors.

"I've always believed that if you put in the work the results will come," he said. "I don't do things halfheartedly because I know if I do then I can expect halfhearted results. That's why I approached practices the same way I approached games. You can't turn it on and off like a faucet. I couldn't dog it during practice and then, when I needed that extra push late in the game, expect it to be there.

"But that's how a lot of people approach things. And that's why a lot of people fail" (Jordan 1998).

Alexander Karelin, winner of 12 consecutive world or Olympic Greco-Roman championships in the 286-pound class, was once filmed as he ran through waist-high snow, dressed in a parka. In the segment, which was televised around the world during the 1992 Olympics, announcer Bob Costas was awed by the training regimen of Karelin and his powerful physique. Costas said that the Russian superstar had been accused of experimenting with muscle-enhancing drugs and that Karelin was unhappy about the charges.

"I wish those who accused me would train once in their lives like I train every day of my life," he said. "The real drug is to train like a madman, really like a madman."

A popular poster made by Culture House in the 1990s captured his words. Thousands of the posters now adorn the walls of wrestling rooms all across the nation. Gracing the poster is a huge photo of Karelin lifting a foe, his face contorted in a grotesque mask of effort. His expression is one of extreme commitment.

"You have to be extreme to be exceptional," said Jim Courier, one of the world's premier tennis players, winner of four Grand Slams.

Many premier athletes have come to understand and embrace this truth.

Two wrestlers are locked in a tense struggle, with the athlete behind trying to continue his control and the athlete in front trying to work himself free. Wrestlers must know the meaning of dedication and hard work toward goals.

MAKING DECISIONS EFFECTIVELY

The best of the best also must have tunnel vision so that they can block out all distractions and focus like a laser beam. But there's more to it than just the physical preparation. Dedication is the key, and dedication comes from making the right decisions along the road.

"Anybody who is successful must be a decision maker. You've got to make up your mind on what you're going to do and how you're going to do it. . . . The successful people seem to have blinders on. Everything is straight ahead. They go forward and know exactly what they're going to do once they've made up their mind to do it, and by God they don't look sideways."

Any great wrestler might have said that—from John Smith to Kurt Angle. But it was actually Jack Nicklaus, regarded by many as the best golfer of all time. Golf and wrestling may seem worlds apart in terms of style and grit, but mentally they are much the same. The same focus and dedication and commitment that marked Nicklaus during his golf reign in the 1960s and 1970s is the same commitment that drove John Smith to six straight world or Olympic titles.

"I was blessed at an early age to know exactly what I wanted to do," said Smith, upon being inducted into yet another hall of fame. "At 19, I gave up my life. I willed it to wrestling."

"I lost in the finals of the NCAAs my sophomore year (to Wisconsin's Jim Jordan, in 1985)," related Smith, "and I said to myself, 'That's it! I'm not losing again. From here on out, it's going to be a different story.

"Joe Seay (the Oklahoma State University coach at the time) wanted me to redshirt, and I wanted to do it, as well. That year off changed me. I found out that I missed the spotlight. I missed being out there in front of the crowd, wrestling. But I also took the time to become a better student of the game, and to analyze what my strengths and weaknesses were.

"I focused in on the mental part of wrestling. And I really studied the sport. You know, a lot of wrestlers say, 'I'm going to be an Olympic champion,' but 99.9 percent of them will never do it. And do you know why? They will give themselves an option out. They will say they got hurt or something interrupted them, or come up with something.

"But I made a true, deep commitment. And after I won my first world championship in 1987, I kept raising the bar. I no longer wanted to be just the best in my weight class, I wanted to be considered the best wrestler in the entire world, at any weight. I kept setting the bar higher and working with all I had to get there.

"I make a commitment that no other wrestler does," said Smith in an interview with the *Los Angeles Times* in 1992. "There are probably a few wrestlers out there who think they make a commitment. But I really make a commitment. Anything that gets in my way, I pretty much eliminate."

He explained that such a lofty commitment involves a high cost.

"I don't have too many close friends," he said. "I don't have too many close relationships. I just can't afford to have them to go where I want to go, to do what I want to do. I really focus on myself. I really figure out and find a way how I can win, how I can beat everybody.

"I'll do whatever it takes. Put it this way: I've never had a girlfriend I've been good to. Because I'd blow them off when it was time to go to work. I'd say, 'Don't come around. I don't want to (see you).' It's been hard on some of those girls. They don't understand it."

And then he offered the essence of his commitment: "But it's like, 'Hey, I'm in love with this more than I am with you.'"

Arnold Schwarzenegger, the man who brought bodybuilding into the mainstream in America through his charm, personality, and movies, was of the same mind-set as Smith when he was in his competitive years, back in the 1970s.

"If you want to be a champion you cannot have any kind of an outside negative force coming in to deflect you," said Schwarzenegger in the film *Pumping Iron.* "I have to cut my emotions off and be kind of cold, in a way, before competition. If someone steals my car, I don't care. I cannot be bothered. I trained myself for that."

"Listen, it's about making choices," said Smith. "I knew early on what I wanted . . . to be the best wrestler in the world, and I was determined nothing would get in the way. Nothing!"

Of course, not every athlete will go to the extremes that John Smith did to compete effectively in his sport. Thousands upon thousands are able to love their sport and still do well without making such sacrifices, particularly in the area of relationships. John Smith devised a formula that worked for him and that allowed him to become one of the best wrestlers ever. But when his competitive days were over, he became a strong family man, marrying and raising children. The same is true of Schwarzenegger.

Jim Gibbons, who was NCAA champion at Iowa State University in 1981 and coached his alma mater to the NCAA team title in 1987, is fully aware of the terrific commitment it takes to be a national champion. He also won three Iowa high school state titles and his brother, Joe, captured four state titles.

"When I was coaching at Iowa State, I would tell my wrestlers, 'Guys, you're going to come to a fork in the road. That's where you figure out what it takes to be successful in this sport. That's when you decide if you're going to pay the price it requires . . . or if you decide it's not worth it.'

"You plant the flag, so to speak. You say, 'This is my territory. This is what I want . . . to be a state champion or a national champion. This is what will define me in terms of who I am as an athlete.' But it comes from your commitment.

"It's a fork in the road that all wrestlers, and all athletes, face at various times in their careers."

That theory applies to wrestlers of all ages, and at all levels. They must constantly evaluate the situation and make their own determination as to the depth of their commitment. It is a very personal decision.

In chapter 19 we will explore in detail how one can find a balance between commitment to the sport and building a fulfilling life off the mat. Many wrestlers have been able to use the lessons they learned in the practice room to help them succeed in a wide range of ventures, from serving in the United States Congress to writing popular books, from working in films to working everyday jobs. Ben and John Peterson, both Olympic champions, are excellent examples of learning to excel both in wrestling and in life off the mat.

One can strike a balance by being aware of the various priorities—even writing them down on a sheet of paper and reviewing them from time to time. But one has to be truthful when compiling such a list, pay attention to the way the priorities are ranked, and then stick to it. That approach will be the key to balancing one's life.

MAKING SACRIFICES

Sacrifice is another word for dedication. All top athletes are aware of what it means to make sacrifices, but none more than those who choose the sport of wrestling. Among scholastic sports, wrestling is alone when it comes to the sacrifices that athletes must make with regard to diet and food.

"You've got to make sacrifices, you can't be the norm," said Dan Gable. "If you're with the mainstream, you will probably achieve average results. It depends on what you want. The amount that you're willing to sacrifice is directly proportional to your desire for success" (Arangio 2002).

Kurt Angle was focused and committed at an early age, as well. That commitment extended off the mat in his lifestyle choices, and it led him to a pair of NCAA titles for Clarion University and gold medals at the world championships in 1995 and the Olympics in 1996.

"If they wanted to get high, they didn't call me," Angle said of his friends in high school and college. "I'm not going to say I never touched alcohol, but I made sure I never smoked dope or took drugs. Nobody ever tried to force them on me, either, because they knew how serious I was about what I was doing.

"You talk to people from my high school days about what direction I was headed and they'll say they knew I was going to do something special like win the Olympics. Years later a lot of them told me they used to say, 'This kid's so focused. Nobody's going to stop him.' Everyone knew I was special except for me. I just thought I was doing my thing. Some kids got straight As; I won wrestling titles" (Angle 2001, 43).

Angle was on a mission to become the best 220-pound amateur wrestler in the entire world, and he dedicated himself as few others ever have.

"There were the countless trips overseas to Russia, Turkey and Bulgaria over the years, grueling odysseys that took as long as 38 hours, one way, with connecting flights, all in search of the world's best competition," he said. "And there were all those insane days of training when I pushed myself to the brink of passing out, weeks and months when I was obsessed with winning a gold medal" (Angle 2001, 43).

Matt Furey is another athlete who understands the principles of sacrifice and dedication. Furey placed second in the Iowa state high school tournament as a senior and opted to try the Hawkeye system. He learned an incredible amount in the Hawkeye room, banging heads with the best wrestlers in America, day after day. After two years, he knew it would be near impossible to crack the Hawkeye lineup with his limited skills and background, no matter how big a price he was willing to pay. So he transferred to Edinboro University, a Division II school in Pennsylvania, and competed for coach Mike Deanna, a product of the Gable system who was a four-time All-American as a Hawkeye. At Edinboro, Furey flourished to the point that he captured the Division II national title at 167 pounds in 1985.

He then began studying all forms of wrestling like few other athletes of the past 50 years. Nearly obsessed, Furey became world champion in kung fu wrestling and the nation's leading expert in the nearly forgotten style of "catch-as-catch-can" wrestling.

Furey expanded on the theme of commitment in a brief article entitled "Excuses vs. Commitment to Success." His writing was inspired by Lance Armstrong's sixth straight win in the grueling Tour de France bicycle race through the mountains.

Furey started with a quote from 19th century writer Rudyard Kipling: "There are six million reasons for failure, but not a single excuse."

"How right Mr. Kipling was, and how often I wish he were wrong," wrote Furey. "But the fact is that once you remove all excuses, all obstacles to your success go away, as well. Before I went to China in 1997, I read George Jowett's classic, *Unrevealed Secrets of Man.* If I hadn't read this book, I don't know that I would have won. It inspired me *that* much; helped me train harder and remove all excuses.

"The following Jowett quote is my favorite. It gives me goose bumps, even today. It goes as follows: 'The MAN INSIDE could not move to fulfill your purpose. That is why you fell down. No other reason in the world.'

"I'm betting that Lance Armstrong is in total agreement. And I'm also betting that the excuse makers will get violently upset at quotes like these. It puts the onus where they don't want it: on themselves. It's always easier to point the finger and say you can't succeed because of this, that or the other thing. But always remember: Excuses don't lead to success.

"Focused action and a firm commitment to success are the keys to a great future. It doesn't matter whether you're talking about fitness or fighting; academics or career success—success starts on the inside and works its way outward, not the other way around."

Paul Brown, a former coach and owner of the Cleveland Browns, is considered one of the most important figures in the long and illustrious history of the NFL. He understood what it took to make it in the NFL as a player, coach, and owner.

"The only thing that counts is your dedication to the game," said Brown. "You run on your own fuel; it comes from within you" (Ferguson 1990, 2-12).

In 1983 one of America's most successful wrestlers decided to try to make a comeback and earn a spot on the United States Olympic team. Russ Camilleri, age 46, was the proud owner of 13 national titles in freestyle and Greco-Roman wrestling and had already been a member of two Olympic teams and five world teams. He had retired to his Missouri farm years earlier, yet he was determined to try it one last time.

"All elite athletes are driven by issues of identity," said Robert W. Grant, a leading sports psychologist and author. "They have literally trapped themselves in their sport. The more of their lives and self-esteem they put into it, the harder it is to let go" (Clarkson 1999, 81).

Camilleri had enjoyed an extremely successful career, yet he was either unfulfilled or had, as Grant says, trapped himself into his sport and was finding it difficult to let go. And he picked the University of Iowa practice room to work toward the nearly impossible goal. There, he came face to face with another such athlete, one who had turned his passion and drive into coaching and was blazing a new frontier.

Camilleri's commitment was inspiring, but his body simply couldn't hold up to the grueling demands. Battered and weary physically, he eventually had to surrender the dream, but not before he had gained the admiration of wrestlers two decades younger who were in the same room, working toward the same goals. When Camilleri left for his Missouri farm, he took with him a large measure of respect and a new outlook on what wrestling had become in his absence, at least at the University of Iowa.

"I have been in programs all over the country for years, but I've never seen anything like Dan Gable," Camilleri said. "He is a genius, the absolute best, ever. He just plain outworks everyone and it carries over to his kids, or anyone who's around him" (Banach 1985, 109).

Camilleri had gained an understanding that many others had come to know through pounds of sweat and yards of tape. This comprehension does not come easily. One who did understand was Mark Mysnyk, who came to Iowa as a three-time state high school champion from New York. A workout fanatic of seemingly unlimited endurance, Mysnyk cracked the Hawkeye lineup but never placed in the national tournament. Few had worked so hard or learned so much, in or out of the wrestling room. When he graduated with his bachelor's degree, he compiled a record that was the envy of every student who ever cracked a book: He had earned As in every single class over four years but one, in which he received a B.

Mysnyk became a physician and stayed in the Iowa City area, where he has given a great deal back to the sport. For years, he ran a successful sport symposium to which he brought experts in every aspect of wrestling, ranging from nutrition to weight training to technique. He also wrote a book titled *Wrestling the Iowa Way*.

Dr. Mysnyk's explanation of the importance of the mind in wrestling is simple and to the point. "Most men stop when they begin to tire," he said. "Good men go until they think they are going to

Terry Brands controls a foe during the 1993 world championships in Toronto. Brands won world titles in both 1993 and 1995 and claimed a bronze medal at 127.75 pounds in the 2000 Olympics.

collapse. But the very best know the mind tires before the body and push themselves further and further, beyond all limits. Only when these limits are shattered can the unattainable be reached."

PERSEVERING THROUGH PAIN

Overestimating the value of commitment to achieving any goals in life would be difficult. For one to accomplish anything out of the ordinary takes commitment to the goal. That dedication is what seems to separate the elite athletes, the true champions, from the rest of the pack. The careers of Arnold Schwarzenegger and Terry Brands provide two excellent examples.

Schwarzenegger was born in humble circumstances in a small town in Austria. His father was the local police chief, his mother was a homemaker, and he had an older brother. The family had little extra money. But young Arnold had a passion. He wanted to excel at something. He tried several sports, but he was hooked when he began to lift weights. He loved the feeling of the blood surging through his veins and pumping up his muscles. In the movie *Pumping Iron*, he compared a pump to having an orgasm.

After he decided to commit himself to the goal of becoming the best bodybuilder in the world, nothing could deter him. He trained with a fanatical approach seldom seen at any level of sport. He once entered a small gym in subfreezing weather and found out the heating system was broken and everyone else had left the gym. Nevertheless, he begged the gym owner to let him stay and work out. The gym owner came back later in the night to find the young Schwarzenegger still lifting hard, bundled up in a parka and blowing steam. He also found little patches of blood on the iron bar where Arnold's hands had stuck to it as he performed his curls.

In the movie *Pumping Iron*, which almost overnight made Schwarzenegger a cultural icon, he explained how important the acceptance of pain is to success in the world of bodybuilding. In fact, bodybuilders seek pain as few other athletes do, because they know that only when a muscle enters the fatigue stage, the painful stage, will growth come about. With the acceptance of pain comes an overall commitment that few elite athletes can look beyond.

"The body isn't used to the 9th, 10th, 11th and 12th rep," Schwarzenegger said, "so that makes the body grow, going through the pain barrier, experiencing pain in your muscles, the aching—just to go on and on and on—the last 2 or 3 repetitions, that's what makes the muscles, and divides one from being a champion and not being a champion.

"If you can go through this pain barrier you may get to be a champion—if you can't go through it, forget it! And that's what most people lack—is the having the guts to go in and say, 'I don't care what happens!' It aches and if I fall down. . . . I have no fear of fainting in the gym, because I know it could happen. I threw up many times while working out. But it doesn't matter because it is all worth it."

Handling pain is one of the key elements to success in all sports, especially in combative sports like boxing and wrestling. When two athletes come together head to head, with the explicit purpose of defeating the other by trying to overpower him or her, stress will inevitably result, both physically and mentally. Twisted fingers, banged-up knees, cauliflower ears, and broken noses are common (and painful) distractions in the world of wrestling.

Terry Brands experienced intense and long-lasting pain in 1996 when he failed to make the United States Olympic team. He and Kendall Cross had battled ferociously for several years to be the best 125.5-pound wrestler in the world. Kendall placed sixth in the 1992 Olympics, and Terry made the world team at that weight for the next three years, winning the gold medal in both 1993 and 1995.

At the 1996 Olympic trials in Spokane, Washington, the two warriors were as evenly matched as any two wrestlers could possibly be, yet their styles were vastly different. Cross was a wide-open, go-for-broke wrestler capable of scoring points in sensational flurries, whereas Brands was a relentless, pounding wrestler who never gave an opponent a moment's respite.

Brands won the first match in the two-out-of-three series, 7-2. Then Cross fought back to take a 7-6 win in the second bout, tying the series. The pressure on both athletes for the final match was overwhelming. Terry's twin brother, Tom, had already made the team at 136.5 pounds with two straight wins over John Fisher, and Terry desperately wanted to join him on the U.S. squad. But Cross was chasing a lifelong dream as well.

In the final bout, before a packed crowd holding its collective breath with every move, the two warriors fought with all they had. Cross emerged with an 8-7 victory. He went on to win the gold medal in Atlanta without a great deal of difficulty. He stated afterwards that wrestling Brands was the toughest part of winning the gold medal and went a long way in preparing him for the Olympic competition.

Holding his weight near the 125.5-pound mark for another four years to have another shot at the Olympics was almost too much for Brands to contemplate or endure. He was recently married and eager to start his coaching career. He had emotional forces tearing at him from every angle. He was already a two-time world champion, two-time NCAA champion, and World Cup champion. Perhaps it was time to move on.

Yet he could not let go of his Olympic aspirations. He had committed himself to that dream years earlier, as a youngster back in Sheldon, Iowa. He and his twin brother, Tom, worked nonstop for 20 years as part of that dream.

Facing incredible odds, he decided to keep wrestling. He took a long break and then began competing again. The toughest moment came at the world championships of 1998. Before the event, Brands collapsed in his hotel room. The strain of pulling down to 127.75 pounds again was too much for his body. He weighed nearly 145 pounds in normal circumstances and was lean and hard at that higher weight. The cut was simply too much to maintain year after year.

Shortly after, Terry Brands announced that he was retiring from wrestling. It seemed that he would never realize the dream.

But 12 months later, he was back. He entered the 2000 Olympic trials in Dallas and fought his way up through the rankings ladder. In the final wrestle-offs, he scored two decisions over Kerry Bouman, the second win coming in overtime, to make the Olympic team.

After the win that clinched his spot on the team, Brands ran from the mat area to the back of the arena. He sprinted 20 yards several times and then collapsed against the wall, his weary body sagging in relief. His brother, Tom, joined him for an emotional embrace. Terry had met one goal—to be an Olympian. He had kept his commitment to himself, overcoming the most demanding situations imaginable.

"It's been a long four years. I'm so pumped up right now," Brands told the assembled members of the press. "But it isn't just me. I owe a lot of people. Without Christ and God, I don't exist."

Like Schwarzenegger years earlier, Brands remained true to himself and overcame the pain, both mental and physical, of training to keep the commitment. Arnold said he didn't care if he passed out or threw up because "it was all worth it." The same was true for Terry Brands and for many other wrestlers who become champions at the highest level.

All great wrestlers have been totally committed to their sport, their dreams, their training, and their preparation. They understood that the extent of their success was directly related to the depth of their commitment.

SUMMARY

Commitment and dedication must go hand in hand with sacrifice when an athlete makes a decision to be the best that he or she can be. First, an athlete has to make a commitment to the sport and the chosen course of action. The commitment is marked by dedication to carry out the necessary workload. Never missing practices and giving each practice everything he or she has are the keys to dedication, but it extends beyond that.

Athletes must dedicate themselves to long-term goals as well as short-term goals, decide what it is that they want from the sport, and then go after it with total commitment. They will need to engage in self-introspection first and then sacrifice to get to the top. Excuses are not part of the program, so athletes must wipe excuses from their minds. They simply don't exist in the world of elite athletes. Next on the agenda is to take a hard look at desire and discipline.

5

Gaining Desire and Discipline

In the popular movie *Troy*, released in the summer of 2004, Brad Pitt starred as Achilles, generally accepted as the greatest warrior of all time. After a particularly hard day of fighting at the Trojan War around 1180 B.C., Achilles returns to his tent and begins a conversation with the slave girl, Briseis.

"What do you want?" Briseis asks Achilles at one point.

He responds in terms that Pete Rose, Larry Bird, Brett Favre, and John Smith would understand: "I want what all men want. I just want it more!" says Achilles.

Wanting something more than anyone else does is a key ingredient to attaining stunning success. Olympic champions have a greater desire for success than their opponents do and are willing to pay a higher price in terms of sacrifice, dedication, and output. Although not an Olympic champion, Arnold Schwarzenegger won the top title in bodybuilding, called Mr. Olympia, seven times. He has been a huge success in everything he has tried—bodybuilding, real estate, acting, and politics—driven by his desire and his discipline to be someone special.

"I dreamed of coming to America and being different from everybody else," he said in his breakthrough movie, *Pumping Iron*.

"Legendary players like baseball's Pete Rose (who was not drafted by a major league team) and basketball's Larry Bird didn't necessarily have legendary physical prowess," wrote Michael Clarkson in his book *Competitive Fire*, "but they made up for it with their motivation to succeed. They *wanted* it more than others did, so they did what it took to get it. They practiced harder, they studied their skills and their opponents, and they worked harder in games. They sacrificed their personal lives and gave up vacations. They took more risks. Their motivation seemed to come from desire, sometimes bordering on manic desire" (1999, 69-70).

For years, a thin, young runner in Wichita, Kansas, was determined to bring the world record in the mile run back to America. Jim Ryun was on a relentless quest, running at odd hours every day, for years, in pursuit of his dream: "The climate in Kansas varies from ice, deep snow, and blizzards in winter to 100-degree heat in summer. Through it all, Ryun ran. Every day, twice a day. Hot or cold, rainy or sunny, he ran," wrote Phil Pepe (Shields 1987). In June 1966 Ryun's dream came true when he set the world record in a time of 3 minutes, 51.3 seconds.

People in elite wrestling circles often say that to become a wrestler of Olympic stature, the athlete must be selfish. Training and dedication to the pursuit and the goal must come before anything else. Personal relationships don't flourish under such a system. Exceptions to the rule exist, of course, but in this case there aren't many.

In addition, an athlete must believe in himself or herself to the point of seeming arrogant and self-absorbed. The athlete must make a total commitment to the objective—something that 99 percent of good athletes cannot do, for one reason or another. Therefore, commitment becomes the great divide between the truly legendary performers and the merely very good performers.

"You have to believe you're great," said Favre, one of the finest quarterbacks in the history of the National Football League and a three-time league MVP. "You have to have an air about you. My success wasn't because I was a great talent, but because I wanted it more than anybody else. Every minute I step on that field, I want to prove I'm the best player in the league."

WILLPOWER

How does one go about preparing for the type of success that Brett Favre is talking about? Preparing for success comes from two sources: (1) the way you practice day in and day out, and (2) the way you compete. Those two factors build the foundation required when desire and determination kick in, taking performance to a new high. At that point, one's desire becomes the propelling element.

Some athletes blessed with sensational physical skills never quite go over the top because they do not have the desire to drive themselves that high. On the other hand, athletes of moderate ability have reached Olympic heights almost exclusively because of their desire to succeed at that level.

"There were times when deep down inside I wanted to win so badly I could actually will it to happen. I think most of my career has been based on desire," said Chris Evert, the winner of 18 Grand Slam singles titles in tennis.

Golfing superstar Tiger Woods believes that "you can never turn a switch on and off. It's got to always be on."

Woods could have been speaking about the Brands twins, Terry and Tom. Few athletes can match them when it comes to dedication, drive, and attitude. As a pair, they won five NCAA titles for the University of Iowa, three world championships, and two Olympic medals, a gold and a bronze. Along the way, they developed a reputation that stretched around the world for their incredible displays of heart and intensity.

When he walked off the mat for the final time at the 1996 Olympics, Tom left a legacy that may be impossible to duplicate in the years ahead—one of total commitment and dedication to the sport he loved. But Tom Brands is quick to say it was more than that which allowed him two win three NCAA titles, five freestyle national titles, the 1993 world championships, and the 1996 Olympics.

"I *willed* it to happen," said Tom, the intensity flowing out of him as he sat in his comfortable home in Iowa City. The lower level of the house provides evidence of the Brands' commitment to working out. It is filled with weightlifting equipment of all types, as well as a mat and sauna bath. Motivational posters dot the wall and the walls of his den. His bookshelf is stacked with inspirational books about some of the most fascinating men in history. He ranks legendary World War II General George Patton among his favorite subjects to study.

"Patton was constantly testing himself, throughout his life," said Brands. "I like that philosophy."

DISCIPLINE PLUS

Pushing themselves to the brink and testing themselves in many ways was commonplace for Tom and Terry Brands for two decades. And inspiration was a huge part of their careers; in fact, Tom said that inspiration was the single most important aspect of his success.

"I remember asking at the very beginning of my wrestling career, when I was maybe 7 years old, what is the very highest level you can get to?" he said. "They told me about the Olympics and Dan Gable. Then I went to a wrestling camp at the University of Nebraska at the age of 12, and Chris Campbell was there. He was talking about how he had made the Olympic team, but President Carter boycotted the games. He was very emotional, and that made a very strong impression on me, even at such a young age.

"At age 12, wrestling and its possibilities hooked me and grabbed me so hard."

Wrestling also grabbed his twin brother, Terry, and the two of them set out in their small town of Sheldon, Iowa, to become wrestling legends. They played other sports, like baseball and football, but they knew they were going to be too small to compete in those sports in college. Besides, they already had an attitude that was perfect for wrestling. They were extremely aggressive.

The twins met with success early, with Terry claiming two Iowa state high school championships and Tom winning one. In a state where two- and three-time state champions are common, they did not stand out from the field. But they were laying a solid foundation for much bigger goals and achievements down the road. And they had to learn how to will themselves to reach the higher levels.

During his sophomore year in high school, Tom heard Dan Gable give a talk about wrestling and dedication. "I was blown away," he said. "I went home and wrote down the words, 'I'm going to be one of Gable's boys.'"

Then he set out to brainwash himself! "We became obsessed," he said, the intensity blazing in his eyes. "We had notebooks, dozens of them."

He wheeled around, dug through file drawers, pulled out a stack of thick notebooks, and threw them on the table. "I still have them, from my high school days," he said. "Look what I wrote." He opened the first of 10 books and threw it on the desk. Page after page after page after page was filled with the same handwriting, and the same message: "I WILL go undefeated this season." Then, a dozen pages later, appeared a new message: "I will win the state title this year."

Ginger Robinson

Tom Brands works for a single-leg takedown during the 1995 world championships in Atlanta, Georgia. Tom won the world title at 136 pounds in 1993, slipped to ninth in 1995, and came back to win an Olympic gold medal in 1996.

The notebooks contained hundreds of pages of such declarations, simple and short. Many of the pages were dedicated to beating a certain wrestler, one he had never defeated before. The books included many other declarations.

"I brainwashed myself," he said, gritting his teeth. "I had dozens of these notebooks, all filled up with messages. So did Terry. We wrote in them every night, to keep our goals clear and in front of us. And it worked for us."

He recounted a story that showed his determination and focus at a very early age. "I got in a fight in sixth grade in the playground. This kid made fun of me because he heard me say I was going to be an Olympic champion some day. So I went after him. I didn't feel he had the right to make fun of my dreams.

"I got pulled into the office of a teacher, who was also the wrestling coach, Galen Nelson. He looked angry and said, 'What's going on with you?' I told him the kid said I couldn't be an Olympic champion. Nelson acted like he was angry and I was crying because I was so upset. But years later he told me he could hardly stop from laughing. He didn't want me fighting but he loved that attitude he saw in a young kid . . . a young kid who had a dream of winning the Olympics."

Even after graduating from high school, Tom found that he had a long way to go to be a champion in college, let alone at the highest level possible. He lost 15-0 in a freestyle match to Dan Knight, an undefeated, four-time state champion from Clinton, a city on the opposite side of the state from Sheldon.

But Gable saw something in the Brands boys that he loved, and he recruited them hard. When they showed up in the fall of 1987 to start college and begin their training under Gable, something magical happened.

"It was an explosion!" says Tom, clenching his fists for emphasis. "Mixing the Brands desire with the Gable philosophy and training methods caused an explosion!"

"When love and discipline come together you have great chemistry," says Rick Pitino, basketball coach at the University of Louisville. The proof of that statement could be found in the Iowa wrestling room for the two decades of the Gable era. It was epitomized by the arrival of the Brands brothers.

The Brands' love of wrestling was matched by an iron discipline that never gave in or bent during their long sojourn through the sport. The Brands brothers responded to the spartan training methods of the Hawkeyes program as few others ever have, or could. The harder the workouts, the more they thrived. At first, they could hardly score on the more senior wrestlers in the room, but they never stopped and never took a backward step.

"The Brands boys were unbelievable," said Randy Lewis, 1984 Olympic champion, years later. "I was out of college wrestling but still training in the room when they arrived. I can remember when they couldn't even score a point in a workout, but they never stopped, ever. They gave all they had, in every practice, every day, every week, and every year. No one ever worked like they did."

The education was nonstop, year around. The Brands wanted all they could get, and then some.

"I remember when Gable drove a group of us out to Colorado Springs in the summer of 1990 to see the world team training there," said Tom. "It was a great experience. It brought into clear focus what we needed to do to get to that level. It educated me.

We got to meet people like Dave Schultz and Bruce Burnett, the national coach. We learned so much, and learned that we had so much yet to learn."

INTENSITY AND EFFORT

The Iowa room had plenty of intensity to feed off, with NCAA champions hanging around the practice room to continue their training. Two other wrestlers who arrived in Iowa City the same year as the Brands boys were a set of twins from North Dakota, Troy and Terry Steiner. They were cut from the same mold.

"The Steiners and the Brands, we were all masochists," said Tom. "The Steiners are great people, great trainers. They trained incredibly hard, all 12 months of the year. We all fed off each other."

Then Brands gave a remarkable insight into his success: "Some people, even some top coaches, think it's all skill and training, but it's not always that. Sometimes, that just isn't enough. Other guys have great skills and are training very hard, too. So what's the difference? How will I beat them? Sometimes, it's solved with plain effort. And intensity."

Intensity made the difference for both Tom and Terry Brands, carrying them from good high school careers to great college careers, and then to world and Olympic titles. For Tom Brands, it started on a playground in Sheldon, Iowa, when another young boy made fun of him for daring to dream big. He took that negative experience and used it to motivate him for 20 years, and then he willed the dream to come true. His is a powerful message for other young boys and girls who aspire to greatness even though their talents may be little more than average. His message resonates all through the world of sport—from wrestling to basketball to golf. Intensity, born of desire, is one of the magical ingredients for success.

"The harder you work, the harder it is to surrender," said Pat Summitt, the superb women's basketball coach at the University of Tennessee.

"To win you must have talent and desire—but desire is first," said golf legend Sam Snead.

"Even when I went to the playground, I never picked the best players (for my team)," said basketball star Magic Johnson. "I picked the guys with less talent, but who were willing to work hard, who had the desire to be great."

SOMETHING EXTRA

Another Hawkeye wrestler, Lou Banach, demonstrated how strong his desire was by making serious adjustments all during his superb career at Iowa. A native of Port Jervis, New York, Lou arrived at Iowa in the fall of 1978 with his twin brother, Eddie. After a redshirt year, both made the lineup as freshmen, but the results could not have been more different by the end of the season. While Eddie won the 177-pound NCAA title in his first shot at it, Lou wound up quitting the team, frustrated by the tremendous amount of weight cutting he underwent to make the 190-pound class.

After some serious soul searching, Lou came back a year later, determined to make the team at heavyweight. At six feet and 220 pounds, he was powerful and had explosive quickness and highly crafted skills. He also had a huge heart and extraordinary dedication and commitment.

After committing to wrestling at heavyweight, Lou developed a specialized training program designed to take him to the top of the collegiate heavyweight ranks. One "area I worked on—and I mean worked—was running," he wrote in his book *The New Breed: Living Iowa Wrestling* (Banach 1985). "I never ran in high school mainly because it wasn't fashionable, or in my training repertoire. Runs of three to four miles every other day soon became a common occurrence in my life. Slowly, but acceptably, I continued the running program, supplementing the distance runs with dashes up the sharp flights of steps at the old field house, real runners' sprints—things all foreign to the average heavyweight."

But there was more for this fired-up young wrestler. "I switched my thoughts to mental toughness. I was a small heavyweight and not the strongest, either, but I felt I was going to be the most determined. I kept telling myself all the running, lifting and technique drilling I was doing would give me the deciding edge in any match. I always tried to do one more rep on weights or one last sprint, or one more minute of hard wrestling than I thought I could. And it paid off many times in the months ahead. Many matches I won were won because I never quit mentally or physically" (Banach 1985, 45).

Usually outweighed by a considerable amount during his next three years, Lou Banach turned in one remarkable performance after another. He captured two NCAA titles and finished third as a junior, losing only 1 match in 16 NCAA bouts during his career.

That one loss came in overtime to Steve Williams of Oklahoma, a tremendously powerful wrestler who outweighed Lou by nearly 60 pounds. In an earlier match, Banach had suffered a separated shoulder but chose to continue competing.

During his career, Lou pinned—not merely beat, but pinned—a number of outstanding heavyweights, including Steve Williams (in the dual meet), Bruce Baumgartner, Tab Thacker, and Wayne Cole. Baumgartner and Thacker would both become NCAA champions, and Thacker weighed 410 pounds to Banach's 220 pounds at the time of his pinning. Cole was fourth and second in the NCAA and usually held a 30- to 40-pound edge on Lou. Banach also scored victories over Russ Hellickson, winner of 12 national freestyle titles and an Olympic silver medal winner, and Dan Severn, two-time All-American from Arizona State who went on to become champion of the Ultimate Fighting Championships (UFC).

But his biggest challenge, literally, came during his senior year at Iowa. In a dual meet, he found himself facing Mitch Shelton, a 400-pounder from Oklahoma State. Never one to hold back, Lou threw his 220-pound body at the much larger man, trying to take him to his back for a quick pin. Instead, Lou wound up on his back, with all of Shelton's 400 pounds bearing down on him. Lou fought off the pin for what seemed like hours before finally hearing the sound of the referee's hand on the mat signaling the pin.

Shaken, Lou had to rethink his entire philosophy of the sport. Like his twin, Ed, he believed in all-out assault. When a friend reminded him of how successful Muhammad Ali's rope-a-dope strategy was against the larger and more powerful George Foreman, Lou still wasn't convinced that he could mentally change to a less aggressive style of match.

"Make it more like a chess match than a slug-out," cautioned the friend.

Meeting Shelton in the semifinal round of the 1983 NCAA championships, Banach wrestled a smart and strategic match. He was no longer preoccupied with pinning Shelton but, rather, with defeating him. The result was a 3-1 victory. "It wasn't pretty, but it was a win," said Banach afterward.

"Sometimes you have to win ugly," said Vinny Testaverde, a longtime NFL quarterback and Heisman Trophy winner.

Banach had used Sam Snead's advice as well, letting his desire to be a champion be the most important ingredient in his victory. He closed out his career a year later by winning an Olympic gold medal at 220 pounds in Los Angeles. He retired from wrestling to become a successful high-level banker in Milwaukee. For many years, he gave credit for his wrestling successes to his dedication and commitment to train himself to become the best heavyweight rather than starving himself to be a good 190-pounder.

SUMMARY

"Many coaches believe that an athlete's success depends on four factors: physical ability, physical training, mental training, and desire or *drive*. The percentages of these four factors may vary from athlete to athlete and even with the same athlete from game to game. Many psychologists say that it is the desire, the passion, and the ambition, that separates high achievers from the rest of the field, even from others with equal or more talent . . ." (Clarkson 1999, 69).

Pete Rose wasn't even drafted by a professional team during his amateur days, but he became the all-time leading hitter in major league history. He did it through an insatiable desire, simply wanting to be a major league player and the best player he could be. Desire took him to the top of the baseball world.

Desire is an extremely powerful force. Desire can be developed, but it must be nurtured to stay strong and healthy. When coupled with discipline, it can move mountains and will result in high accomplishments for an athlete.

6

Adding Intensity and Effort

One day in 1997, a sportswriter from a major newspaper on the East Coast was given an intriguing assignment. He was to travel to Indiana and find out why the Hoosier state is so preoccupied with basketball, journey down to Texas to answer the same question about football, and finish up in Iowa to unravel the mystery of the state's long-lasting love affair with the sport of wrestling.

He didn't know anything about wrestling but was determined to get to the heart of the matter. He arranged an interview with several Iowa newspapermen who he felt could offer some insights and then spent several days in Iowa City. The trip changed his entire perspective of what sports are all about in America.

"It was an incredible experience," the journalist said later. "I was totally unprepared for what I saw in the Iowa practice room. I saw Tom Brands, Lincoln McIlravy, Joe Williams, and guys like that working out in conditions I had never dreamed of. The pain, the determination, the commitment were amazing. I had never seen anything like it in sports. They are like warriors from a bygone era.

"But most of all, it was the intensity. The intensity was so thick in that room hour after hour, day after day, that it drained me, just watching.

"I went back to my newspaper and told the entire sports staff that the greatest untold sports story in the country is taking place in Iowa City, Iowa, and hardly anyone knows it. It was an incredible experience for me."

The intensity of the Iowa wrestling room is not for the faint of heart. Athletes who entered the room during Dan Gable's tenure as coach and expected to survive a workout had to have some degree of mental preparation for what they could expect. Even a fanatical trainer like Kurt Angle, in the midst of his preparations for the 1996 Olympics and in superb shape, was shocked by what he experienced.

"If I really wanted to punish myself, I'd go to Dan Gable's wrestling facility in Iowa," he wrote. "He's known for holding the most intense practices in the country. I worked hard on my own, but Gable had a way of pushing you beyond what you thought you were capable of doing. As a coach, he'd pound you into the mat to where you couldn't walk, and then he'd pound you some more.

"He'd put us through a series of drills, then have us do some live wrestling. Then we'd do sprints, climb ropes, a series of calisthenics. And then we'd wrestle live some more. It was nonstop for two and a half hours, with nothing but a 30-second break for a drink once in a while."

Angle describes a certain day when the workout was incredible. Everyone was about to break. "After a while I started looking at the other wrestlers. But they're all scared to death of Gable. He's got that aura about him. They're like, 'Just keep going.'"

After more torture, Angle said, "I wanted to die right there. I had nothing left and I had to wrestle for another 40 minutes straight. But that was typical Dan Gable. Guys know what they're getting into when they go to wrestle for him" (Angle 2001, 86, 87).

The University of Iowa doesn't have a monopoly on intensity, of course, although many feel that Gable took the intensity to new levels at both Iowa State as a competitor and at Iowa as coach. Jack Brisco, who won the NCAA 191-pound title in 1965 while at Oklahoma State and then went on to become one of the most popular world heavyweight professional champions of all time, told of the intensity in the Oklahoma State room. His workout partner much of his junior year was Joe James, a phenomenal athlete with a tremendous physique, one of the most impressive ever seen on a collegiate wrestling mat.

"Joe had the widest shoulders and the smallest waist of any athlete I have ever seen," related Brisco. "Joe was about six foot three and weighed 220 pounds of pure muscle. He had no fat on him. He made all the guys in those muscle magazines look as if they were sick. He was about as cut as anyone who ever stepped on the mat. The most amazing thing about Joe was that he was all natural; he never lifted a weight in his life, back then.

"And this was the guy I would have to face for two hours every day. One day at practice, he threw me hard. My leg caught a corner of the cinder block wall and I ripped open a huge gash in my leg that required 10 stitches. I was back on the mat two days later at practice and Joe threw me again. I hit the same corner with the same leg, broke open the stitches and had to have 10 more.

The intensity of wrestling shows on the face of this athlete as he charges into his foe, attempting to score a takedown.

"When we would hook up, Joe would always hold his hands out and try to interlock fingers as a test of strength. I would challenge him for a while but the strength in his hands was tremendous. He would crush my hands to the point that I couldn't close my hands after practice. Joe thought this was funny; I didn't. As much as I would try to avoid it he would always find a way to lock up my fingers. It got to the point that I was so frustrated that I told him, 'Damn it, Joe, cut it out. I can't even close my hands. The next time you do it, I am going to do something about it.' Joe said, 'OK, Jack, I'm sorry, I won't do it anymore.' He had promised me before and never kept it. Like I said, Joe was tough and he thought it was funny.

"We locked up and Joe grabbed my fingers again. I threw my head back and head-butted him, catching him square in the mouth. I split both his lips, bloodied his mouth and knocked out one of his front teeth. He let go of my hands, bent down and picked up his tooth from the mat, placed it on a ledge and locked up with me again. He never said a word about it, he just wrestled. However, he never did mess with my hands again" (Murdock 2004, 29).

During his years there as a competitor, John Smith said he would push himself and teammates in the Oklahoma State room to the point that they would begin throwing fists. Fistfights happen in other rooms around the country as well, but probably not as often as they did at Iowa when the Hawkeyes were winning 15 NCAA team championships in 21 seasons. The stories that have escaped from that overheated, intense room have become part of wrestling folklore.

When the Banach brothers, Ed and Lou, wrestled at Iowa (1979 through 1983), Coach Gable eventually installed a punching bag at the far end and often ordered Ed and Lou to go slug the bag when their tempers grew too spirited during brotherly work-outs. The Banachs won five national titles and two Olympic gold medals between them. After the Banachs left the room, the Brands brothers moved in shortly after with much the same results—five NCAA crowns, three world titles, one Olympic gold medal, and one Olympic bronze medal—and the same intensity took over.

Emotions can influence how one prepares for a sporting event, of course, and one's ability to psych up for the competition ahead. The two extremes of mental state are arousal, which occurs when an athlete is in a hyped state of excitement, and total calm, which comes when an athlete is completely confident that he or she has prepared perfectly for an event and is at peace with himself or herself.

Two of the best examples are the state of high arousal that Cassius Clay (now Muhammad Ali) showed at the weigh-in for his career-making fight with champion Sonny Liston in 1964, and the total peace that Evander Holyfield showed while he walked down the aisle to meet the ferocious Mike Tyson in 1996. Although Clay and Holyfield were at opposite ends of the scale, both turned in stunning upsets.

MAINTAINING CALM UNDER PRESSURE

Intensity can often create tremendous pressure. So can other factors, such as high expectations from fans, from teammates and coaches, and from the athlete himself or herself. The ability to comprehend the many intricacies of pressure and to handle them properly is crucial to athletic success. Not all athletes have the same reaction to pressure. Take the case of Evander Holyfield.

Few athletes in the past 50 years have faced as much pressure as Holyfield did on November 9, 1996, in Las Vegas. Although most boxing experts considered Holyfield one of the 10 best heavyweight champions ever, nearly all felt that he was long past his prime the night he faced Mike Tyson, one of the most feared sluggers of all time. Yet Holyfield was strangely serene in the days building up to the fight. Just before the event, he was seen in his dressing room listening to a spiritual song and singing along, smiling and bouncing, almost as though he were in a trance. Walking to the ring, he was calm and poised. Tyson, on the other hand, was like a caged tiger in his corner, stalking back and forth, rolling his tremendous shoulder muscles, glaring at the ringside spectators and Holyfield.

During the brief instruction period, Holyfield continued to give the appearance that he was about to engage in a friendly game of checkers rather than in one of the most savage pugilistic contests of modern times. The minute the bell rang, Holyfield took command of the fight. He peppered the charging Tyson with beautiful left jabs and stinging combinations. Halfway through the fight, fight fans around the world were stunned. It appeared that Holyfield just might win.

Then, in the sixth round, he decked Tyson with a beautiful left hook. Tyson rose, staggered physically and shaken to his core mentally. Holyfield was in complete control from that point on. Five rounds later, the referee stopped the fight to save a thoroughly beaten Tyson from being severely injured. Holyfield had shocked the world with a brutal and convincing technical knockout over a nearly invincible foe. He had dealt with the incredible mental pressure and had succeeded far beyond all expectations, except his own.

"Pressure bursts pipes," he said later. "I thank God for giving me peace of mind to overcome pressure. The difference between winning and losing is when pressure hits."

His peace of mind, which sprouted from total confidence in his preparation, carried him to victory that night. His execution of his game plan allowed him to be calm and poised and helped him avoid becoming embroiled in the overpowering emotional tug of the night.

"You don't win on emotion, you win on execution," Tony Dungy, head coach of the Indianapolis Colts, once said. Holyfield proved that true on the night he whipped Tyson and stopped him in the 11th round.

Although most wrestlers rely on arousal to prepare themselves, much can be said for the calm state of mind as well. Arousal is not always the secret to victory. A case in point is the incredible Ultimate Fighting Championship match between then-champion Tito Ortiz and former champion Randy Couture in 2003.

Ortiz entered the caged ring as though he were about to catch on fire. The glare from his eyes was stunning, and he began leaping up and down in a state of arousal that was chilling to watch. His technique had gone a long way in ensuring his dominating victory just months earlier in a sensational performance against Ken Shamrock, one of the most respected UFC fighters of all time. In that match, Ortiz had entered the cage in a near frenzy of emotion. His arousal techniques were awesome, and their effect showed on Shamrock's face as he watched the champion go through his paces just a few feet away. Ortiz dominated the fight from the outset, and the referee finally had to stop the match after Shamrock had taken a pounding.

But Couture, at age 40 a good 10 years older than Ortiz, was the picture of total calm as he walked toward the cage. He smiled faintly, nodded at fans chanting his name, and climbed into the ring to see Ortiz in a wild state of arousal. While Ortiz fixed him with a stare as cold as has been seen since the days of Sonny Liston, Couture merely smiled faintly at him and then turned his back on Ortiz and looked out into the crowd, smiling at friends. The inner athlete had taken over Randy Couture's persona.

Couture had considerable wrestling skills to draw on. He was a two-time NCAA runner-up at 190 pounds for Oklahoma State in the early 1990s and won four national Greco-Roman championships. In addition, he made four world teams and competed in four Olympic trials. In the match, Couture made use of his wrestling skills. He constantly took Ortiz to the mat and dominated him for five rounds, winning a unanimous decision.

Couture gives credit to both his personality and his mental training routine for allowing him to change his attitude since becoming a fighter.

"I tend to be a laid-back type of guy to begin with," Couture explained, "but the most important thing is the way you approach a fight mentally. When I was wrestling, I wanted to win so badly that I placed way too high expectations on myself, and too much pressure. It all built up inside me and sometimes it would leave me too tense to perform up to my best.

"When I started the mixed martial arts contests, I decided at the outset it was going to be mostly for fun. I analyzed what it was that was holding me back in wrestling—I was top-ranked in two of my four Olympic trials but didn't make the team either time—and I changed my attitude.

"I realized that the worst thing that could happen to me was to get knocked out, and also that if that was the worst thing that happened in life, well then I was doing OK. I knew my wife would still love me, that my mom would still love me, that all my friends would still feel the same way about me. So, it was no big deal.

"That way, I was able to alleviate a great deal of stress. I came to terms with the 'little voice' inside that controls what and how we think, and makes us who we are. I learned to control that little voice and to just relax and enjoy the experience. Just have some fun out there."

PSYCHING UP AND PSYCHING OUT

During his days as a top amateur wrestler, Couture had the opportunity to work with sports psychologists from time to time, and he knew the basics about controlling his thoughts and emotions. But it wasn't until he began the mixed martial arts events that he really was able to control them.

"The nature of the sport (of mixed martial arts) and everything that goes with it is so electric, with all the hype and huge crowds, that we really try to be relaxed in the dressing room," said Couture. "We tell jokes, listen to some music, keep it light. If I'm relaxed and enjoying the experience, I know I'm going to compete well and that's all I really care about. Competing as well as you can is the goal."

Something else that Randy Couture cares about is the respect that wrestling has gained from the success of all the wrestlers who have entered the mixed martial arts competitions around the globe.

"One of the things that I set out to do when I started was to represent the sport of wrestling in a class manner and with a great deal of respect. I love the sport of wrestling and wanted to do all I could to let people see how great it is."

Besides competing in tournaments, Couture offers seminars around the country, teaching mixed martial arts. He incorporates a great deal of wrestling technique, of course. Wrestling is a huge part of who he is as an athlete and the key to his tremendous success in his new sporting endeavors.

Bill Koll had discovered a powerful kind of controlled arousal five decades earlier in the quiet of his dormitory room on the campus of Iowa State Teachers College. With the window shades pulled down and sitting alone with his innermost thoughts, Koll could construct any vision he wanted to motivate himself. He could also control the power of the visions and how they acted on his psyche. He entered his matches with a calm demeanor that belied the inner storm, and he had a focus that was on the highest plane possible for athletic competition.

Few boxers ever fought with the ferocity of Stanley Ketchel. Known as the Michigan Assassin, he tore through the middleweight ranks in the 1905-1910 era, compiling knockout after knockout. The kid from Battle Creek, Michigan, was one of the most feared fighters ever to step in a ring. He lost only 4 of 61 fights and scored

50 knockouts. In one stretch, he knocked out 14 in a row, including some of the toughest fighters in the world. His method of psyching up was similar to that used by Bill Koll decades later.

"He would spend a couple of rounds psyching himself up to a fever pitch by imagining that his opponent had insulted his mother. With this finally fixed in his mind, and with his power of attention sufficiently accumulated, he would suddenly become transformed into a tiger and tear mercilessly into his foe" (Zabriskie 1976, 94).

And then there is Gable.

In the sport of wrestling, controlling one's emotions can be as important as controlling the opponent.

"Gable has spent a lifetime possessed by demon wrestling," wrote Douglas Looney. "Even Mack Gable (Dan's dad) says that after Dan won in Munich, 'They gave him all sorts of special dope tests, and I don't blame them. His eyes were glassy, and he was so psyched up. Getting psyched that high isn't good for you'" (Looney 1984, 500).

Neither was it good for his foes. Facing a psyched up Dan Gable, John Smith, Dan Hodge, Bill Koll, or Tom Brands wasn't much fun for their opponents, no matter what part of the planet they came from.

"And miraculously, Gable is able to take this intensity and transfer it to others," added Looney. "When he greets you and says, 'Good morning,' you have a sudden urge to run through the nearest wall or at the very least pin somebody."

Psyching out an opponent is another major part of any sports competition, particularly the one-on-one combative sports. Wrestlers like Gable and Smith were masters at it, as were Bill Koll and Dan Hodge. They raised the ante to a point that others capitulated before the match even began, most often without even realizing it.

A wrestler facing Koll in the late 1940s knew that he was going to tangle with one of the most ferocious competitors ever seen on a mat. Having returned from World War II as a man who had experienced life at its worst, Koll believed that wrestling was nothing to be timid about. He would demand that his opponent meet his level of tenacity and commitment or be in for a very tough night.

Hodge's strength and determination were legendary throughout the sports world. His hand strength was such that he was known to crush apples and snap the handles off pliers. When he wrestled Gary Kurdelmeier, a powerful Iowan who was to become NCAA champion the year after Hodge graduated, Hodge's fingers gripped Kurdelmeier's arms with such power that Kurdelmeier had black and blue spots on his arms for days afterward.

"When you knew you were going to wrestle Hodge, you didn't get many good nights of sleep," confessed Kurdelmeier decades later. "I think he scared most of his opponents into a form of paralysis."

Those lining up against Gable knew that Gable would test their endurance to its absolute maximum. He broke people mentally, because they could not pay the price that Gable would demand of them. Like Koll and Hodge before him, Gable was a devastating pinner, working his foes into exhaustion and then flopping them to their backs. All three of them—Koll, Hodge, and Gable—pinned their way through the NCAA tournament at least once in their careers. John Smith, on the other hand, dazzled his foes with a style that was nearly impossible to defend. His low single-leg attack, developed through his incredibly flexible hips, sent shivers of apprehension through his foes. But, like the other three, he was also a punishing, aggressive style of wrestler.

"Anyone who doesn't think John Smith was a physical and punishing wrestler never wrestled him," said Tom Brands, a three-time NCAA champion and 1996 Olympic gold medalist. "The first time I wrestled him in a freestyle tournament, I was young and unprepared for what hit me. He leg-laced me with such force and power that my legs were sore for a week!"

The physical style of wrestling of a champion can cause mental trauma for a foe. No one looked forward to wrestling Mark Churella in the late 1970s. A third-place NCAA finisher for the University of Michigan as a pure freshman, Churella won three straight NCAA titles. He won twice at 150 pounds and then moved up to 167 as a senior, pinning Iowa's multitalented Mike DeAnna in the finals.

"He was a very physical guy, one of the most punishing wrestlers of all time," said Mark Johnson, a two-time All-American on the same Michigan team at 177 pounds. "Every practice was a brutal session. You didn't want him to get the legs on you, no matter what. I think he had a psychological edge on a lot of guys before they even stepped on a mat with him."

Building a reputation for a punishing style of wrestling is an extremely effective form of psyching out an opponent. Down through the decades, such stars as Robin Reed, Bill Nelson, Tom Peckham, Cary Kolat, Mike Sheets, and many others have used such a reputation to advantage.

Few used it with such efficiency as Reed, who exploded on the athletic scene in the early 1920s. A tough and skinny kid from Oregon, he learned how to wrestle as a form of self-preservation. He ran away from home at an early age and prowled the docks and back streets of Portland, learning how to survive by using his wits and his wrestling skills, when needed. He developed a brutal hold known as a double wristlock, forcing foes to make a choice between going to their backs or having their elbows dislocated. Nearly all of them chose to be pinned.

Reed never lost an amateur match any time, any place, to anybody. In the 1924 Olympic trials, he weighed in at 134 pounds and won the trials in four weight classes. On the ship passage to the Olympic Games in Paris, he pinned several other Olympic teammates, including Harry Steele, who won the gold medal in the heavyweight division!

Reed then wrestled professionally for many years, traveling around the country and learning more joint lock submission holds from such legends as Farmer Burns and John Pesek. Many of his foes were psyched out the moment they knew they had to face him.

"You knew when you climbed into the ring with Reed that he was out to get that double wristlock on you, and that he would use it to its fullest extent," said Earl Conrad, an old-time wrestler from Reed's era, with over 6,000 matches to his credit. "It wasn't much fun if you valued your elbow and your arm. He was very intimidating. He psyched out most of his foes before they ever tied up with him."

Psyching an opponent out is a major part of any sports competition, particularly the one-on-one combative sports. But it can even extend into esoteric sports like bodybuilding. In the film *Pumping Iron*, Arnold Schwarzenegger is preparing to defend his coveted Mr. Olympia title in Pretoria, South Africa, in 1975. He works continually on the premeet mental state of his archrival, Lou Ferrigno, until at last Schwarzenegger declares, with a wry grin, where he is coming from: "He will be ready to lose. I will talk him into it," said the king. And, of course, his prediction came true. Schwarzenegger won his fifth straight title, with Ferrigno placing third, behind French star Serge Nubret.

"Most great athletes acknowledge state of mind as the key to success in sports," write the authors of *Sports Psyching*. They quote Patti Johnson, an Olympic hurdler: "Once you are physically capable of winning a gold medal, the rest is 90 percent mental," and baseball Hall of Famer Maury Wills: "It's all mental" (Tutko and Tosi 1976, 11).

"Emotions run the show in sports." That's the viewpoint of James E. Loehr, a sports psychologist who has worked with top stars in tennis and speed skating.

"But it's a delicate process, very intricate," he added. "Some emotions, like fear and rage, are disempowering and move you away from your optimal performance level, your ideal performance state. Others are empowering, like challenge and determination, and they move you towards it" (Clarkson 1999, 59-60).

SUMMARY

Psyching up, or preparing oneself mentally to compete, is one of the primary essentials of sports. Intensity and psyching up are two sides of the same coin. Intensity is the long-term drive and desire that the athlete is focusing into the thought process of competing, whereas psyching up is generally referred to as the short-term effect for an immediate match. Athletes need to recognize their own emotional characteristics, learn what techniques work for them in both areas, and then apply them.

When an athlete is able to reach a high state of anxiety or arousal and then focus on the task ahead, he or she will do well. But the athlete must recognize the danger of becoming so aroused that he or she loses focus and allows anger or anxiety to take over, forcing him or her to make errors in judgment or to shut down. Intensity and psyching up lead to true mental toughness.

7

Achieving the Right Mind-Set

Those who want to become great wrestlers can learn invaluable lessons from the best athletes in other sports. Cross-training has its purpose not only in the physical world but in the mental world as well. When it comes to being the absolute best, the principles are often interchangeable from one sport to another, especially in the areas where one goes to find the characteristics that allow athletes to push the barriers to the uppermost levels.

Arnold Schwarzenegger carved the greatest physique of his era through obsessive determination. But he also developed a game plan according to his own physical profile. He knew he had to work harder on some body parts than he did others because of his genetic makeup. The same is true of great boxers. Joe Frazier and Muhammad Ali fought three of the most sensational fights in history, but they were completely different in body type and ring style. Because Ali was taller and much faster than other heavy-weights, he preferred a style of stick and move, using his great natural quickness to stay out of harm's way. Frazier was built like a bull; he charged in full steam ahead, willing to take three punches to land a big left hook. They trained differently because they were completely different in both their styles and their approaches to the sport.

Obviously, wrestlers bring many different styles and physiques into competition. The same is true of their mind-sets. Some wrestlers are mean by nature and enjoy pounding on their opponents. Others love the technique side of the sport. Although some look on wrestling as a sport, others see it as a controlled fight. Wrestlers use different approaches and styles of preparation. You should establish a goal to identify your mental qualities and determine what style of preparation will work best for you.

Two of the great contrasts in preparation in boxing history are the approaches of Rocky Marciano and Muhammad Ali. Marciano retired undefeated in 1956 after fashioning a record of 49-0, with 43 knockouts. He was all ice water before a big fight. While his brothers and handlers worked themselves into a near frenzy discussing an upcoming battle, Marciano often slipped away to find a secluded spot to sleep.

Ali was the extreme opposite. He would work himself into a state of near hysteria, shouting at his opponents and making up names for them. His first fight against Sonny Liston, one of the most feared fighters in boxing history, is part of boxing folklore. Ali, then known as Cassius Clay, was a brash, fast-talking 21-year-old, whereas Liston was in his late 30s and liked to paralyze his foes with a hard, angry stare. Ali yelled at Liston and called him "the big ugly bear," shaking his fist at him. Many sportswriters thought that Clay had lost his mind with fear. Yet when fight time came, Clay entered the ring calm and composed, and he completely outclassed the feared champion from the opening bell. He outjabbed and outhit the powerful Liston, puffing an eye and frustrating him. When Liston refused to answer the bell for the eighth round, a new era in boxing had begun.

Ali used a form of self-arousal to take himself to the peak level of alertness.

Athletes take different physical characteristics into competition, and the same is true of their emotional qualities.

In a chance meeting on Highway 64, somewhere between Taos and Raton, New Mexico, Wayne Baughman and his wife stopped to check out a sculpture gallery that featured Indian and wildlife art. There he met a man who left a lasting impression on him.

"We were greeted by a guy who appeared to be in his 60s but in great shape," said Baughman. "He was hard and lean; I guessed about five foot nine and 165 pounds or so. He moved with a slow and deliberate confidence and grace but no swagger or strut. He was dressed in typical Southwest boots, jeans, and chambray shirt. He'd obviously spent a lot of time in the sun with a dark tan and deep 'laugh lines' that would turn into deeper wrinkles.

"But the prominent features that caught my attention were a crooked broken nose and cauliflower ears. I said, 'It looks like you've done a little boxing or wrestling in your time.' He gave a little embarrassed smile and explained he'd been a carnival boxer–wrestler–no rules fighter for many years before he figured out he could make an easier living as an artist-sculptor. He said the carnival would travel from town to town and he would take on all comers, any size under whatever rules they imposed. Some were wrestling matches to a fall or decision on points or went on to include win by submission or unconsciousness by choke. Some were boxing matches with gloves and were won by decision, knockout or by 'throwing in the towel.' Some were just an out-and-out no-holds-barred brawl.

"The higher the risk, the greater the entry fee and admission charge and the higher the prize money. Most opponents were just strong country kids or the local town tough that had little or no training or technique. He had the advantage of some training and over the years developed a lot of experience. He said he won the great majority of the matches over the long haul but every now and then would 'get his clock cleaned.'

"I asked him about injuries. He said he'd sustained quite a few over the years but mostly minor things that rarely kept him out of competition but made the competition just a little more difficult. That reminded me of myself. I never really got hurt or injured enough to get me out of anything, just enough to make it more miserable.

"That's when he stated, 'You know, it don't hurt you to get hurt,' and I nodded an affirmation of his observation.

"My wife looked at us like we were idiots and I could see the wheels turning in her mind. I understood and agreed with exactly what he was saying but for most people it is beyond comprehension! Come to find out, he was in his late 70s and was part Hispanic. He said his ethnicity made his carnival competitions more of a draw, especially for people with prejudices."

Baughman had met a man who was truly tough, both mentally and physically. The man was not afraid to test himself in any type of combative situation, and he had conquered the fear of pain and injury. He was a man at peace with himself. He had acquired a quiet confidence in himself and his abilities. He had found the right mind-set.

The wrestler on the right is using head control of his opponent to set up his takedown attempt. Young wrestlers need to learn the proper techniques early on in their careers and practice them over and over for years.

MIND OVER MATTER

The opposite side of arousal is, of course, total calm. Arousal is not always the secret to victory, as we saw in the preceding chapter in the recounting of the mixed martial arts career of Randy Couture. On the contrary, Couture had to struggle to learn how to control his arousal so that it didn't control him and inhibit him as a wrestler. Once he learned how to relax before his matches, he became a highly successful athlete in one of the most emotionally charged of all sports.

The March 1989 issue of *GQ* magazine included what seemed an unlikely story for readers of such an upscale publication. Titled "The Last Pure Sport," the article took a long, serious look at the sport of amateur wrestling. Deep in the story, writer Kenneth Turan provided *GQ* readers a concise analysis of the sport at the NCAA tournament level.

"With wrestlers at this competitive peak, physical condition-ing—often determined by who will tire first under the match's incessant strain—is not usually the deciding factor. Everyone does the roadwork, the endless stairs, the weight training, the uncounted hours practicing moves again and again. The difference here—and the key to what makes wrestling so riveting to watch—is that it's all in the mind. 'At this level, it's the only thing,' says Jim Gibbons (Iowa State coach at the time). 'If you're focused, you're going to win most of your matches. If you're not, you're lost out there'" (Turan 1989, 278).

The contribution of the athlete's mind to performance in upper-level sports has been a hot topic of conversation for the past decade or more. As sports in general become more sophisticated and as coaches strive to learn what will make the difference between winning and losing for their teams and athletes, all avenues are explored. Increasingly, the mind is being looked at as the dividing point.

Nobody recognizes that fact more clearly than Dan Gable does. Looking into the mind of young athletes has been the key to his recruiting ever since he became the head coach at Iowa in 1976. He often passed up wrestlers with almost perfect high school records to select a wrestler who may not have had near the credentials but had a hunger burning deep inside him.

THE MENTAL GAS TANK

For another example of preparation, consider the perspective of Wade Schalles, one of the greatest wrestlers in American history. He has spent decades studying the philosophy and mechanics of the sport. Schalles has developed a fascinating theory about mental toughness. He has applied that theory to the genius of Gable and his performance at Iowa.

"Gable trained the Iowa wrestlers to be boxers, not sprinters," said Schalles in 2003. "They slug away and pound away at you, constantly boring in, forcing you to keep their pace. The Gable philosophy is to never let up and to put almost unbearable pressure on the foes."

Constant and tremendous pressure is what makes lesser opponents break and give way. Many great wrestlers have used that style of wrestling through the decades, going all the way back to Frank Gotch in 1908 and extending through the collegiate stars of the 1940s and beyond. Bill Koll was an excellent example of one who used unrelenting pressure. After returning from World War II, he was a changed man, more mature both physically and emotionally. He tore into opponents with an aggression that no one had seen before on a collegiate mat. He won three NCAA titles without a defeat and was twice named the outstanding wrestler.

Gable still had the task of getting the Iowa wrestlers to buy into his philosophy, says Schalles. They had to come to understand that training the Iowa way, the Gable way, would pay huge dividends in the end.

"But how many athletes can pay that price continually, day after day, month after month?" asked Schalles rhetorically. "Not many, of course. Not even many elite athletes can do it without running out of mental gas. The amazing thing about Gable is for 10 years—when the Iowa teams were at their very best—you could put 10 Hawkeyes on the mat and take an all-star team from all the rest of the teams around the country and still not beat 'em.

"Why? Because Gable was able to instill that kind of work ethic there. He had mental gas stations set up everywhere, either by design or by the power of his impact on the Iowa scene.

"Every time you work out you are losing gas from your mental gas tank. Eventually, I burn out, and say, 'Screw it, I've had enough!' In college, there are all sorts of things that can drain the mental gas tank—studies, girls, friends, pressure from within and without.

"What Gable set up, either knowingly or unknowingly, was a series of mental gas tanks. There were newspaper stories, teachers in classrooms, students, and fans—all sorts of things providing feedback and filling up the mental gas tank.

"When you walk out in an arena with 14,000 people cheering for you, that fills the mental gas tank up, so that when you are out running and ready to quit, you envision that arena full of fans cheering for you and think, 'I may be tired, but I'm not going to go out there and lose in front of 14,000 fans, that's for sure!' And you have just gotten a big boost in your mental gas tank, and you keep running.

"In my opinion, Gable set up more mental gas stations than any other coach ever has. He did it in the work ethic language, as well. I like to say Gable spoke wrestling Latin—and he looked for wrestlers who spoke the same language. In other words, he looked for the type of athlete who would welcome his very demanding approach to the sport. Once he found those athletes, the program was off and running, and no one could catch them."

SUMMARY

Wrestlers display many different styles and physiques in competitions at all levels. The same is true of their mind-sets. Some wrestlers are mean by nature, and they enjoy being able to physically dominate an opponent. Others love the technique side of the sport. Some view wrestling as a sport; others see it as a controlled fight. Approaches and styles of preparation vary. You should establish a goal to identify your mental qualities and determine what style of preparation will work best for you. The "mental gas tank" theory can provide a new perspective about what you can do to help stay on track toward your goals.

One thing is certain in wrestling: You will eventually face adversity, either in the area of cutting weight or injuries. Understanding that adversity is simply part of the overall package will help you deal with it when it appears.

8

Getting in the Zone

For decades, sportswriters and fans have pondered why super athletes continue competing far past their prime when they seem to have all the financial security and adulation that they could possibly need. Why do many great boxers fight way beyond their peak? Why do many professional football players continue to play the game when the physical injuries pile up to the point that they will never be able to lead normal lives?

Perhaps they are desperately searching for that "landmark in memory for what life should be like." That thought may be the powerful motivational tool lurking in the deep subconscious of every great athlete who has ever climbed into a ring, pulled on a football helmet, or stepped onto a wrestling mat!

The path begins when a young person first ponders what sport he or she will invest time, energy, and devotion to. The path goes through the following stages: building confidence, coming to terms with dedication and commitment, learning the essence of competition, and developing the will to win. Then he or she will work on desire and discipline, learn the art of preparation, and study the power of heart.

The path continues with the study of the attacking mind-set and how to pay the price of excellence. The athlete will want to understand the link between mental and physical toughness and come to terms with intensity and preparation. He or she will need to know how to deal with adversity and how to face odds that can, at times, be daunting.

After doing all that, the athlete may be ready to move into "the zone," and to experience flow. What is flow? It all starts in the mind.

"The battle that will make you a champion is fought in your mind, not on the mat," writes Steve Knight (2003) in his book *Winning State*.

The final step in the evolution of a great champion who has come to grips with the mental part of any sport is when he or she enters what is commonly called the zone.

"A person's long-standing personality traits are less relevant to producing good athletic performances than are the individual states of mind, like anxiety or excitement, that the athlete can bring about at particular times for the purpose of readying," wrote David R. Kauss in his book *Peak Performance* (1980). The state of mind that he was talking about has become known as the zone—a place where athletes go mentally to reach an optimal stage of performance and to allow their bodies to go beyond what normally may be expected of them.

The most successful athletes in all sports seem to have one trait in common—the ability to get into the zone when the need arises. Of course, it is not necessary to go there for all levels of competition. If one can win without going there, then nearly all athletes will choose to do just that—win without going into the zone. But there are occasions throughout a career when the athlete simply must elevate his or her mental state to another level of awareness to claim victory. From Chris Evert to Muhammad Ali, from Dan Marino to Michael Jordan, the ability to push oneself into the zone is the key to attaining the highest level of success.

"Ninety percent of my game is mental," said Chris Evert. "It's my concentration that has gotten me this far. I won't even call a friend on the day of a match. I'm scared of disrupting my concentration. I don't allow any competition with tennis" (Ferguson 1990, 5-38).

Evert was protecting herself so that she could concentrate on the game ahead, another way of getting into the zone.

"You get into the feeling like you are in a zone," said Dan Marino, the NFL's all-time leader in passing yardage, while talking about his best games with the Miami Dolphins. "You can't be stopped. It's a good feeling but it never lasts. People catch up to you and that's when you have to do something different."

Like Marino, Ahmad Rashad had a long, successful career in the National Football League. He has remained in excellent shape many years past his football days by playing high-level tennis. He has also had the opportunity to observe many of the world's finest athletes compete through his job as a television sports announcer and sidelines commentator.

"In sports, the more you can stay inside yourself, the more chance you have to win or to be successful," he said. "As soon as you start dealing with the player on the other side of the net, you've got a big problem."

Perhaps that is just another way to define the zone—which is to say that the athlete who can remain inside himself or herself and wrestle the match to perfection, regardless of what the foe can do or is doing, will have the best chance to succeed.

A perfect case of that example—and one of the best examples of entering the zone in all sports history—occurred on February 25, 1964. On that night a young, fast-talking heavyweight contender named Cassius Clay took on Sonny Liston, one of the most feared heavyweight champions in boxing history. Liston had an aura of invincibility and a formidable appearance that unnerved even veteran boxing observers. He had won the title with a devastating first-round knockout of Floyd Patterson and then had defended his title with another brutal first-round knockout of Patterson.

Going into the fight, Clay was 19-0 but a seven-to-one underdog. He had been taunting Liston for months, calling him names and saying that he was too ugly to be champion. At the weigh-in, Clay appeared to have lost his mind completely, yelling, screaming, and waving his finger in the face of Liston, who regarded him with cold contempt.

"The famous scene at the weigh-in was something out of the Mad Hatter," wrote famed sports commentator Howard Cosell years later. "Sugar Ray Robinson restraining him, Drew Brown, one of his trainers, who called himself Bundini, restraining him. All the while Clay going through this act of apparent insanity, gesturing and screaming at Liston. The blood pressure was way up. Everyone who saw him wondered if he had truly popped his cork, out of fear" (Chapman 1981, 55).

It was later reported that even those closest to Clay were extremely worried about his outburst, thinking that he had gone over the edge with fear of facing Liston. Several observers suggested the fight be postponed until Clay could gather his emotions. But it was all a ruse by Clay, the master tactician. He had studied

Liston for years and gotten a solid read on his personality. Clay's plan was to work himself up into an incredible state of arousal and challenge Liston's manhood. He figured that Liston would enter the ring in a state of rage and fight with uncontrolled anger, exhausting himself emotionally.

An hour before the fight, Cosell saw Clay standing at the back of the arena, calmly watching his younger brother in a preliminary bout. Cosell approached him, shocked at how composed he was. When he asked Clay about the incredible change in his demeanor since the weigh-in, Clay told him that it was all an act, a way to intimidate Liston and prepare himself.

When the fight started, Clay came out fast, firing his jabs and making Liston miss with wild swings. By the end of the first round, Clay was composed and controlled, and gave Liston a lesson in boxing. In the fifth round, he opened a cut under the champion's left eye and sent blood pouring down his face. Unaccustomed to fighting past the first three or four rounds, Liston grew disheartened and then became physically and emotionally weary. Clay had defeated him mentally with his arousal techniques and then physically in the ring. Liston surrendered between the sixth and seventh rounds, sitting on his stool—and Cassius Clay was the new heavyweight champion of the world.

"In the moment of truth, the great athletes lose total self-awareness and even lack of consciousness of what's going on," said Bruce Ogilvie, sports psychologist (Clarkson 1999, 39).

Was Ali there, in the zone, inside that "moment of truth"? Many wrestlers have found their home in that moment—from Milo in ancient Krotona, to Robin Reed in Paris in 1924, to Dan Gable in 1972, to John Smith in 1992, to Tom Brands in 1996. But the question is, how do they get into the zone? Do they reach flow and then ease into the zone without being aware of it? Or do they consciously set a goal of getting into the zone?

A book written by Stephen Holland (1983) called *Talkin' Dan Gable* contains a fascinating glimpse into Dan Gable's psyche. In the book, Gable expressed what he felt when he walked into a wrestling room:

"You're in a trance. You're in another world. It's just like you're on drugs. I don't know what drugs are like but it must be something like that. Once I step into the wrestling room I change completely from one level to another. I'm gone. My body tingles. And I've got to shake all the time. All of a sudden, I've been in a state of hyperness for almost four hours. When it's done, I can't get out, I'm so drained" (Holland 1983, 1).

Perhaps Gable's mind and body are so tuned into the sport that he enters some form of the zone every time he walks into a wrestling room, and then goes into a higher level of the zone when it's time to compete. Or maybe it's just his amazing intensity boiling over. After all, his intensity has become a part of wrestling folklore around the world. They talk about it in Russia and England, in California and Illinois, in Florida and New York, wherever people discuss wrestling. After winning an Olympic gold medal at 125.5 pounds in Los Angeles, a Japanese wrestler came to Iowa City to train. "I want to learn the Gable spirit," he said.

REMOVING BARRIERS TO THE ZONE

But entering the zone is not a cut-and-dried mechanical procedure. "I don't know anybody who knows how to get into the zone. It's more a matter of how to remove the barriers that keep you out of the zone," said Nancy Haller, a sports psychologist.

Dick Butkus was an expert at removing those barriers. He is widely considered one of the toughest men ever to play football, one of the toughest games devised by man. As a three-time All-American at the University of Illinois and as a many time All-Pro with Chicago Bears, no. 51 personified what toughness was all about. In the first of the *Rocky* boxing movies, Sylvester Stallone's character named his bulldog Butkus.

"The name Butkus has come to be virtually synonymous with pro football violence," wrote Bob Rubin in the book *Football's Toughest Ten* (1973). Rubin wrote that even Mike Ditka, as hardnosed a player and coach to ever visit the NFL, was in awe of Butkus' ferocity and mind-set.

"With the highest respect, I've got to say Dick is an animal," said Ditka once. "He works himself up to such a competitive pitch that on the day of the game he won't answer a direct question. He'll grunt" (Rubin 1973, 23).

Like Ali and Butkus, Michael Jordan was able to use unique and specific arousal techniques to enter the zone and excel. "Jordan admits to fabricating stories to trick himself into an angry state against opponents, but that doesn't surprise sports psychologist Bruce Ogilvie, who said that a former NFL defensive end would get himself motivated by pretending that an opponent had raped his wife" (Clarkson 1999, 137).

The great Bill Koll, referred to earlier, used a similar technique during his sensational career at Iowa State Teachers College in the late 1940s. The stories of Bill Koll's accomplishments are legion, stretching from coast to coast. No one who ever saw him wrestle will ever forget him, and his influence was felt for decades, particularly in Iowa, where great wrestlers are looked upon with the same awe as Babe Ruth or Rocky Marciano.

Koll was a skinny, scrappy kid when he enrolled at Fort Dodge High School, a town of 20,000 in north central Iowa, a hotbed of wrestling. He made the team his junior year and proceeded to lose every single dual meet he participated in. Nonetheless, he was making progress. By the end of the season, he managed to place third in the Iowa state tournament of 1940, at 125 pounds.

Bill Koll, a three-time NCAA champion, was undefeated during his entire collegiate career at Iowa State Teachers College in the late 1940s. Working for the pin here, Koll was known for his tremendous mental approach to the sport.

As a senior in 1941, Koll won the state title at 135 pounds. But the depression had ravaged his family's finances, as well as the economic well-being of much of the nation, and college didn't seem possible. Still, he scraped up enough money to enroll at Iowa State Teachers College in the fall of 1941. Dave McCuskey, the head coach, was early in a career that would stamp him as one of the finest wrestling mentors of all time.

Koll won the NCAA championship at 145 pounds in 1946 and gave up the only takedown in his entire career in the finals, when he defeated Oklahoma State's Edgar Welch by a score of 7-2.

He won the NCAA title again as a junior, in 1947, without a close match all season. He was also voted the outstanding wrestler of the tournament. He repeated in 1948, in sensational fashion. Because 1948 was an Olympic year, the tournament was held under free-style rules, and Koll was 7-0, with seven pins! He was voted the outstanding wrestler award again, the first wrestler ever to win the honor twice.

After the 1948 college season, Koll sailed through the final Olympic trials, made the team at 147.5, and was voted the outstanding wrestler award again. His punishing physical style of wrestling was known far and wide, and he was the most feared wrestler of his generation. His swooping double-leg takedown was nearly impossible to stop. He would elevate his foe and slam him hard to the mat, often dazing him, and sometimes knocking him senseless.

What was the secret behind Koll's transformation from being a good high school wrestler to becoming the most feared wrestler of his generation? The answer is found in his arousal techniques and the way that he applied them. For him, the art of arousal was the same as being in the zone.

"It was during the freshman season when I was working against outstanding talent in the practice room that I also realized that directing and controlling one's arousal to competition could be as important as learning skills," wrote Koll many years later. "I discovered that if I would focus my anger towards some incident, object, event or person that my state readiness and overall performance was increased. My strength, speed and ability to think were increased tremendously by just sitting apart from the action prior to the match and getting into a state of controlled anger.

"The key is that I was always in control of the arousal and never allowed it to control me" (Chapman 1981, 128).

Koll's arousal technique has become part of wrestling legend. Bob Siddens, who was to become one of the greatest high school coaches of all time and who coached Dan Gable at West Waterloo High, was Koll's roommate in college. He clearly remembers what it was like to be with Koll on the day of a meet.

"He had a fierce attitude," said Siddens. "If we were wrestling on a Friday or Saturday night, he would pull the shades down in the windows of our room and sit in the dark for hours, getting mentally ready for the match that night. He really would work at getting psyched up for the matches."

Siddens said there were two Bill Kolls—the genial college student off the mat and the fierce warrior on the mat. He was able to combine the two into one person but separate them at the appropriate time.

"He could be nasty on the mat, though he was a really sweet guy off the mat," said Siddens. "I can still remember he wore saddle shoes in those days, and I would actually see him skipping from class to class. Honestly!

"He was a gentleman off the mat, but it was a different story on the mat. Slamming was allowed in his era . . . and they put a rule in that if your knee touched at the same time as your foe came down, you could slam. Well, I can remember clear as a bell this one time Bill slammed a foe to the mat so hard the fellow was nearly unconscious. Bill shook him when he was on top, so it looked like the guy was trying to escape, and the referee called a pin. The referee raised Bill's hand, but the poor guy just laid on the mat. They had to carry him off.

"They changed the slam rule after that. . . . They changed it because of Bill Koll," said Siddens.

Fifty years after wrestling at Iowa State Teachers College, Bill Weick was still in awe of his famous mentor. Weick was an Illinois state champion from Chicago who came to Cedar Falls two years after Koll's final season and won two NCAA titles himself. Koll was still in graduate school and was in the room working out. Weick was able to observe him in action and digest the many stories. Weick then became one of the most successful coaches in American history, both in high school and at the international level.

"Koll was something else, in a class by himself when it came to psyching up," said Weick in 2004, during inductions into the

Glen Brand Wrestling Hall of Fame of Iowa. "I remember one time when I was coaching at San Francisco State College. A couple of my wrestlers and I ran into him in a bar. I asked Koll to show the guys how he would get ready for a match. He started twitching, pushing at his glasses, squirming in his chair like he always did. He looked around the room and fixed on one guy in particular, a big, tough-looking guy.

"'See that guy over there?' said Koll, twitching and jerking. 'I could work myself up into a fever pitch right now, just thinking about him. I could make myself get ready to go over there and take him out.'"

Weick laughed, recalling the incident from the security of five decades later. "He scared the heck out of my wrestlers. They looked at me like, 'Who is this guy? . . . Is he some sort of madman?' But that was just Koll, getting ready to compete. Oh yeah, he was something else when it came to mental preparation."

Bill Koll was an expert at entering the zone and at moving out of the zone when the competition was over.

Another physically intimidating wrestler was Dan Hodge, generally acknowledged as the strongest wrestler in collegiate history. Hodge never lost during his three-year career at the University of Oklahoma, winning NCAA titles at 177 pounds in 1955, 1956, and 1957. In his junior year, he won the NCAA title, the national AAU freestyle title, and the national AAU Greco-Roman title with 15 consecutive pins. During his senior year in college, he was 16-0 with 15 pins. Like Bill Koll, he was twice voted the outstanding wrestler at the NCAA tourney.

Hodge's hand strength was such that he could crush apples and snap the handles off pliers. He also was an accomplished boxer, winning the national Golden Gloves heavyweight title in 1959 and posting a 21-0 record as an amateur boxer.

Despite all his accomplishments and his awesome reputation, Hodge admitted he would get highly nervous before college matches.

"I would break out in a rash and even get chills down my back before a match," said Hodge in 2003. "Yes, I would get nervous, but it was a good thing because it got the blood flowing. I could control the nerves."

His nervousness was a form of arousal, and Hodge wasn't the only sensational athlete to suffer from nerves. According to Michael Clarkson's book *Competitive Fire* (1999), one of the greatest basketball players who ever lived was not immune from such attacks of anxiety, and Clarkson offers a reason:

"Former track coach Brooks Johnson believes the best athletes learn to change fear and other 'negative' emotions into potent forces. 'Some people are able to take the negative feelings they have and concert them into energy,' he said. 'It creates this sort of electricity and they take it and focus it on their event. Bill Russell got so nervous before [NBA] games, he'd lose his lunch [throw up], then he'd go out and turn that nervousness into a marvelous performance. It's yin and yang, an awesome pressure. . . . All the great ones have the ability to do this. You cannot get to a certain level without this mentality'" (Clarkson 1999, 184-185).

Ali, Jordan, Koll, and Hodge all shared one characteristic, and that was the ability to use arousal to enter the zone.

TUNNEL VISION

The career of Dan Gable has caused some experts to wonder how long an athlete can be in the zone. According to those who were his teammates at Iowa State and who competed in the Olympics with him, Gable seemed to be in the zone for a good part of his active career.

In a 2004 interview by Mike Finn of *W.I.N. Magazine*, Gable admitted that he was so focused through his college years that he did not realize that others were watching his incredible training methods with a touch of awe.

"Why could I go to high school and go to class and have ankle weights on my legs in biology class and be doing leg lifts?" he asked. "Why could I walk in college to class with a weight vest on and run to class with my street clothes on, sweating all over? I didn't even know people were looking at me. That's how focused I could be."

Gable told Finn it wasn't until years later when he saw a documentary on his career that he discovered how people reacted to his unique lifestyle. "It never crossed my mind that they were looking at me," he said. "I was a man on a mission."

While competing in the U.S. Pro Championships one year in Philadelphia, Lance Armstrong discovered what it was to enter the zone. He wrote about the experience in his best-selling book, *It's Not About the Bike: My Journey Back to Life* (2000).

"With about 20 miles left, I went (took off). I attacked on the most notoriously steep part of the hill and as I did I was almost in a rage.

I don't know what happened—all I know is that I leaped out of the seat and hammered down on the pedals and as I did so I screamed for five full seconds. I opened up a huge gap on the field.

"By the second to last lap, I had enough of a lead to blow my mother a kiss. I crossed the finish line with the biggest winning margin in race history. I dismounted in a swarm of reporters, but I broke away from them and went straight to my mom, and we put our faces on each other's shoulders and cried" (Armstrong 2000, 59).

Armstrong had been raised by his mother in Texas without his biological father anywhere around, and the two of them have a special bond. They lived and worked for one another, and Lance loved winning for her. He wrote "I don't know what happened," but it seems that he was in the zone, in the flow, all at once. The pain of the race was removed from his mind because he was at harmony with the race.

At another point in the book, Armstrong equates losing with dying. But that is only because he has never experienced death. If he had, he would never be able to race again. After losing, he can race again, many times. So losing and dying are obviously not the same, even if Armstrong has brainwashed himself into believing that they are.

The value in Armstrong's thinking that way is that it allows him to give the race all that he has—not just 98 or 99 percent, but 100 percent. At some point in the race, he is probably even willing to give up his life to win, once he is in the zone. And that belief can make the difference in winning or losing if the competition is close physically. If it is, mental toughness and emotional commitment will decide who wins.

John Smith was of a similar mind-set during his days as a collegiate star at Oklahoma State University, in Stillwater. He remembers being isolated to the point that he went long periods without speaking to his parents, who lived just an hour's drive away, in Del City.

"I had some serious, serious tunnel vision," he recalled. "I can remember times if any little thing went wrong, I was off the wall. If someone took me down (in practice), they better duck because I was throwing punches. Over a takedown.

"I've hit a lot of guys in workout rooms. I can remember a particular time in the room where me and this other guy spent 15 minutes working out and an hour and a half fighting. One would sit on the other one until one cooled off. Things would be all right but then, before you knew it, we were back at it again. There have been a lot of battles in that room" (Wojciechowski 1992).

Fights were not confined to the Oklahoma State workout room. The practice room at the University of Iowa, during the 21-year coaching career of Dan Gable, was legendary for the fights that broke out, so deep was the intensity.

The Banach brothers, who won five NCAA titles and two Olympic gold medals between them, were such fierce competitors that Gable finally decided to install a heavy punching bag in the far corner of the room, and he often had to lead either Ed or Lou over to it to work out their anger on the bag. In addition, the piece of apparatus known as the Adam, a solid figure with arms and legs used for practicing moves on, was battered relentlessly by angry and frustrated wrestlers in Iowa City, and elsewhere around the nation.

"The fights of the Brands boys are part of Iowa's wrestling folklore," said Mark Johnson, who was an assistant coach at Iowa for eight years before resurrecting the program at the University of Illinois. "Fights broke out often in the room, all due to the incredible intensity and competitive spirit."

THE ROLE OF FLOW

The zone overtakes athletes when they are so caught up in the moment that they are no longer aware of where they are, only of the immediate task and the sense of what they must do to soar, or even survive. Another term, flow, offers an understanding of a place that is similar to the zone. In fact, flow may be the same force under another name. Alternatively, flow may simply be a new concept of a state of mind that has always existed but has just recently been discovered, like some new quasar on the far reaches of the universe.

The fascinating book *Flow* (1990) is subtitled *The Psychology of Optimal Experience*. In the book, author Mihaly Csikszentmihalyi, a professor at the University of Chicago, discusses his two-decade-long study of what he calls flow. He states that the goal of life should be to find and secure happiness. But, he quickly adds, that search is extremely difficult. Even Aristotle, one of the greatest thinkers in all of history, couldn't get a grasp on it, says Csikszentmihalyi.

He builds the case that nearly everything we face in life is out of our control, from the force of gravity to the era we are born in to the genetic makeup that we receive from our parents. Because we have little control over such circumstances, "It is not surprising that we would believe that our fate is primarily ordained by outside experiences," he says.

But there is more to the situation. Much more!

"We have all experienced times when, instead of being buffeted by anonymous fortunes, we do feel in control of our actions, masters of our fate," he writes. "On the rare occasions that it happens, we feel a sense of exhilaration, a deep sense of enjoyment that is long cherished and that becomes a landmark in memory for what life should be like" (Csikszentmihalyi 1990, 3).

© Human Kinetics

The wrestler on top has his foe in an awkward position as he works for near-fall points. Turning a foe to his back can lead to as much as three points in scholastic wrestling and can eventually result in a match-ending pin.

In that statement, Csikszentmihalyi has defined the incredibly powerful lure of sports and of performing at the very highest level: It provides a "deep sense of enjoyment that is long cherished and that becomes *a landmark in memory for what life should be like.*"

He adds: "The best moments usually occur when a person's body or mind is stretched to its limits in a voluntary effort to accomplish something difficult and worthwhile. Optimal experience is thus something that we make happen" (Csikszentmihalyi 1990, 3).

In his book *Sports Psyching*, Thomas Tutko writes, "The real reward (of sports) was 'flow,' an altered state of being that occurred when people were enjoying their activity the most" (Tutko and Tosi 1976, 129).

That certainly describes what many top-level wrestlers seem to feel when they are at the very heights of their sport.

GOING INSIDE TOUGH

To those who saw him in action during the 1984 Olympic trials, and in the Los Angeles Games, Steve Fraser was the epitome of wrestling tough. He entered the Greco-Roman tryouts with one of the most determined mind-sets in American wrestling history. He battled through one of the roughest weight classes imaginable, beating 1980 Olympian Mark Johnson, one of the strongest men ever to step on a mat, and Mike Houck, who a year later would become the first Greco-Roman world champion in American history.

At the Olympic Games itself, wrestling in the Anaheim Convention Center, the former University of Michigan star faced one of the toughest fields. Despite the Soviet Union-based boycott, the best Greco-Roman wrestler in the world at 198 pounds was there. Frank Andersson of Sweden owned three world titles when he arrived in Los Angeles, and he had a huge cheering section, which included the king of Sweden. With movie-star good looks, Andersson was a crowd favorite and the man most fans felt would win the class. But in the quarterfinals, Fraser simply overwhelmed the Swedish star with a relentless and pounding attack and came away with a stunning 4-1 triumph. In the finals, he pulled out a 1-1 criteria decision over Ilie Matei of Romania. With five victories to his credit in five matches, Steve Fraser had become the first American ever to win a gold medal at the Olympics in the time-honored style of wrestling known as Greco-Roman.

As the honors poured in, Fraser took a long look at where he wanted to be in life. He had worked hard to earn his gold medal and knew that he still loved the sport of wrestling. Although he was employed by Domino's Pizza in the public relations department and enjoyed giving speeches around the country and inspiring other athletes to try to reach their potential, he finally decided to take a position as Greco-Roman national coach with USA Wrestling, the sport's national governing body. Stressing the same values of physical preparation and mental toughness that he employed himself in the early 1980s, he guided the United States to a fourth-place finish in the world in 2001 and helped prepare Rulon Gardner for his incredible triumph over Alexander Karelin at the 2000 Olympics in Sydney.

At the world championships in 2003, Fraser was so impressed by the performance of several of his wrestlers, and one in particular, that he wrote the following column for *W.I.N. Magazine*. He titled it "Are You Tough Enough?"

> What does being tough really mean? Is it having the "Killer Instinct"? Is it being mean or cold? Is it being hard, insensitive, callous or ruthless?
>
> In a previous issue of *W.I.N. Magazine* in Wade Schalles' column, Wade identified what, in his mind, were some tough, hard-nosed wrestlers. He mentioned Doug Blubaugh, Wayne Baughman, as well as the Brands brothers. I think most people would agree that these individuals all fit the bill of "tough."
>
> So, would we describe these tough wrestlers with the adjectives above or do words like flexible, responsive, relentless, strong, resilient under pressure come to mind? Although they all have some of the above attributes (i.e., "Killer Instinct"), I think the latter words better represent what tough really is and these men are definitely all that.
>
> Toughness is the ability to perform at your "Ideal Competitive State" no matter what the competitive circumstances are.
>
> What is your "Ideal Competitive State"? Your "Ideal Competitive State" is your personal state of being that allows for you to wrestle with the greatest potential. It is a state of being where you feel most energized, most confident, and most strong. It is when you are generating positive emotions that help you to be most alert, instinctive, responsive and creative. It is

when you have that positive fight—when you are having fun and enjoying the battle. When all these positive emotions are flowing you are going to wrestle to your greatest potential.

Toughness is being able to create these positive emotions upon command thus enabling you to bring all your talent and skills to life at that moment.

Emotion is very important in wrestling and all competitive sport for that matter. The positive emotions mentioned above will empower you with great action and attitude. But some emotion can disempower you, blocking your potential. Negative emotions include such feelings as fear, confusion, low energy, fatigue and helplessness.

Which brings us back to toughness . . . being truly tough means no matter what is happening that might be considered negative, you continue to operate in your "Ideal Competitive State" generating positive emotion. This means during the match when you make that big mistake, you can refocus and be right back on track. When you get thrown to your back or taken down, you can refocus and get right back at it. When the referee makes that bad call against you, you can refocus and get back to business.

Being tough means that if your girlfriend breaks up with you, your mom is on you about keeping your room clean, your teachers are hammering you about your school work, it doesn't matter . . . when you step on the mat you kick into gear, rising above all of the problems. You can adjust your mind-set and voila . . . you are in your "Ideal Competitive State." Nothing can break you. Nothing can stop you. You are resilient. You can bounce back. You are one tough cookie!

Toughness is physical, mental and emotional. Being tough involves all three of these areas. And make no mistake—toughness is learned. If you are not tough, it is just because you have not learned and practiced enough yet. Just like any wrestling technique or skill . . . toughness can be developed, practiced and honed to perfection.

Adapted by permission of Steve Fraser.

MEASURING TOUGHNESS

So how tough are you? Before you can improve your toughness, you must be able to face the truth. And if you are unsatisfied with what you see, you must be willing to take full responsibility to change it. So let's look at the truth.

On a score of 1 to 10 with 10 being the best (strongest), rate yourself on some of the following issues:

Resilient	_____	Confident	_____
Disciplined	_____	Focused	_____
Self-reliant	_____	Patient	_____
Responsible	_____	Motivated	_____
Committed	_____	Relaxed	_____
Coachable	_____	Physically fit	_____

Be honest with yourself in how you rate in those areas. Remember, in the heat of the battle, when push comes to shove, you'll tend to break at your weakest points.

For example, suppose that your weakness is discipline. In a tough match when it really counts for you to be disciplined—say you are ahead 3-2 with 30 seconds to go in the match—you must stay disciplined at keeping to your game plan of "sticking and moving" (not stalling) to burn seconds off the clock and secure the victory. But because your discipline is weak, you second-guess yourself, change your strategy, and start backing up. Boom—your opponent takes you down to win the match.

To improve your toughness, you should focus your training on your weakest areas. For that reason, you must know the truth about yourself and your needs for improvement. Getting feedback from your coaches is vital here. You need to be open minded about what your coaches see. This objectivity will help you get to the real you.

To address your needs for improvement, take two areas that you score low in. Now let's create a toughness training plan to improve these areas. Here are some suggestions.

1. State your needs for improvement in writing in a positive fashion. For example, for discipline, write "I have tremendous discipline." For resilience, you might write "I love being in a close match in which I must come from behind to win."
2. For the next 30 days make these positive statements the most important issues in your wrestling life.
3. Post these positive statements in your locker, near your bed, or on your bathroom mirror.
4. Write a one-page summary on how you will improve in each of these areas.
5. Just before you go to sleep and when you first wake up take 30 seconds to visualize yourself being successful at improving these issues. Take the time to really feel it.
6. For the next 30 days track your progress in these areas. Note in your training journal the days during which you feel you improved and the days when you did not.
7. At the end of 30 days take two new areas in which you feel you need improvement and repeat the process.

Remember, you must take control of your wrestling career and commit to making changes. The sooner you take full responsibility for your actions and hold yourself accountable, the better.

No matter how old or young you are, how weak or strong you are, you can get tougher. Never believe that you cannot achieve because you are not talented enough, not smart enough, or that you did not receive the gifts that you need to succeed. Your future depends much more on the decisions you make and what you do than it does on your genetic makeup. And believe me, the level of toughness that you acquire through your focused training efforts will be the most powerful force in your wrestling career and your life.

As always, expect to win!

Adapted by permission of Steve Fraser.

SUMMARY

The mind is the key to just about everything in life, and that includes success in sports. Countless athletes win because they are able to enter into a higher state of awareness, often referred to as the zone. Another intriguing concept of mental competition is flow, which is best understood as the place in the mind where people go to find an optimal state of happiness. Certainly, victory in athletics is one of those optimal states.

Many experts feel that personality traits are not as important as the state of mind that an athlete occupies when he or she competes. One of the best examples of the zone in wrestling history is Bill Koll, who never lost a match during his three years at Iowa State Teachers College and was known everywhere for his ferocious approach to the sport. He was a perfect example of an athlete in the zone.

Physical preparation can only take an athlete so far, and then the mind kicks in. But most athletes don't understand how that happens, why it happens, when it happens, or how to get into the zone. The ability to get in the zone may be the difference between the world's finest athletes, like Olympic champions, and the rest of the field. One of the best ways to understand the zone and learn to employ it is to study the careers of athletes who have been there.

9

Paying the Price

"The moment of victory is much too short to live for that and nothing else," said Martina Navratilova, winner of 54 Grand Slam tennis titles and one of the best tennis players of all time.

Winning the way Martina Navratilova did in tennis or Bruce Baumgartner (13 world or Olympic medals) did in wrestling, demands far too much from the athlete to live only for the moment of victory and nothing else. An athlete must pay a tremendous price over many years, so the reward must be more than just the moment of victory. And there are further rewards, of course. The payoff comes in many different ways—from a sense of self-worth to family and community pride, to a sense that one can accomplish anything that he or she wants in life—if the person is willing to work hard enough, if he or she is willing to pay the price.

Two essential elements of paying the price can be found in the work ethic of highly successful athletes and in understanding how crucial the basics of a sport are.

"I can pay the price" to be great, say millions of athletes. What they really mean to say is, "I can pay a certain price, but don't ask me to go beyond what I think I am capable of doing." Ninety-nine percent of athletes will come up to a line in the sand and halt. Once a person has entered into the pain threshold of severe training, he or she naturally tends to shut down.

"OK, that's it," is what most of us tell ourselves. "I'm hurting, I've worked hard enough and put in enough hours. I've paid the price." At that point, however, we are just knocking on the door of paying the price.

Paying the price in hard work is a familiar idea, but not many people really understand what the term *hard work* really means.

Few men have observed as much of the total athletic scene around the world as Jim McKay did during his long and successful television career as a broadcaster. He traveled the globe watching the best athletes in the world in his job as sports broadcaster for ABC's *Wide World of Sports*. And he came to understand what it took to be the very best.

"I believe there is a price tag on everything worthwhile, but it is seldom a monetary one," he said. "The price is more often one of dedication, deprivation, extra effort, loneliness. Each person decides whether he or she wants to pay the price" (Ferguson 1990, 3-5).

Paying the price has been the key behind the best wrestling programs in the country, from junior high through college and to the postgraduate level. Of course, the price to be paid is limited at the earliest levels as young athletes decide which sport is theirs and begin to educate themselves about the sport and what it takes to excel. As their education advances, so does their commitment, at least for those who are on that path. Sometimes, coaches, athletes, and parents begin looking for secrets and shortcuts to paying the price. If they do, they come away disappointed.

"Coaches would always come to Iowa to try and figure out what Gable did differently—what his secret to success was. It was hard work," said Troy Steiner, NCAA champion and four-time All-American during his Hawkeye days. "But, like Gable always said, most people do not know what hard work is."

Nor do they understand what paying the price truly means. One athlete who does is Ed Banach. He came to the University of Iowa from Port Jervis, New York, with his twin brother, Lou. After a redshirt year, Ed captured two straight NCAA titles at 177 pounds. Going for a third, he was defeated by Mark Schultz of Oklahoma in one of the greatest showdowns in American wrestling history.

In his senior season, 1983, Banach moved up to 190 pounds and ran into Mike Mann of Iowa State, a tough and talented three-time All-American who was determined to claim his first NCAA championship in his final shot. In their first two meetings of their final season, Mann scored decisive victories over Banach. It looked to some as if Ed was destined to close out his career with two straight misses after claiming national crowns as a freshman and sophomore.

"It was after I lost to Mann in the dual meet in January by a 13-8 score," recounted Banach in 2004. "I went up to Gable and said, 'Coach, what do I need to do to win nationals?' I was willing to do about anything."

Banach had a plan of his own, wrapped up in asking his coach's advice. "The year before, my junior year, the coaches told me what to do to beat Mark Schultz, but I didn't listen," said Banach. "I thought to myself, if I listen this year and still lose, then I have a built-in excuse; I can blame Gable."

The Hawkeyes were already holding two punishing workouts per day leading up to the NCAA championships. What Gable proposed to Banach was a third grueling workout. Banach's first thought was natural: "When?" The Hawks were already working out at 7 in the morning and in the late afternoon, and recovery time was required for such taxing workouts. Gable's answer was to meet in the wrestling room at 5 a.m.!

In this extra predawn session, they stressed takedown technique, primarily the high crotch, over and over and over, pounding it into Ed's psyche. The two men, coach and pupil, began their sessions eight weeks before the nationals.

"Gable wanted me in the room at 5 a.m., dressed and ready to go," said Banach. "We did it three times a week. After it was over, I would go to the small trainer's room at the back of the wrestling room and take a nap before the 7 a.m. practice."

In short order, several other Hawkeyes decided to join them. While most of the Iowa City community and the civilized world was fast asleep, a small and determined band of wrestlers was paying a huge extra price to try to achieve their lofty goals.

"We worked mostly on getting mentally tougher," said Banach. "I remember one morning a worker brought in 50-pound bags of rat food that had to be taken to a laboratory for rats that was on the top floor of the field house, right next to the wrestling room. They were keeping rats there for experiments conducted by the university hospital. Gable saw the guy and said, 'Hey, we'll take those bags up for you.' Of course, this worker was delighted, and Gable and I ran up the three flights of stairs carrying those 50-pound bags of rat food.

"After a couple of sessions, J Robinson (assistant coach) began showing up too, and we started studying films, as well.

"The key was the high crotch (takedown) off the Russian two-on-one tie-up," said Banach. "I began doing it 75 times a day, five days a week, for eight weeks. That would be around 3,000 times. I did it over and over and over until it became second nature to me."

It was an incredible commitment by coach and athletes; how many other coaches and athletes would be willing to pay such a price? When the NCAA tournament rolled around in Oklahoma City, Ed Banach and Mike Mann both made it to the finals. Then, in an incredibly tense, hard-fought battle, Banach scored the only takedown of the championship match, a high crotch, of course, for a stunning 4-3 triumph and his third NCAA title. In addition, 9 of the 10 Hawkeyes earned All-American honors, and Iowa won the meet by a 53-point margin over second-place Oklahoma State.

"The price of greatness is not cheap and there are few willing to pay it," said Jack Spates, head coach at the University of Oklahoma and author of *Mat Snacks*. "Ed Banach was and it paid off" (Spates 1999, 17).

"I think the difference in the last match was the training Gable put me through," said Banach. "What Gable was able to do was focus on mental toughness. He put us in the sauna at the end of practice for the last 15 minutes to get us mentally tough. There's no doubt in my mind that the extra time I put in, getting up at 5 a.m., was the key. I knew I was in great shape and could go all out every second of the match. That gave me the edge I needed."

What was it called? Paying the price, big time!

WHAT HARD WORK IS

Of course, many other world-class athletes have paid the price by working incredibly hard during their careers. Herschel Walker, Heisman Trophy winner and former pro superstar, used to tie a rope around his waist, connect it to a tire, and then run like a deer until he couldn't go any longer. Arnold Schwarzenegger, on his way to building his sensational physique, would work so hard in the weight room that he would sometimes vomit. While riding his bike, Lance Armstrong pushed himself to the point that the pain would become almost unbearable, yet still he pushed himself harder and harder.

Walter Payton laid out a course in the sand near his hometown of Columbia, Mississippi. He would run sprints in the hottest part of the day, pushing himself to the limits of tolerance. "You stop, throw up, and push yourself again," he said. "There's no one else around to feel sorry for you" (Ferguson 1990, 3-5).

"The dictionary is the only place success comes before work," said Vince Lombardi. "Hard work is the price we must all pay for success. I think we can accomplish anything if we are willing to pay the price."

Until you truly understand what hard work is and accept it as part of what it takes to be one of those champions who rise above the crowd, you are not likely to achieve your goals. Success is all about wanting something enough to pay an extraordinary price to get it.

Many wrestlers have expressed that attitude, verbally or otherwise, in their quest for Olympic honors. Wanting something more than did the rest of the soldiers who fought at Troy is what

© Sport the Library

The wrestler on the bottom has found himself in an uncomfortable position, and risks losing near-fall points and being pinned.

distinguished Achilles from them. Wanting something more than others did is what distinguished wrestlers like John Smith and Bruce Baumgartner from their peers.

Another key part of paying the price is understanding how crucial the basics are and then drilling on them over and over and over. The basics are what make your skills work. And you learn the basics by drilling, by paying the price to drill over and over and over and over.

"Fundamentals were the most crucial part of my game in the NBA," wrote Michael Jordan. "Everything I did, everything I achieved, can be traced back to the way I approached the fundamentals and how I applied them to my abilities. They really are the basic building blocks or principles that make everything work. I don't care what you're doing or what you're trying to accomplish; you can't skip fundamentals if you want to be the best" (Jordan 1998).

J Robinson took over a struggling program at the University of Minnesota in 1986 and molded it into a national power. The Gophers won back-to-back NCAA championships in 2001 and 2002, and defeated archrival Iowa in several dual meets. Along the way, they regularly brought in crowds of 10,000 or more, including the NCAA record of 15,646 in 2002.

A 1972 Olympian himself and a former ranger in Vietnam, Robinson understands what paying the price means. He has stressed technique and fundamentals at all levels he has coached, including an eight-year stint as assistant coach at Iowa.

"The way you win is to improve your skills and eliminate your mistakes," he said. "We work with our guys one-on-one. We actually keep a book on them, charting their progress.

"Winning is an abstract . . . you can't really practice winning. What you *can* practice is your skills and improving them. Our philosophy is actually pretty simple—if you can refine your skills and eliminate your mistakes, you *will* start winning. That's the price you must pay to be successful in wrestling, and in most aspects of life.

"Learning is the same for geometry or piano lessons or wrestling. Practice it over and over and over and over, make adjustments, fine-tune it. It is a process of eliminating mistakes. Over the duration of the season, you will eliminate the mistakes if you are working on technique. You drill these skills over and over and over and over, just like playing the piano.

"Do it right and you'll do it the rest of your life that way. Do it wrong and you will spend the rest of your life trying to do it right. It's all about building skills."

THE WILL TO PREPARE

The key to reaching that state rests with your ability to accept what it takes to win at the highest level. Then, it's making yourself pay the price to do what is necessary, no matter how boring or uninspiring it may seem. To reach the top, you must have the will to prepare adequately, at all levels.

Nearly all athletes—young and old, big and small, male and female—believe that they have the will to win, at least on some level. But very few have the will to pay the price for victory. That difference is often the separation point between the athletes who *seem* to have it all and the athletes who *win* it all. The levels of winning are sometimes so miniscule—like a tenth of a second in a race or an inch in a leaping touchdown catch—that a tiny extra bit can make the difference.

So it is with the will to win. Suppose that two athletes are evenly matched all the way down the line in physical skills, that they spend the same amount of time training, and that both are operating at 98 percent of their ability. If one then kicks it up a tenth of a point, that small movement can make the difference in coming home with an Olympic gold medal and coming home with nothing.

In the 2004 Olympics in Athens, Joe Williams of the United States and Gannadiy Laliyev of Kazakhstan were deadlocked at 2-2 in their third-round match at 163 pounds. They went into the overtime locked up in the dreaded clinch.

The two battled for every square inch while chest to chest, arms around each other and locked tight. According to the rules, the first man to unlock his hands would lose the deciding point, unless he immediately tried to drive the other man from the mat. When Laliyev's hands broke apart first, nearly everyone watching at home in America on television felt that Williams had won the match. But the mat official raised Laliyev's hand, sending him into the medal rounds and sending Williams into the lower rounds where he could no longer win a medal.

It was a shocking moment. Phone lines lit up all around the country as fans tried to call their local television stations to see what had happened. In Des Moines, Iowa, the largest sports talk show in the state spent considerable time showing the move and discussing how Williams had lost the all-important match on an incredibly poor call by the officials.

But the call was the correct one, according to freestyle coach Tom Brands and USA Wrestling coach Kevin Jackson, both Olympic champions in their own right. "It was the right call," said Brands. "There's no excuses and Joe knows that."

Jackson said the American team had even trained for that precise situation. "He had a lapse in his concentration," said Jackson of Williams' failure to fight off the attack for a mere second or two.

The key, said Brands and Jackson, was that Joe relaxed for just a split second on the edge of the mat when he felt Laliyev's hands break apart. If the former three-time NCAA champion would have resisted Laliyev's efforts, then Williams would have earned the point and would have advanced.

That situation shows how miniscule the difference can be between finishing fifth (where Williams wound up) and taking the silver medal for second (Laliyev's eventual finish). An athlete can train for 20 years and see it all come down to a decision made on the edge of a mat in overtime on the other side of the world, and lose a medal in the blink of an eye. It can happen in any sport.

The mental training can be just as essential. An athlete can be so tuned in and mentally tough that he or she simply refuses to break under any circumstances. That was the case with Doug Blubaugh in 1960.

Gray Simons was one of the finest collegiate wrestlers of all time. He claimed seven national titles in college, winning four NAIA championships for Lock Haven State and three NCAA championships. In addition, he was voted the outstanding wrestler in six of those seven national meets. In 1960, he earned a spot on the freestyle Olympic team, where he became a teammate of Blubaugh, one of the most mentally tough wrestlers ever to step on a mat.

"The Olympic team was training in Colorado, up in the mountains," said Simons. "I arrived in camp late and saw how hard the coaches, mostly head coach Port Robertson, were working the guys. We were running all the time—long, hard runs with weights on our legs in the high altitude. Some of the guys were about dying. At one point after a long run, I could hardly breathe and I saw Blubaugh standing off by himself, hands on hips, his glasses all fogged over.

"I went up to him and said, 'Hey, Blubaugh . . . What are they trying to do out here, kill us?' He looked at me with sweat pouring down all over his face and his shirt soaked all the way through, and said, 'Simons, they can't make it tough enough for me. I love this! Give me more!'"

Simons was in awe of his friend's attitude at the time and still was four decades later when retelling the story in 2000. "That tells you where Doug Blubaugh was coming from," said Simons. "That guy was so tough mentally that it's hard to believe!"

Blubaugh was so charged up that he relished the challenge of the severe workouts, to prove to himself, the coaches, and the world that he could take it all and come back for more. He was willing to pay any price that the coaches could ask of him, without complaining. His willingness to train at an extremely high level was all part of building the mental confidence that we talked about in chapter 3. He wanted to enter the Olympics knowing that he had survived the most intense camps possible and was ready for literally anything that would come his way.

As a young college wrestler at Oklahoma State University, he would sometimes run all the way from Stillwater to his home in Ponca City, a distance of nearly 30 miles. As a young high school wrestler, he had once set out to run down a horse in a corral.

"That horse was a mean one and wanted to run away all the time," said Blubaugh. "I put him in a corral once and told him to take off. I ran alongside him the entire time and finally tired him out. He just stopped, and quit. We got along good after that."

The 1960 Olympics were held in the ancient coliseum in Rome, where gladiators had once fought to the death. There, Blubaugh showed once again what mental toughness is. He won all seven of his matches, five by pin, and earned the gold medal in the 160.5-pound class. He was working so hard that he actually weighed in at 156 pounds, almost 5 pounds under his weight class. That kind of disparity was unheard of in an era when wrestlers were giving all they had to make weight, sometimes losing 10 pounds a day.

In the fifth round he found himself up against Email Habibi of Iran, a five-time world champion. Habibi was one of those rare wrestlers who come along every decade or so who are considered unbeatable by their peers and the fans who follow the sport closely.

In the early going, Habibi twice took Blubaugh down and put him in precarious positions. But Blubaugh never panicked.

"I wasn't worried either time," said Blubaugh 40 years later. "I knew I wasn't in danger of being pinned and I knew I had the conditioning to come back. I had worked so damn hard for 10 years to get to that point and I wasn't going to give up without the fight of my life."

Halfway through the match, Habibi tried the same move that had scored two takedowns for him. This time, Blubaugh was ready. He caught the fabled Iranian in a crushing pancake and threw him straight to his back. Habibi bridged like a wild animal, trying to avoid the pin. But Blubaugh, fueled by years of intense workouts and a desire that knew no boundaries, tightened up on him. Slowly, Blubaugh forced Habibi's shoulders into the mat to score one of the most sensational pins in Olympic history.

After winning the gold medal, Blubaugh returned to a simple life as an Oklahoma farmer. "I was actually out in the field plowing when my mom told me I had received a box from overseas," said Blubaugh. "I came in from the field, opened the box and there was a medal from FILA (the sport's international governing body), saying I had been named the outstanding wrestler in the world. I just gave it to my mom and went back to the plowing."

Blubaugh coached in several colleges for decades and was the top assistant when Michigan State University won the NCAA title in 1967, the first Big Ten Conference school to win it all. He also coached several international teams and had a huge influence on many of his athletes, including one Olympic gold medal winner from 1972.

"Doug Blubaugh taught me a lot about self-discipline," wrote Dan Gable. "Doug grew up in a lifestyle that demanded a hard-work ethic. Every day he did farm chores early each morning, ran five miles into school, attended classes all day, went to wrestling practice and outworked everyone on the team, ran back home, worked on the farm until dark, and then did his homework before bed. This example of self-discipline had a lot to do with my training and my philosophy about what it takes to excel.

"Doug's wrestling style was just as unique as his amazing work ethic. Doug couldn't see very well, but that didn't keep him from using a straightforward, aggressive style. One time I saw Doug wrestle right into the front row of bleachers and people say that he once tackled a referee by mistake" (Gable 1999, 6-7).

Culture House, a company that promotes the sport of wrestling and some of its heroes, produced a poster titled "The Epic Struggle" in the mid-1990s. The poster is a huge photo of Blubaugh pinning Habibi. Nearly 5,000 have been sold to date, most of them hanging in wrestling rooms around the country. Blubaugh's dramatic victory has served as an inspiration to countless wrestlers of all ages for decades.

SUMMARY

Preparing oneself for competition is an art form. Effective preparation takes real commitment to physical activities, including a great deal of cross-training—wrestling, running, weight training, and diet control. Once the physical side is properly trained, the mental side begins to adjust as well. The mind understands that the physical price that has been paid will result in high-level performance.

The greatest athletes know that victories are won primarily during the training process. The will to prepare is what separates the champions from the also-rans. The willingness to pay a tremendous price is usually the line between the best and the rest. The ability to deal with adversity goes hand in hand with the concept of paying the price.

10

Dealing
With Adversity

Dealing with adversity of all types and forms is a major part of both life and sport, and it is certainly a significant part of wrestling. Anyone who devotes considerable time and energy to wrestling will eventually have to deal with pressure and setbacks.

One form of stress unique to wrestling among all scholastic sports is the often intense pressure of cutting pounds to fit into a certain weight classification. No other scholastic sport places such emphasis on athletes' body weight. In fact, among professional athletes, only boxers, martial artists, and jockeys must deal with both the scales and their opponents.

The necessity to cut weight is the most vulnerable target of wrestling among those who dislike it; it is, in fact, the Achilles heel of the sport. Yet it will always be a part of amateur wrestling because athletes are divided into weight classifications to make the competition fairer. Another dimension to cutting weight is often overlooked, according to J Robinson, a world-class competitor who as a coach has taken the University of Minnesota to the pinnacle of the collegiate world. Under his direction, the Gophers won back-to-back NCAA titles (in 2001 and 2002) and set a national record for attendance at a dual meet, with 15,645 fans at the Minnesota–Iowa meet.

"You can slice it any way you want, but cutting weight makes you mentally tough," said Robinson. "There are hundreds of stories of good wrestlers who just couldn't cope with cutting weight. They had the physical skills but weren't mentally tough enough to handle it. Cutting weight is a part of wrestling and one of the things that makes it different from other sports and builds so much mental toughness.

"I have heard that the number one guys who make it as navy seals or rangers are ex-wrestlers, and there are reasons for that. What you are looking for in the special operations units are people who are very disciplined, can work at a high level while deprived of basics like food and sleep, are individuals by nature but can function very effectively for the good of the group when that is called for. That's what wrestling is all about."

Robinson wrestled at Oklahoma State University in the late 1960s and then went into the army. He graduated from ranger school with high honors and spent two and a half years in the program, serving in Vietnam.

"Wrestlers spend most of their lives learning how to function under stress and in denial of the basics like food and sleep," he said. "They can cut weight, suck down, and still go out and perform at a high level. Lack of sleep and food don't hold them back because they are trained to endure it. Everything in life is a 'learned skill development'—whatever skills you have you have learned through experience."

With 40 years in the sport, Robinson has seen numerous inspirational examples of weight cutting. "One of the best examples of mental toughness I can think of is the way Bruce Kinseth cut weight at Iowa," said Robinson, a tinge of awe in his voice. "We called him 'King of the Cutters' because of the way he could do it. He would cut 10 pounds in an hour, then go out and wrestle at an extremely high level.

"He could do it because he was in such incredible physical shape that his body could handle it. But what really allowed him to cut that much was his mental toughness. He was really, really tough mentally."

Weighing around 180 pounds in the off-season, Kinseth wrestled at 150 pounds his final two seasons at Iowa. He was NCAA runner-up in 1978 and then entered the zone for nearly his entire senior season. He pinned his way through the Big Ten tournament and then pinned his way through the NCAA championships of 1979. He was named outstanding wrestler at both tournaments, and Gable and others still use him today as the supreme example of a wrestler who paid an incredible price to reach his goals.

"Looking back at what Bruce accomplished is amazing," said Jed Brown, a teammate and close friend. "Most of his teammates were in awe of Bruce and his training methods. I've never seen anyone who could cut weight like that. And yes, it was his mental toughness that allowed him to do it."

But even the toughest wrestlers have been shaken to their core by cutting large amounts of weight over a prolonged period. One of the best-known stories is that of Barry Davis, the irrepressible star of the Hawkeye program during the early 1980s. A three-time Iowa state champion at Prairie High School, Barry was to become a three-time NCAA champion and four-time All-American at Iowa. He would eventually be named Big Ten Male Athlete of the Year in 1985 and would go on to win a silver medal in the 1984 Olympics and a silver medal in the 1987 world championships.

Davis was known for his total commitment to wrestling, to the Iowa program, and to the demands of the sport. He was enthusiastic, driven, disciplined, and uncomplaining. He simply loved the sport as few others ever have. Yet Barry Davis broke under the pressure of cutting too much weight over a prolonged period. No one saw it coming—not the coaches, not the teammates, not the fans. Yet it happened.

Barry won the first of his four Big Ten titles in 1981 and earned All-American honors as a freshman at the NCAA tournament.

"Davis began the 1981-82 season in typical Davis fashion, rolling over foe after foe," wrote Lou Banach. "All the time, he was paying an immense price, struggling to keep his weight at the 118-pound limit. Even the best machine will fatigue itself with overuse, however, and Davis overworked his body" (Banach 1985, 66).

Early on the morning of March 1, 1982, the morning the Iowa team was to leave for the Big Ten tournament in Ann Arbor, Michigan, Davis arrived at the Iowa workout room at 3 a.m. All alone, he pulled on his cold sweat clothes and climbed onto the stationary bike, desperate to cut a few remaining pounds. But several minutes later, he crawled off the machine. He walked to his locker, dressed, and wrote a note to head coach Dan Gable, the other coaches, and the team, saying that he simply could not cut the weight and was leaving the team. He wished them well, saying that he was sure they could win without him.

When the Hawkeye team filed in an hour later, teammate Dave Fitzgerald found the note and handed it to Gable. The coach read it and immediately set out to find his missing star, taking several teammates along. They found Barry in the checkout lane at a local grocery store, a bag of pastry in his hands.

Gable walked up to him, put his arm around him, and played the role of concerned parent and coach. They missed the plane to the tournament but booked another one. Gable stayed at the side of his prize pupil the entire time, working out with him, sharing the misery with him, helping him survive the combined mental and physical torture. Davis made weight, won his second Big Ten title, and won the NCAA championship that year. He finished at 46-1, setting a record for most victories in a season by a Hawkeye.

"He had weathered the storm and become a stronger wrestler," wrote Banach. "More importantly, he became a stronger man, for he had learned how to deal with adversity without buckling under it. It has taken a giant of a man to quit, to admit things were not going right and that a change of direction was needed, but it took an even bigger man to come back with the style and grace that Barry exhibited" (Banach 1985, 69).

Numerous such stories mark wrestling's long history. Robinson recalled the efforts of several Hawkeyes, back when he was the assistant coach, who cut huge amounts in 1984 to help the team win the NCAA championship.

"We had two top wrestlers at 134 pounds that year in Mark Trizzino and Greg Randall," said Robinson. "One of them had to go down to 126. Mark made the sacrifice and when he made weight you could see all the veins in his chest. It was amazing. Tim Riley had been at 126 and at the start of the season, he told me, 'There's no way I'm going back to 118 (where he had been an All-American the year before) so don't even ask.'

"But Riley finally dropped to 118 and with Mark at 126, we won the nationals. We all know wrestling is an individual sport, but it is also a team sport. These individuals make unbelievable sacrifices for the team. You see that over and over in wrestling."

At Iowa State, Joe Gibbons pulled a huge amount of weight to win All-American honors at 126 pounds in 1983. After he made his final weigh-in, he took his workout clothes out into a parking lot and burned them, letting everyone know he was through cutting that much weight!

Rick Sanders, perhaps one of the best pure wrestlers of all time, was also a weight cutter of legendary stature. Far off his weight class of 114.5 pounds at the Greco-Roman world championships in 1965 in Finland, he was ready to throw in the towel. But three of his teammates decided to take matters into their own hands.

"Larry Kristoff, Russ Camilleri and Bobby Douglas locked him in a sauna overnight and he looked like a prune the next day," said Wayne Baughman. "We carried him to weigh-in in a laundry basket and piled him on the scales. He barely made weight. He was one of the first matches up, less than three hours later. He lost two high-scoring matches to the eventual first- and second-place finishers but wrestled great in the only time he ever competed in an international Greco competition.

"I guess he also had a close call making weight the last day at the 1969 world freestyle championships," said Baughman. There, in Mar del Plata, Spain, Sanders and his coaches worked nonstop to get him to 114.5 pounds again, and he responded by winning the first gold medal ever for the Untied States in a world championship.

Baughman, one of America's most traveled competitors and coaches, saw many other great American wrestlers struggle terribly to make weight.

"Gene Davis making weight at the 1976 Olympics was something," he said. "If he'd had a little more time between weigh-in and competition or the officials hadn't screwed him, he would have definitely been a gold medal winner instead of bronze."

He also cited Chuck Yagla's making weight at the 1979 world championships and Mark Schultz's losing 11 pounds in 90 minutes before the 1988 Olympic trials and then beating the great Mike Sheets a short time later.

One of the best-known weight-cutting stories concerns Kendall Cross at the 1996 Olympic trials in Spokane. He had a terrible time making 125.5 pounds, and one official even declared it "a near-death experience." But he made the cut and then showed remarkable courage and durability by beating Terry Brands, two-time world champion, in one of the most exciting tryouts in American history. Cross dropped the first match but fought back to make the team with a pair of one-point wins.

In the Olympic Games in Atlanta, Cross was sensational. He plowed through the field without a close match on his way to a gold medal. Afterward, he gave credit to Brands for his help in making him so focused and tough in his preparations. He repeated the compliment in 2004.

The list could go on and on. Making weight is still one of the greatest challenges in all of sport, and then having to wrestle a short time later demands toughness that only those who have been through it can understand.

"You do what you have to do, but it takes mental toughness of the highest degree," said Robinson. "It's about paying the price to be a winner. In this dumbed-down society, where we even have five valedictorians at some places, wrestling is still a sport where there is just one champion per weight class."

THE ALTERNATIVE TO WEIGHT CUTTING

John Smith takes an entirely different view of weight cutting. He believed in disciplining himself year-round to keep his weight near his 136.5-pound weight classification. Year-round workouts and diet control were the keys for him.

"I was disciplined and I never bought into all that cutting weight stuff," he said in 2004. "I knew what I needed to do in my career and I avoided the kind of things that would burn me out on the sport, like cutting too much weight. In my opinion, guys who cut too much weight hate wrestling at the end of that and take three or four months off, and that's when they should be learning and drilling.

"Weight cutting can destroy your longevity in the sport," he continued. "It's a mental drain that you simply don't need. You shouldn't have to give your weight much thought. Some guys make the scales the enemy. I didn't have to deal with any of that because I kept my weight under control. I was tall and I could have wrestled 149 pounds, but I chose to keep my weight down so I could go at 136 pounds."

Smith's program worked well for him. Discipline was one of the foundations on which he fashioned a sensational career, particularly in the field of international wrestling.

One of the best arguments against cutting weight is the post-college career of John Peterson, who won an Olympic silver medal in 1972 and a gold medal in 1976.

Courtesy of Paul Jensen, The Gazette, Cedar Rapids, Iowa

John Peterson lifts a foe in preparation for a turn during competition in the 1970s. Peterson and his brother, Ben, were one of the most successful brother acts in American sports history, making five Olympic teams between them.

After graduating from college at Stout State in Wisconsin, where he placed fifth in the NAIA tournament at 167 pounds, John traveled to Ames, Iowa, to train with his brother, Ben, who was NCAA champion at 190 pounds for Iowa State. There, John began working out with the Cyclones in the off-season. He was thinking about entering the tryouts for the world championships but was hesitant to do so because he didn't feel that he could make the long cut to 163 pounds.

But one of the men he was training with, Dan Gable, convinced him that he could do well at 180.5 pounds.

"Dan said I shouldn't be trying to cut to 163, that I should just train hard, lift weights to improve my strength, and wrestle at 180.5," recalled John years later. "That was a new way of thinking for me. I was only weighing about 175 pounds and it was hard to adjust my thinking to not trying to cut to 163. But I took Dan's advice."

Gable was wrestling at 149.5 pounds and was hardly cutting any weight at all, because his incredible training regime was keeping him within 5 pounds of his competition weight all year long.

At the trials, Peterson surprised just about everyone by making the U.S. team at 180.5. A year later, again without cutting weight, he astonished the wrestling experts when he emerged from the tryouts as the 180.5-pounder on the 1972 Olympic team, while Ben made the team at 198 pounds. John and Ben were not cutting weight; they were simply training so hard that they had no excess weight on their lean, muscular bodies. And they decided to compete at their "regular" body weight. The results were stunning, as both men came home from Munich with medals.

"The fact is that rather than starve myself into a 163-pounder, I built myself into a 180-pounder," said John three decades later. "Ben did the same thing. He was always struggling to keep his weight up around 198 pounds. If I hadn't been at 180, he probably would have tried to cut there himself and I doubt he would have done near as well in Munich as he did by staying up at 198.

"Gable got us in such great shape. His philosophy was that mentally you're making weight every day. His mentality was if you don't work out, you don't eat. Ben and I wanted to eat, so we worked out two and three times a day so that we could eat. We ate all we wanted, every day, until a couple of days before a major event, and then we would cut back on food intake and liquids. But I didn't miss meals. Neither did Ben."

The Petersons won numerous national and international honors over the next decade and stamped themselves as two of the finest wrestlers in U.S. history, and they did it all without weight cutting. In fact, they often weighed in at less than their weight class and were serious weight trainers during their long careers.

"I think not cutting weight was one of the keys to our success," said John. "I've never been an advocate of cutting much weight."

WRESTLING WITH PAIN AND FATIGUE

Pain is another adversity that wrestlers must learn to live with. Pain comes in many forms—from broken fingers, to cauliflower ears, to torn knee ligaments. Pain is a constant companion in a sport where athletes are plowing into each other without pads, banging heads, gripping fingers, and dropping to their knees in takedown attempts.

For the most part, wrestlers have learned to accept pain. Some even wear their bandages with a sense of pride, and cauliflower ears have become a badge of honor for many wrestlers. When the ears become swollen with blood, an athlete can choose to have the ear drained with a needle, but in many cases the problem will return throughout the season. Most wrestlers just learn to live with the enlarged ears and even come to appreciate them as a proof of their involvement in one of the roughest sports known to man (and now to women).

And then there is the pain of fatigue. One key element of the Iowa success story during the Gable era was the price that Iowa wrestlers paid in fatigue. Of course, they forced their opponents to pay the same price if they were to have a chance to win against them.

"There's no limit on pain in the practice room," said Tom Brands, who spent 17 years in the Iowa program, including 5 as an athlete and 12 as a coach. "You keep doing one more, one more, one more. You'd actually black out sometimes and find yourself still going several moments later.

"Once I was wrestling so hard and was so exhausted that I blacked out in the middle of a move. But suddenly I was on top and riding the other guy. I don't even know what happened, but I just kept wrestling. That was trained into us. Many times, we made other wrestlers quit during the match, not because they wanted to but because they had to."

Their opponents simply weren't trained the same way and weren't accustomed to paying the price. The Iowa program taught its wrestlers to keep going and going and going, despite the pain and intense desire to stop. Hawkeye wrestlers were trained to go through the pain barrier and to keep paying the price. Years after their careers were over, many were still in awe of what they had endured.

"I'd rather do time (in prison) than go through that again," said Royce Alger, the two-time NCAA champion who was known for his never-say-die, straight-ahead, relentless attacking style.

The world's finest athletes understand that slamming up against the ultimate wall of the pain barrier in the training process is one of the keys to incredible athletic success.

"Just because your muscles start to protest doesn't mean you have to listen," said Dianne Holum, Olympic speed skating champion.

"I like the 1,500-meter race the most," said Eric Heiden, winner of five gold medals in Olympic speed skating, "but I've got to prepare for the pain. The only way you can win is by suffering a lot—by working through the pain" (Ferguson 1990, 6-17).

"You learn pain in practice and you will know it in every race," said Don Schollander, winner of five Olympic gold medals. "As you approach the limit of your endurance, it begins coming on gradually, hitting your stomach first. Your stomach feels as if it's going to fall out—every kick hurts like heck—and suddenly you hear a shrill, internal scream. It is right there, at the pain barrier, that the great competitors are separated from the rest" (Ferguson 1990, 6-16).

They were expressing a philosophy that Arnold Schwarzenegger understood while becoming the most successful bodybuilder of all time in the 1970s. The sport of bodybuilding demands tremendous pain tolerance, because the muscles don't grow to superhuman size unless put under tremendous duress. Pain is the constant companion of all high-level bodybuilders, a point that Schwarzenegger stressed when making the popular documentary *Pumping Iron*.

Both Dan Gable and Tom Brands have said one of their secret desires is to work out so hard in the practice room that they simply cannot leave the room on their own. Gable admits that he came close several times while training at Iowa State and for the Olympics but somehow could always manage to stand and stagger out.

"It was my goal to have to crawl out of the room, but I never quite made it," said Brands in 2004. "That always disappointed me."

Jim Courier, winner of four Grand Slam titles in tennis, summed it all up: "You have to be extreme to be exceptional."

The philosophy outlined by Courier, Schwarzenegger, Gable, and Brands is indeed extreme. But so were their accomplishments!

Success can be a double-edged sword when a champion wrestler thinks that he can win at the highest level without training as hard as he did to get to the top. Lou Banach learned that lesson after he won the NCAA heavyweight crown as a sophomore in 1981.

"I was gaining something that would cause problems—vanity," he wrote. "As long as I was considered the best, I thought that I would enjoy it. I began to rely more on my credentials than on the ingredients that had made me a champion. I figured that a champion doesn't need to work out, to lift weights and to run 'all that much.' After all, at Iowa, all you really had to do was think and believe that you were the best, and would be. It went with the territory" (Banach 1985, 51).

Banach discovered the truth in time to pull out of a possible tailspin. He rededicated himself to the training program that had made him a champion. The adversity that he faced was double-sided in nature, working at both a physical and an emotional level.

SHUTTING OUT SELF-DOUBT

Another form of adversity that all athletes have to face at some time in their career is self-doubt. At one time or another in their careers, all wrestlers have faced self-doubt when they stepped onto a mat. Perhaps they were less skilled, less prepared, or less motivated than they wanted to be or knew they should be. Perhaps they had started the sport much later than the foe had and had less knowledge and experience to call on. Maybe they were not as physically gifted or as mentally tough. Maybe they even got scared or choked.

"Anybody who has played sports and says they have never choked is lying to you," said Pete Sampras, who won Wimbledon seven times.

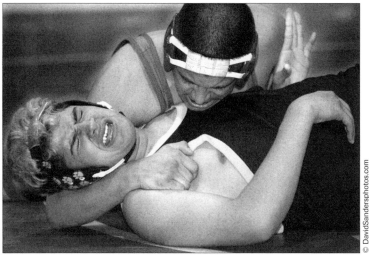

This pin is the ultimate form of victory (and defeat) in wrestling. Here, one wrestler nears the ultimate victory while the other is experiencing the agony of defeat.

"The real tough guys get scared, everyone gets scared a little," said Kim Wood, former strength trainer of the Cincinnati Bengals. "But it's that period of time when you decide to take it up several notches, and it's lightning quick when you need to make that decision. It comes from being prepared at all times for what may happen."

Randy Couture said that the first time he entered a mixed martial arts competition, he experienced a strong mixture of both excitement and fear. Mark Kerr, a former NCAA wrestling champion who had tremendous success early in his combat career, said that he was plain scared before his initial match. And Gable admits that Larry Owings' statements that he came to the 1970 NCAA tournament to beat Gable placed doubts in Gable's mind and played a large role in his first loss after 181 consecutive victories.

"It's been said that existence reveals itself by surprises," added Wood. "Well, that means you have to be prepared all the time. That is the real essence of the warrior's training. You have to know how to deal with surprises and diversions. I think that's maybe why Dan Gable lost to Larry Owings in his final college match. He was still young and had never been there before, in a situation where he was losing. He fell behind quickly, then went into what looked like a kind of shock.

"But he was fighting back at the end. If there had been 20 more seconds, he probably would have won. And I'm sure he learned a lot about himself, and the importance of preparation in all instances, in that match.

"You have to train so that if you lose the battle you can still win the war. That's the key. And that takes preparation!"

Thomas Tutko obviously agreed with the sentiment when he wrote the following: "Many of their experiences in the so-called 'arousal zone' of peak performance seem related to a need to defend their ego and self esteem, resulting occasionally in a type of 'fight or flight' on the playing field. These insecurities often leave them with a strong need to prove themselves, driving them through years of rigorous training . . ." (Tutko and Tosi 1976, vii).

Jeff Blatnick became a folk hero of sorts by overcoming considerable adversity before the 1984 Olympics. Diagnosed with Hodgkin's disease, a form of cancer that attacks the lymph nodes, it seemed that his athletic career was over. But he was determined to fight the disease and ultimately came back strong and healthy to make the Greco-Roman team in the super heavyweight division. Then, in

Los Angeles, he defeated the 1982 world champion from Yugoslavia in the first round before losing a narrow match to a wrestler from Greece.

Facing Thomas Johansson of Sweden—a foe whom Blatnick acknowledged was younger, heavier, and stronger—for the gold medal, Blatnick decided on a strategy that would capitalize on his own superb conditioning, attacking from the outset. He wore down the Swedish star and scored two points in the closing minutes for a dramatic 2-0 victory. The photo of Blatnick sinking to the mat, hands clasped in prayer, was shown around the world, and his Olympic teammates voted him the huge honor of carrying the American flag in the closing ceremonies.

But he had to fight a much larger battle before he could even dare to think of wrestling in the Olympics.

"In the spring of 1982, I was in the best shape of my life, both physically and emotionally, working toward my goal of making the 1984 Olympic team and winning a medal," he said. "Primed, focused and determined, I was defending national champion when my world was again upended and slammed to the mat" (Naber 1999, 47).

Five years earlier, in 1977, he had suffered a huge blow when his brother, David, who had introduced him to wrestling, was killed in a motorcycle accident. His brother's death had been a devastating loss. Now he learned that he had Hodgkin's disease.

"Here I was, a six-foot, two-inch wrestler, stopped at the peak of my career by an almost invisible, yet frequently fatal disease. I felt I was no longer the master of my destiny; cancer was now in control. This was way more than a wrestling match. How in the world was I going to remain focused on winning an Olympic medal while I sparred with this unfamiliar opponent? My life had changed."

But Jeff didn't waste much time and energy feeling sorry for himself. Instead, he resolved to find solutions. He drew upon his wrestling experiences to help.

Chris Campbell is another who was determined to prove himself at the Olympic Games and, as a result, overcame adversity to win an Olympic medal.

He was indisputably one of the two or three best wrestlers in the entire world in the early 1980s. A two-time NCAA champion at the University of Iowa at 177 pounds, he was on track to win a gold medal at the 1980 Olympics in Moscow. Just a year later, in 1981, he breezed to the gold medal in the world championship and was named the world's best technical wrestler.

But he, like hundreds of other top athletes, was denied the opportunity to win an Olympic gold medal the year before when President Jimmy Carter announced that the United States would boycott the games in Moscow as a means of protesting the Soviet Union's invasion of Afghanistan.

Campbell retired from wrestling after winning the world championship in 1981 to pursue a law degree. But 11 years later, in 1992, he decided to try out again for the Olympics. He was now 37 years old and well past his wrestling prime. But Campbell was a man of immense skills and immense pride, and he made the team at 198 pounds. Then, to top it all off, he won five matches in Barcelona and returned home with a bronze medal. Campbell had shown the world how to overcome stark adversity by dreaming big and exerting a powerful will.

SUMMARY

Dealing with adversity is a major part of life and an integral part of sport. Overcoming adversity is certainly a significant part of wrestling. Anyone who wrestles for a prolonged period will have to deal with the pressures and setbacks of the sport. Wrestlers must contend with the unique pressure of cutting weight. They must be able to wrestle with pain and fatigue and have the ability to overcome self-doubt.

PART II

The Essence of Wrestling Tough

11

The Link Between Mental and Physical Toughness

"The thing that makes winning so difficult, and I mean winning anything, even a five-cent ring toss much less the Tour, is that the mind and the body almost never work together cooperatively," said Lance Armstrong, six-time winner of the Tour de France, in his autobiography. "Mostly we are at odds with ourselves . . ." (Armstrong 2000, 281).

Few athletes understand pain to the degree that Armstrong does. Riding the Tour de France demands every single ounce of mental and physical toughness that a person can summon up. It's a tortuous three-week race of more than 2,000 miles, up and through the mountains, down steep grades at speeds of 70 miles an hour. Riders pound the pedals for hours at a crack with no letup.

"Cycling is so hard, the suffering is so intense, that it's absolutely cleansing," added Armstrong. "You can go out there with the weight of the world on your shoulders and after a six-hour-long ride at a high pain threshold, you feel at peace. The pain is so deep and strong that a curtain descends over your brain."

For the mind and body to work together, the athlete must understand pain. If they ever hope to be winners, wrestlers must recognize the huge difference between pain and injury.

ACCEPTING PAIN

One man who clearly understood the difference and became a legend through conquering pain was Harry Houdini. The greatest magician and escape artist of all time, Houdini was an American icon in the early part of the 20th century. Born in Budapest, Hungary, as Ehrich Weiss, he adopted the stage name Houdini. By the early 1920s he was the talk of the nation. He thrilled huge crowds by dangling hundreds of feet in the air wrapped up in a strait jacket and then wiggling free as the crowd held its collective breath far below.

Houdini was a genius at escaping from any set of handcuffs, any jail or prison. He once was submerged in the icy Hudson River in New York City, entombed in a coffin that was securely locked on the outside. On the inside, he was wrapped in chains. When he escaped from the coffin, he was to grab the supporting chain from which the coffin was suspended and follow the chain up to the large hole in the ice to safety. But the chain holding the coffin broke as the coffin was submerged, and when he escaped from the coffin, he had no way to find the hole in the ice.

A crowd that included his wife watching from a bridge over the river began to panic. After half an hour had passed, almost everyone gave him up for dead. Nearly two hours later Houdini finally emerged, shivering uncontrollably. His body temperature was so low that he was near death. He had freed himself almost immediately but could not find the hole in the ice. Houdini had drifted along in the freezing water, sucking pockets of air from under the ice while trying to find the exit hole. His miraculous escape was credited to his incredible poise and his ability to tolerate pain. He did not panic and lose control but methodically searched for the opening, fighting off the numbing effects of the frigid water.

Houdini died at age 52 in 1926, but his legend has endured for eight decades. Part of the secret of his escapes and tricks was his incredible physical condition. Houdini was a fitness fanatic, and he knew that his body needed to be in extraordinary shape to endure the hardships that he would put it through. Another huge key to his success was his ability to accept pain. He knew that pain was part of the lifestyle he had chosen, and he ignored it and accepted it.

Dr. Robert J. Albo, a sports doctor who has worked with a number of top professional teams, made a powerful point in a television special on Houdini that appeared on the Discovery Health Channel: "Soldiers run across battlefields and get shot and not even know it until afterwards due to the adrenaline rush. Athletes are much the same," said Albo. He compared the situation to Houdini's ability to ignore pain: "He had learned to live with pain."

Wrestling is replete with stories of men who have blocked out intense pain to compete at a high level. Three standard ways of measuring the price that a wrestler must pay to attain success are (1) dealing with pain, (2) dealing with the various distractions that all athletes face, and (3) cutting weight, often drastic amounts of it. We'll talk about dealing with pain here; chapters 7 and 10 discussed dealing with distractions and cutting weight.

In the first area, Wayne Wells provided an excellent example of an amazing juggling act. Wells was a three-time All-American at the University of Oklahoma in the 1960s and won the 152-pound NCAA title in 1968. He is one of just nine wrestlers to win the NCAAs, the worlds, and the Olympics. After claiming his gold medal at 163 pounds in Munich in 1972, he retired from wrestling and became a highly successful attorney. Wells is one of wrestling's finest role models, showing that it is possible to excel in both wrestling and academics at the same time. And he did it while facing tremendous pressure, both on and off the mat, and by enduring considerable pain.

"Wayne Wells wrestled through the entire tournament and won the 1972 Olympics with a separated and displaced rib and an enlarged spleen," said Wayne Baughman, a teammate at the University of Oklahoma. "He also wrestled in the 1971 Pan Am Games with a major knee injury that required a complete reconstruction immediately following the competition."

At that point, Wells decided to follow his doctors' advice to forget wrestling and concentrate on finishing law school. But Bill Farrell, head coach of the 1972 Olympic freestyle team, talked him into reconsidering. Wells rehabilitated his knee, finished his last semester of law school, studied for and passed his bar exam, and won the national freestyle championships, the Olympic trials, and the Olympic Games, all in a period of about 90 days.

Wells knew about paying a price and about overcoming both pain and distractions in pursuit of his dreams.

TYING TOGETHER PHYSICAL AND MENTAL TOUGHNESS

"The mind and the body are one," said expert Jim Loehr, who is founder of LGR Performance Systems, a motivational training center located in Orlando, Florida. "Mental toughness is not just something you can sit in a room and visualize and all of a sudden you are mentally tough. The ability to handle physical stress takes us right into the ability to handle mental and emotional stress" (Tolson 2000, 41).

All wrestlers have experienced pain at various levels, mentally and physically. Often they are tied together. Wrestlers must deal with countless injuries, ranging from twisted fingers to broken noses, from damaged knees to separated shoulders. No athlete who has been in the sport for long will escape an injury of some type. They come in all forms and shapes, and in various degrees of discomfort and seriousness.

Ronnie Clinton was one of the most gifted wrestlers of his era. Coming from Ponca City High School, he made a name for himself at Oklahoma State University with his surfer-style good looks and his smooth mat style. As a sophomore in 1960, he was NCAA runner-up at 167 pounds. But the Oklahoma State lineup was packed from top to bottom with tremendous wrestlers, and in his junior year he could not crack the lineup at his regular weight. He jumped up two entire weight classes and finished third at the 1961 NCAA championships at 191 pounds. His ability to compete effectively nearly 23 pounds above the spot at which he wanted to be was testament to his resolve, commitment, and mental toughness.

But the truest test to Clinton's toughness didn't come until the final match of his senior year. Back at 167 pounds, he was on target for the NCAA title that had thus far eluded him. The NCAA championships were on his home campus in Stillwater, Oklahoma. In the Saturday night finals, he was facing Terry Isaacson, a talented athlete from Iowa who was also a star quarterback on the football team for the Air Force Academy.

On the night before the finals, a freak accident almost put Clinton out of the tournament. While he was shaving, his hand slipped and fell onto a mirror, shattering the glass. The result was a badly cut palm on his right hand, one that required numerous stitches. Less than 24 hours later, Clinton was on the mat, facing Isaacson, and facing his last chance to become an NCAA champion. Ironically, Isaacson had sustained a two-inch eyebrow cut in a previous round, and the cut reopened in the match with Clinton. Both Clinton and Isaacson were bleeding profusely, and the match was stopped numerous times for extended periods for both to be treated. Discussion occurred in both corners and with the official about injury default and extended injury and blood time.

Clinton could hardly squeeze his hand during the entire match. With blood soaking through his bandages, Clinton posted a narrow, hard-fought victory. He had shown that he was not only a slick and exciting wrestler but also a mentally tough and determined one. He had wrestled extremely tough when the need arose, blocking out the physical pain and mental doubts that must have accompanied him on the mat, to perform at his highest level.

"I believe each wrestler thought the other would give up and throw in the towel but neither did," recalled Wayne Baughman. "It was a gutsy match. I remember it well because I was warming up just one more match away from my final and my anxiety level was being prolonged by their match."

In 1988 Rob Koll of the University of North Carolina was facing his final opportunity to become an NCAA champion, following in the footsteps of his famous father, Bill, who won three titles in the late 1940s at Iowa State Teachers College. Rob had placed third the previous year and was determined to go out on top. But he severely injured his knee in a first-round match at the NCAA meet in Ames, Iowa.

"I heard a tearing sound and it really swelled up," Koll admitted later. "But I said they'd have to tear my leg off to make me quit."

Instead of folding, he got tougher as the tourney wore on. Battered and limping, he scored a pin in the finals and received his first-place medal from none other than his father, who was asked to present the awards to all those in the 158-pound class that year.

"Records also are frequently the product of playing through pain," wrote Thomas Tutko in *Sports Psyching*. "In track and field events, and in swimming particularly, an athlete's high pain threshold may be as significant as his basic ability" (Tutko and Tosi 1976, 24).

Six-time world and Olympic champion John Smith became familiar with pain during his sensational freestyle career. He suffered from broken fingers, sprained ankles, torn rib cartilage, a separated shoulder, damaged knee ligaments, cauliflower ears, and extremely painful hip pointers. But Smith knew, as do other high-achieving wrestlers, that injuries are part of the game and that a wrestler must learn to live with them and block them out.

While covering the 1988 Olympics for the *Chicago Tribune*, writer John Husar captured what winning a gold medal can cost a wrestler like John Smith.

John Smith, who overcame several injuries throughout his wrestling career, is intent upon turning his opponent for back points during this match in the 1988 national freestyle championships.

"His nose had been broken Tuesday by the Bulgarian and Smith said he had never bled so much," wrote Husar. "His bent and stubby fingers that had been broken four or five times apiece were jammed anew and swollen, and his right shoulder was crying for arthroscopic surgery. But none of that hurt as much, he said, as the rawness on his backside, where he wore away the skin sitting nightly in his rubber suit on the stationary bike."

"'Aw, it's nothing, really,' he assured a knot of incredulous reporters. 'All athletes go through this type of stuff. Aches and pains come with sport. You've just gotta adapt to 'em'" (Husar 1988, 12).

Adapt he did, and again in 1992, when he was searching for his second Olympic gold medal. This time, Smith was facing a different type of injury.

"I had a staph infection hit me in January and it tore me up," said Smith in 2004. "My whole head was swollen, and I had bald spots on my head, too. It just gradually got worse. I suffered from fatigue. After just 15 minutes of drilling, I would be exhausted.

"During some practices, it felt like my head was going to explode. It took everything I had to mentally get through the Olympic trials and the Olympics. It would have been easy for some guys to just walk away at that point, to settle for something less. But I couldn't do that.

"I remember writers coming up and acting surprised that I could keep going, and I thought, 'What's the big deal? It comes with the territory.' I've just always assumed injuries are part of the game."

In that respect, he was akin to Dan Gable, who entered the 1972 Olympics in Munich with a severely damaged left knee. In the first match, Gable's foe from Yugoslavia headbutted him, opening a gash that required seven stitches to close.

"Sure, it hurt," said Gable years later. "But so what? The point of wrestling is that it hurts and you overcome that. It never occurred to me that it wasn't supposed to hurt."

Pain is part of the game at the highest levels. The finest athletes have learned to accept it and to ignore it, in many respects.

"All of the great athletes I have known have an almost unlimited horizon for pain," wrote photograph-artist Roger Riger in his memorable book *The Athlete*. "Pain is their enemy, but they never admit it, never discuss it. Athletes at the height of their power must endure pain beyond their imagination and what they thought was their capacity for suffering in order to achieve their maximum performance" (Riger 1980, 152).

DISTINGUISHING PAIN AND INJURY

All athletes must learn at some point in their careers how to deal with pain. Just as important, they need to learn how to differentiate pain from injury. Knowing the difference could be essential to their achieving their goals.

Athletes feel the pain of preparation when they push themselves physically and mentally to a new level of awareness and acceptance. A completely different type of pain comes from injury. Randy Lewis, one of the best wrestlers in American history, knew firsthand about the pain of preparation from years of work in wrestling rooms around the country. But the pain that he ran into on a cold winter night in January 1981 was of a kind that he had never conceived of before, let alone experienced. Nearly 10,000 wrestling fans poured into Hilton Arena in Ames to see the annual showdown between two of the nation's premier wrestling powers, the University of Iowa and Iowa State University.

Dan Gable coached the Hawkeyes of Iowa, while Dr. Harold Nichols, who coached Gable during his superstar years at Iowa State, led the Cyclones of Iowa State. The fans were noisy and animated as the meet got under way. Iowa won the first two matches and held an 8-0 lead when the 134-pounders stepped onto the mat.

Lewis, one of the most exciting wrestlers of the modern era, represented Iowa. He was 89-0 with 83 pins in high school in Rapid City, South Dakota. He had won the junior world championships in 1977 with a pin in the gold-medal match. He already owned two NCAA championships and was riding a streak of 74 consecutive wins in college. His foe in the cardinal-colored uniform was Jim Gibbons, a three-time state champion from Iowa well known as a scrapper who never gave up. He was a returning All-American, having placed seventh the year before. Lewis, having beaten Gibbons on several previous occasions, was the favorite, but Gibbons had been coming on strong during the season and was nearing the top of his game.

The two battled nonstop, trading moves and counters. Midway through the second period, Lewis held a 4-3 lead when the unimaginable happened. In the midst of a wild scramble for the takedown, Gibbons lifted Lewis and drove him forcefully to the mat. Lewis extended his left arm to cushion the fall—and a terrible noise was heard. Suddenly, Lewis was writhing on the mat in stunning pain while the referee gaped at the injured Hawkeye. Coaches Gable and Nichols stumbled onto the mat but then backed away, shocked by what they saw.

It was then, and remains today, one of the worst injuries ever to occur on a collegiate wrestling mat.

"Jim used to hit a high crotch (takedown) on me a lot, but I had two counters for it," recalled Lewis 23 years later. "One was to extend my left arm, post and reverse him all at once.

"That time, he hit me with this high crotch and I hit the mat. I remember thinking, 'Why didn't I score? I should be on top now.' And then the pain hit me. It was terrible. I looked over at my left arm and couldn't see the part under the elbow. It was pushed so far back that I couldn't see it at all. I thought my arm was broken off at the elbow."

His arm wasn't broken off, but it was severely dislocated, going the opposite way God intended it to bend. When the huge crowd discovered what had happened, the arena went dead quiet. Officials carried Randy off the mat to the trainer's room in the back of the arena. He thinks he was in shock.

With three Big Ten titles and two national championships already under his belt, Lewis faced a sudden and devastating end to his great college career. To get to the NCAAs in Ames, he needed to place in the top four at the Big Ten championships, just six weeks away. The question in everyone's mind was whether he could recover quickly enough to place in the Big Ten meet.

"They never told me how bad the injury was until the season was over," said Lewis. "Gable didn't want me to know. It was a mental thing."

How Lewis responded is a testimony to both his mental toughness and his physical toughness. Few athletes have ever exhibited more raw courage after such a severe injury.

"I was ready to wrestle by the time the Big Tens rolled around, at least mentally," he said. "I won my first two matches to make the finals, and then got beat by Dalen Wasmund of Minnesota, 17-8. I was doing OK early on and even was ahead at one point. It wasn't that my arm hurt so much as it just tired out. I had damaged all the ligaments and blood vessels badly and the arm just wasn't the same yet.

"I had won before the injury by being both mentally and physically dominant," he said. "I only knew one way to wrestle, and that was all out. I hadn't yet learned how to wrestle with injuries like this, so I didn't know how to pace myself. Years later, after suffering other injuries and learning to cope with them, I knew how to wrestle differently."

Although he didn't win his fourth straight Big Ten title, he qualified for the nationals again. He had placed second in the NCAA meet as a pure freshman. As a sophomore in 1979 he completed an unbeaten season by winning the 126-pound championships. As a junior he moved up a weight to challenge the defending NCAA champion, Darryl Burley of Lehigh, and beat him three straight times, including a victory in the NCAA finals of 1980.

The 134-pound class was loaded in 1981. The class included two NCAA champions (Lewis and Burley), a future NCAA champion (Jim Gibbons), a future Olympian (Buddy Lee of Old Dominion), and stars like Derek Glenn of Colorado, Harlan Kistler of UCLA (and, later, Iowa), and Thomas Landrum of Oklahoma State.

Lewis won his first two matches and found himself in the quarterfinal round against Gibbons. The Cyclone posted a victory, putting himself into the semifinals and Lewis into the wrestle backs for the first time in his collegiate career. Lewis wound up in seventh place, becoming an All-American for the fourth time.

Looking back from the perspective of 23 years, Lewis sighs when asked how he prepared mentally to step back onto the mat after such a severe injury in just six weeks.

"I really don't know how I handled it," he said finally. "I knew there were certain things I couldn't do, because of it. But I've never felt like I lost because of the injury. I really don't. I lost because I didn't know how to be mentally tough enough to overcome the injury. I was just 21 years old and had never experienced anything like that.

"Facing that adversity made me better in the future, because I learned how to be mentally tough enough to deal with injuries. I think if that injury would have happened later in my career I could have recovered better and quicker mentally."

And then he said something incredible, further evidence of his mental toughness: "I don't look back on that match and say I wish it never happened. My regrets in my career aren't about that match at all. They are more about the times officials stepped in and changed the outcome of matches, like in the world championships of 1982 when I was given a win over the world champion from Bulgaria, and then the decision was reversed hours later. That's the sort of thing that angers me, not the matches I was injured in."

That philosophy of acceptance—that injuries are part of the sport and that dwelling on them is pointless—made Randy Lewis a supreme competitor and a prime example of wrestling tough.

Two native Illinois wrestlers displayed the same kind courage three decades later, also in the NCAA finals. One achieved victory; the other lost in overtime. Both earned tremendous accolades for their inspiring efforts against unbelievable pain, both physical and mental.

John Kading was a two-time high school state champion in Illinois. He proved himself a warrior all the way through his college career at the University of Oklahoma. He was an All-American at heavyweight as a freshman and at 190 as a sophomore, and he won the 190-pound NCAA title as a junior. But his senior year turned into a nightmare of pain and frustration.

Early in his final season, he severely strained a hip flexor, missing a number of matches. After returning to action, he tore the anterior cruciate ligament in his knee. He was fitted with a cumbersome knee brace that hindered his movement. Then, a few days before the Big Twelve championships, the qualifying tournament for the NCAA, he tore both the lateral and medial cartilage in the same knee.

"We diligently sought to secure a wild card (a spot that would allow Kading to wrestle in the NCAAs without qualifying in the Big Twelve meet) since even training to make weight (at 190 pounds) seemed impossible," said Oklahoma coach Jack Spates. If John could have at least made weight and stepped on a mat before forfeiting, the conference coaches could have voted him a wild-card entry into the NCAA meet.

"The day before the Big Twelve tournament, John informed us he was going to wrestle," said Spates. "We were astonished. There was no way he could wrestle . . . but he did and he won!" (Spates 1999, 61).

Kading showed up at the national tournament with his leg so heavily wrapped that he looked like an escapee from *The Mummy* movie location. He reinjured his knee in the first match and at one point literally crawled back to the mat to resume wrestling.

Incredibly, Kading won four consecutive matches. After each win, many of the fans left the arena shaking their heads in amazed respect for the valiant Sooner, who was obviously wrestling in torturous pain. Years later, Spates admitted that he even considered throwing in the towel during one of the matches but said, "If you throw in the towel on John Kading, he picks it up and belts you over the head with it."

Kading and Lee Fullhart, a powerful and intense sophomore from Iowa, battled to a tie in regulation time in the finals. Kading lost the coin flip in overtime and was faced with riding Fullhart for 30 seconds to secure the win. Fullhart escaped, and the battered Kading had to settle for second place and a thunderous ovation from the more than 15,000 fans in attendance, who rose to their feet to salute the young athlete who had shown everyone what courage is all about.

In the following weeks, letters and phone calls poured into the University of Oklahoma wrestling office from fans wanting to tell John Kading how much his performance meant to them. Several said that he had changed their lives with his display of raw courage.

"John's performance, even in losing, was a celebration of the human spirit," said Spates. And that it was!

Eric Siebert enjoyed a tremendous high school career at LaSalle-Peru High School, wrestling for his dad, Mark—one of the state's top coaches. Known for his lightning-quick moves and power attacks, Siebert set a new Illinois state record with 40 consecutive pins and ended the season with a 46-0 mark, 42 pins, and the state title at 145 pounds. He also won the junior nationals that summer.

He was injured much of his time at the University of Illinois. Still, he managed to place fifth in the NCAAs at 150 pounds in 1997. He entered his final season with high expectations, but they all came tumbling down during the Big Ten championships. In the quarter-final round, Siebert tore his rib cartilage. He defaulted out of the tournament with a sixth-place finish, which was good enough to qualify him for a spot in the NCAA championships two weeks later. A sense of gloom descended on the Illinois wrestling room.

"In my experience, a torn rib cartilage is not a real serious injury but it is one of the most painful injuries you can get," said Illinois coach Mark Johnson. "You can barely move without intense pain. It was a terrible situation because we had thought before the injury that Eric could win it all."

Siebert could not wrestle or even run for the 10 days between the Big Ten tournament and the NCAAs. He was in such severe pain that he was restricted to swimming, and even that was tremendously uncomfortable.

"We thought it was going to be extremely difficult for him to even place in the tournament," said Johnson. "He didn't wrestle once prior to the meet. He would go into the swimming pool and also do some stationary bike riding. That was it. But we had a game plan."

Coaches Johnson, Jim Heffernan, and Steve Marianetti and trainer Scott Frisbee met several times to consider their options. The coaches trained Siebert to score at the end of each period. Finally, they decided that he could take shots of lydocaine before every match. They brought in a huge needle to inject him an hour before each bout began.

When the Illinois contingent arrived at the NCAA tournament, Johnson couldn't wait to see the brackets. "I said to myself, please, don't let us get a rat tail at 150 pounds. And when I opened up the brackets, there it was . . . we get a rat tail at 150 pounds." A rat tail is an extra match at the start of a tournament used to even out a weight class. Siebert would have to win six straight matches, instead of the normal five, to claim the NCAA title. It looked like an impossible task.

Having lost his edge by not wrestling for nearly nine days before the meet and with intense pain, Siebert gained the finals with five consecutive wins. All had been close and hard fought. In the championship match, he was facing a tough adversary, Chad Kraft of Minnesota. They had been ranked one and two all season long. The hill looked as if it might be too tall for Siebert to climb at the very end, but Kraft suffered a severe ankle injury in the opening moments of the match. Suddenly, two injured warriors were on center stage.

Siebert emerged with a hard-fought and extremely courageous 7-3 win. In the media room afterward, he was both relieved and gracious in his comments.

"I knew I wasn't 100 percent going into the match," he said. "Obviously, (Kraft) suffered a pretty good injury to his ankle and it definitely hindered his performance. You could see it. I just tried to really focus on what I had to do, wrestle hard and just concentrate.

© Sport the Library

A wrestler (bottom) gives it everything he has within him as he tries to turn his opponent for back points. A combination of physical and mental toughness is at work here.

There's no way I could have gotten here without my coaches, my teammates, my parents, my family, the doctors, the trainers. They knew I was hurting."

He then announced that he was retired from official competition. He walked away a battered and bruised wrestler, but he was the ultimate winner for all he had endured. Years later, Mark Johnson still found it hard to believe what both Kading and Siebert had endured in their stirring quests to become national champions.

"What both of them did was amazing," said Johnson, a member of the 1980 Olympic Greco-Roman team. "I thought what Eric did was one of the most courageous things I've ever seen in wrestling. In fact, we've named an award after him at Illinois. And anyone who saw what John Kading did has the utmost respect for him, and the way he faced incredible adversity."

USING ADVERSITY AS A STEPPING-STONE

Of course, countless other wrestlers have overcome severe injuries and dealt with pain. The chances of being injured have increased dramatically through the years because of the greatly increased number of matches and the introduction of throwing moves that can send a wrestler to the mat under wild conditions.

"Rarely does a wrestler have the luxury of training or competing completely free of injury or illness," related Wayne Baughman, one of the most successful wrestlers in American history. Baughman was NCAA champion for the University of Oklahoma at 191 pounds in 1962 and owns a total of 16 national titles in collegiate, freestyle, Greco-Roman, and sombo wrestling. He also was a member of three Olympic teams.

"When he does have a day when everything feels good, he'd better really enjoy it and 'make hay while the sun shines' because those days don't appear often. Even on those rare occasions of no injury or illness, there is the pain of exhaustion or of cutting weight or just getting and staying out of your comfort zone in order to improve or 'move it up a notch.'

"Almost anyone can be successful or win when everything is going right, they are feeling good and have no problems," Baughman added. "The real champions are the ones who can come through when they are really hurting, everything is going wrong and the sky is falling all around them. Whether it's an injury, illness, a tragedy in the family, a business failure, academic problems or any other kind of adversity, true champions seem to overcome and even thrive on the challenge, using the adversity to make them better."

In the first several decades of collegiate wrestling, a complete season was often around 16 to 18 matches. By the end of the year 2000, a wrestler could wrestle 50 or more times in a single year. In 1957 Dan Hodge finished his entire career with a 46-0 record; in 2002 Cael Sanderson closed out at 159-0, meaning that he had more than three times as many chances to suffer an injury.

"There is a difference between 'hurt' and 'injury'—or, more accurately, a matter of degree when a hurt becomes an injury," said Baughman. "You can wrestle hurt but it's difficult to impossible to compete when you are injured. The tough call is how hurt or injured you can be and not just compete, but compete effectively. Going out with an injury so serious that you have no chance of being successful will be seen as admirable or tough by some and stupid or delusional by others. Ultimately, the decision has to be made by the individual involved if they can compete well enough to be effective, if the risk is worth the reward."

Baughman was known as a wrestler who would go all out in every match. He was always in superb condition, and his mental approach to the sport was second to none. A gentleman and Air Force officer off the mat, he ran marathons without extra training just to test himself and his mental toughness. He was a fierce combatant on the mat. He asked for no quarter in any match, and he offered none.

"I always wrestle to hurt my opponent but never to injure him," he explained. "There is a definite difference in hurt and injure. If my opponent is distracted by pain, he is not thinking clearly about what else I am doing to him or what he is going to do to me. I will not jeopardize a joint if a person can't turn to relieve the pressure but if they can turn to neutralize the pressure or pain then it becomes their choice."

Baughman listed three other examples of wrestling tough that he has been witness to in his four decades in the sport:

- Yojiro Uetake-Obata's winning the 1968 Olympic gold medal with one arm totally incapacitated. Uetake had been an undefeated, three-time NCAA champion at 130 pounds for Oklahoma State University, but won two Olympic gold medals for his native Japan. That was probably the greatest display of courage or wrestling tough that I have ever witnessed. Yojo was as slick and tough as they come.

• Dan Gable's knee and eye injuries at the 1972 Olympics. I was on the sidelines screaming at Bill Farrell (head coach) and the USA team doctor to quit screwing around trying to get the cut to stop bleeding and just pad and pressure wrap it and get him back out there. Fancy methods take too long and usually don't work for long. They used so much time that there was little or no time for another time-out if needed and the foreigners would have loved to have seen Gable injury defaulted out. Of course, the doctors told Dan that he needed knee surgery shortly before the Games and that he'd never make it without it. . . . And the rest is history.

• Larry Kristoff sustained a major ankle sprain in practice just prior to departing for the 1964 Tokyo Olympics. I am sorry to admit that I was the one who injured him (see story on page 46 of my book). He had a single and I had a whizzer and a wrist. I did the desperation cutback-swing—my planted foot behind and try-to-take-him-backward move. His foot hung up in the mat and popped his ankle. His ankle and foot swelled to the same size as his calf, which was not small. He had trouble getting a wrestling shoe on his foot. He wrestled well, beating Wilfred Dietrich of Germany among others but was not close to his true potential.

"My own personal injuries never came at a very opportune time," said Baughman. "With rare exceptions, they were never serious enough to get me out of training and competition; just bad enough to make it more miserable."

Of course, wrestlers aren't the only athletes to compete with multiple injuries. Most football players can't get through a college or NFL season without some form of serious injury and have learned to suffer though and endure the pain. Kurt Warner, MVP of the Super Bowl champion St. Louis Rams, played most of an entire season with a broken finger on his throwing hand. Brett Favre of the Green Bay Packers is legendary for often playing at his best while injured.

Nancy Lopez, one of the finest golfers of her generation, understands what it takes to overcome injuries when she said, "A winner will find a way to win. Winners take bad breaks and use them to drive themselves to be that much better. Quitters take bad breaks and use them as a reason to give up. It's all a matter of pride."

SUMMARY

With few exceptions, pain is a constant companion of all athletes who stay in wrestling for long. They sustain minor injuries like twisted fingers and broken noses, as well as more serious injuries such as torn rib cartilage and damaged knees. Cauliflower ears are also part of the sport. Athletes who aspire to wrestling success must come to terms with injuries and learn to accept them.

Coaches and athletes must know the difference between pain associated with fatigue and pain associated with injuries. According to Dan Gable, fatigue pain is routine and to be expected in wrestling. Athletes simply must learn to cope with fatigue pain and work through it. Injury pain is completely different and must be treated as such. Injury pain can not only force the wrestler to the sidelines but can also lead to serious long-term damage and, if not properly dealt with, prolong the recovery period. Studying the art of preparation is the next building block, and we will look at such concepts as drilling, shadow wrestling, and visualization.

12

The Art
of Preparation

How big a role does luck play in sport performance? Luck can certainly be a factor from time to time, but over the long haul it tends to disappear into the woodwork. Athletes who consistently find victory at the highest level are the ones who have prepared themselves to win at that level. Preparation is the key.

"I don't believe in luck," said Dan Gable. "Winning the lottery is luck. You can depend on getting lucky in life or you can make things happen. When I was on the University of Iowa coaching staff, the wrestling team won the Big Ten championship 25 years in a row. This is not luck" (Arangio 2002, 29).

Practice sessions are often, but not always, the key to how one competes. The challenge for each wrestler is to find out what works best for him or her and then prepare in that vein.

In any regard, the preparation for competition takes place in the practice room. If you are a wrestler who likes to loaf during practice and work hard only in spurts, chances are that you are training yourself—both mentally and physically—to compete that way. The way you practice, according to wrestling legends like Dan Gable and John Smith, is the way you will compete, for the most part.

Jim Zalesky won three NCAA titles for Iowa under Gable in the 1980s and then became Iowa's head coach when Gable retired in 1997. Zalesky once referred to the Gable formula as magic.

"He makes us believe that the most important thing we do isn't the winning but the effort we put into winning. It's magic" (Looney 1984, 509).

"I always practice as I intend to play," said Jack Nicklaus, one of the greatest golfers of all time and a man known for his iron resolve and sensational ability to focus.

"If I don't do what I need to do to win, I won't win, no matter who is on the other side of the net," said long-time tennis star Andre Agassi.

Tom and Terry Brands competed with such ferocity during their four-year careers at Iowa that many fans were either stunned or turned off by their aggressive, nonstop style. They were intent upon breaking their foes mentally during every single match. Tom won three Big Ten titles and three NCAA titles. Terry won two NCAA titles and three Big Ten titles. Tom's winning percentage was .952, and Terry's was .951.

Each time the goal of the Brands brothers was to make their foe surrender mentally. Probably 90 percent of the time, it happened.

They trained the same way they competed. "They went all out, every practice, every minute," said Randy Lewis, 1984 Olympic champion who preceded the Brands at Iowa but worked out with them many times. "There was never a moment's break. And that's how they wrestled every match. But I don't know many others who could compete at that level of intensity. Maybe no one else."

Muhammad Ali also realized how important proper preparation was in his three-title reign as heavyweight boxing champion of the world. "Before I get in the ring, I'd have already won or lost it out on the road," he said. "The real part is won or lost somewhere far away from the witnesses—behind the lines, in the gym and out there on the road long before I dance under those lights."

There are exceptions to any rule in sports, and intense practices aren't necessarily what works for everyone. Two notable exceptions were Greg Strobel and Brad Rheingans. Both gained tremendous success without going all out in practice every day, in terms of intensity and competitiveness.

"I was much better in meets than in practice," said Strobel. "I've never been able to figure out what the difference is. As a coach, you play the mental game, trying to figure out what motivates different athletes. For me as an athlete, it was very hard to get up for every single practice. I wanted to have some fun, test things out, and so on.

"Sometimes I liked situation wrestling—start with a certain move and go for 30 to 60 seconds, as hard as you can go, and see what works. Some people have to back off just to survive the mental

Mike Chapman Collection

World champions Terry (left) and Tom Brands race up the steps at Carver-Hawkeye Arena in Iowa City. The twins from Sheldon, Iowa, won five NCAA titles between them at the University of Iowa and were Olympians, Tom winning a gold medal in 1996 and Terry a bronze medal in 2000.

pressure. Terry Brands was one who never backed off once, in any practice."

Brands is confident that his physical training and mental commitment would have served him well in other sports, as well. "I think I would have been just as good in boxing, or any sport where combat is involved," he said. "That's what I love about wrestling, the combative nature of it. I believe in doing all phases of your training with total effort—and then you know you are more prepared than anyone on the planet."

Brands belongs to a select group of athletes who actually liked the preparation stage as well as the competition, if not better.

"I probably have a different mental approach to swimming than most people," said Dawn Fraser, Olympic swimming champion from Australia. "I actually enjoy training" (Ferguson 1990, 2-18).

"The game I don't need, the 18,000 people screaming and all the peripheral things," said Bob Knight, one of college basketball's biggest names. "To me, the most enjoyable part is the practice and preparation" (Ferguson 1990, 2-18).

"What I miss the most is the routine, the workouts, the practice room," said John Smith, reflecting back on his six world and Olympic titles, the last coming in 1992. "In 1996 I thought briefly about coming back. It wasn't because I wanted to compete so much as I missed the practice part, the routine, the workouts, pushing yourself so hard."

Athletes have different personalities. Not everyone fits into the same box. Gable recognized that truth as a coach early on, and he considers that one of the reasons that he was able to coach so effectively at a young age. He would have needed different coaching styles for athletes like Terry Brands and Brad Rheingans, who had completely different approaches to the sport.

Rheingans was a standout all-around high school athlete, winning all-state honors in football, wrestling, and the shot put in track and field. At North Dakota State he was a four-time conference wrestling champion and Division II NCAA champion. He really hit his peak after college, winning seven national titles in Greco-Roman. On the international level, he made two Olympic teams, placing fourth at 220 pounds in 1976 and being the favorite to win America's first-ever medal in Greco-Roman competition before President Carter boycotted the 1980 Games in Moscow.

Rheingans won a bronze medal in the 1979 world championships and gold medals in two Pan American Games, as well as the World Cup in freestyle. In addition, he never lost a Greco-Roman match to an American during his entire career.

He turned to professional wrestling and became one of most respected pros of all time, winning the world tag-team championships with Ken Patera, an Olympic weightlifter. In 2004 Rheingans was inducted into the Professional Wrestling Hall of Fame, which is housed in the International Wrestling Institute and Museum in Newton, Iowa.

"I loved wrestling, but I was out there to have fun, too; it wasn't life and death for me, it just wasn't," said Rheingans in 2004. "To me, practice was a time to do just that . . . to practice moves and techniques. Once in a while I would kick it up a couple of notches, but it just wasn't a part of my temperament to pound on guys— friends, really—in practice.

"But I had no trouble at all turning it on when it came to matches. When you go out on the mat is when the mental part kicks in. I was never best of friends with my competitors, because it was different than in practice. I understood that was the mental part—to bring all the training and practice together at the time to really compete."

Rheingans then provided a penetrating insight into his mental commitment and his mental toughness. "Here's the thing," he added, choosing his words carefully. "I don't want to abuse anyone out there, but I want to win. And I want to win *more* than I want to worry about abusing someone. All of the weight cutting, all of the training, all of the competition, it's the accumulation of it all, the final product. It's about bringing it all together to be a winner, not just in the won-lost column but in life itself. It prepares you to win at life."

WEIGHT TRAINING

Through the decades, a number of wrestlers have not done well in practice but have reached another level once the lights came on. People are not all alike, and they don't all practice the same way. The mark of a champion is knowing how to turn it on when the competition starts.

Wrestlers can train physically in many different ways, besides the time they spend on a wrestling mat. Athletes of today are so determined and so dedicated that they spend countless hours each week running, lifting weights, and seeking ways to strengthen their bodies in preparation for the matches to come.

"I started weight training the day I started wrestling, way back in fifth grade," said Tom Brands. "My junior high coach said for us to always do our push-ups on our fingertips and that's the way I've done them ever since.

"I think strength training goes hand in hand with the mental aspect. We had Mark Johnson in the wrestling room at Iowa, and

Mark is an expert. We lifted weights at Iowa with the same intensity that we wrestled."

A two-time NCAA All-American at the University of Michigan and a 1980 Olympian, Johnson was as dedicated a weight trainer as there has ever been in amateur wrestling. He was written about in national strength magazines, particularly for his ability to curl 250 pounds for 10 reps, an astounding feat. He won several physique contests while training for wrestling. After eight years as an assistant coach at Iowa, he became head coach at Oregon State for two years, leading his young Beavers team to the Pacific Ten title. He then pumped new life into the University of Illinois program, making it a top 10 team year after year. Everywhere he has gone, Johnson has placed tremendous emphasis on strength training.

"It's a basic part of wrestling," he said. "Strength will seldom do the job all by itself, but it can make the difference in almost every match. Weight training is now an essential element of all wrestling programs that are at the top. If you want to be an NCAA champion or postgraduate champion in this day and age, then you have to be a weight trainer. It's as simple as that."

Before weight training became popular, the prevalent theory was that weights could make athletes muscle bound or tighten them up so that they could not be flexible and quick. In the 1940s and 1950s, wrestlers often used other exercises to build strength.

Throughout the years, stories about Bill Koll and his workouts were favorite topics of conversation in the wrestling world. An undefeated, three-time NCAA champion at Iowa State Teachers College (now the University of Northern Iowa) in the late 1940s, Koll could walk the length of the football field on his hands, and he was often seen going up the steps of the football stadium on his hands. On occasion, he ran to class backward or moved in a duck waddle between classes, his textbooks strapped to his back, exercising his legs.

Dan Hodge, another undefeated three-time NCAA champion (at the University of Oklahoma), never trained with weights during his career, but he employed a trick to strengthen his fingers and hands. He would take a newspaper section and begin wadding it up in one hand. By exerting finger strength, he would crunch and roll, over and over, until he had worked the entire section into a tight little ball of paper. Then he would continue squeezing it until his fingers cried out for mercy.

A small number of wrestlers weight trained in the early years of the sport, paying no heed to the myth that weights would tighten the muscles and make them inflexible. The first was George Hackenschmidt, who burst onto the professional wrestling scene in the early 1900s when the sport was still a legitimate contest. Known as the Russian Lion, Hackenschmidt was a devout weight trainer who became the toast of Europe for his physique. At age 21, he could clean and jerk 365 pounds overhead, working with stiff barbells that did not rotate as the weight was moved upward. He had huge, thick muscles and became undisputed heavyweight champion of the world.

In the 1940s Henry Wittenberg of New York won over 400 wrestling matches in a row and eight national AAU titles. He made the United States Olympic team in 1948 and won the gold medal in London. Four years later he earned a silver medal at the Helsinki Olympics. He attributed a great deal of his success to weight training.

"I was one of the first weightlifting wrestlers," he said five decades after winning his gold medal. "I lifted because I felt strength gives wrestlers an edge. I had weights at home and lifted very seriously, several times a week.

"Art Griffith (the long-time coach at Oklahoma State University) was the coach of the 1948 Olympic team, and he told the team he didn't want any of us lifting weights because it would make us muscle bound," said Wittenberg. "I told him I was going to lift anyway, and he said, 'OK, but don't let the other guys see you doing it.'"

Wittenberg also was a proponent of hard running, but he used a different style than most. He liked to run the stairs in the football stadium at City College of New York. His approach was revolutionary back in the 1940s.

"Matches were 15 minutes long back then. I did a lot of stair running. I didn't just run the steps, I ran over the seats," he said. "That made me lift my legs higher and work harder."

Wittenberg's approach had two vantage points. First, the fact that he was lifting weights and running stairs gave him a physical edge over the other wrestlers of the era. Second, the awareness that he was doing something that others weren't gave him a psychological edge. The two go hand in hand, of course. Extreme physical training can provide a wrestler with both a mental edge and a physical edge over an opponent.

Dan Gable worked that principle to absolute perfection 25 years later. Gable used weights consistently during his career, but he never lifted for maximum poundage for a single repetition. Instead, he would take a weight that he could lift for 20 to 30 reps and rush through the set, taxing his recuperative strength as well as his basic strength. His goal was to build muscular endurance rather than one-time lift power.

DRILLING

What do sports legends like Vince Lombardi, Michael Jordan, and John Smith have in common? An important characteristic that the three men share is their awareness of the importance of drilling the fundamental aspects of their sports.

Repetition, or drilling, is one of the keys to athletic success. An athlete must work a technique repeatedly, for hours on end, week after week, year after year. The goal is for the technique to become second nature, a pure reflex action that will kick in when the need arises during a match. Time spent drilling was the key to many gold medals for top wrestlers around the world and the key to success for the world's greatest basketball players.

"The minute you get away from fundamentals—whether it's proper technique, work ethic or mental preparation—the bottom can fall out of your game," said Michael Jordan, who led his Chicago Bulls to six NBA championships in his remarkable career (Jordan 1998, 27-28).

The same philosophy rings true on a football field. The great Green Bay Packers teams of Vince Lombardi were known for their superb execution. The Packers excelled in that area. But not all athletes are willing to spend thousands of hours working the same move repeatedly in the quest for perfection.

"Now, I think everyone can be taught to block. The question is whether they will block or want to be taught," said Vince Lombardi. "This is the crux of it to me. Anyone can be taught, but if he doesn't have the desire to block and will not block, then he has no place on my team, regardless of who he might be. Our blocking success on the Packers is due to endless repetitions and practice with our line" (Riger 1980, 55).

The basics are the key to high-level athletic performance.

"You need to have your convictions," said Don Shula, one of the most successful coaches in NFL history. "You can't get away from the basics. Many times you get away from what you know and that's when you don't do well."

Pele, considered the finest soccer player of all time, said, "Everything is practice" (Riger 1980, 69).

One of the best female tennis players of all time knew that the key to her sport was practice. "Tennis is a game of angles," said Billie Jean King. "You never have time to figure the angles. It's practiced. It's so practiced that it becomes an instinct. You just know where to put the ball. You just feel it. It has been computed into your brain so many times—it is there" (Riger 1980, 76).

Such is the case in wrestling, of course. What separates the great athletes from the very good ones is the willingness to learn and to practice as long as it takes to be the best. John Smith is an excellent example of one who paid strict attention to this aspect of winning.

As a sophomore at Oklahoma State in 1985, Smith made it to the NCAA finals at 134 pounds and then lost to Jim Jordan of Wisconsin. The loss taught Smith a lot about wrestling in general and about what he needed to do in particular to go to the next level.

Smith took a redshirt year and then came back with a vengeance. He won two NCAA titles and 90 consecutive matches. Between his junior and senior years, he entered the 1987 world championships and came home with a gold medal in the 136.5-pound class. That success was the start of the most amazing international streak in American history. Smith would wind up with six consecutive world or Olympic titles, closing out his sensational career with a gold medal at the 1992 Olympics in Barcelona, Spain.

One writer called Smith's six-year string the most unbreakable record in American wrestling. "Just making six straight world or Olympic teams is a feat in itself," wrote Mike Chapman in *W.I.N. Magazine*. "But winning six straight gold medals is unbelievable. This is the no. 1 unbreakable record in amateur wrestling, like Joe DiMaggio's 56-game hitting streak in the major leagues of baseball."

One of Smith's secrets was his commitment to drilling. He would often slip into old Gallagher Hall on the OSU campus late at night and go down to the Cowboy wrestling room. There, in the darkness and stillness of the room, he would shadow wrestle against the wall, shooting hundreds of takedowns against an imaginary figure, for hours on end.

"Drilling is the key to wrestling success and to longevity in the sport," said Smith. "Drilling has to become habit forming. Drilling wasn't natural for me, I'd rather just go in a room and spar hard. I just wanted to shake hands and go!

"But drilling has to take place for you to get better. I couldn't do a better leg lace or gut wrench without breaking down the move, seeing how it works, studying it and drilling it, over and over and over. That's when you improve your techniques. Someone who doesn't spend time doing that and drilling isn't going to improve."

Live wrestling, or sparring, is what 90 percent of wrestlers prefer to do in a practice session. The act of wrestling, taking on a foe and seeing what one can do with his or her moves, power, and speed, excites most athletes who choose wrestling as their sport. That makes sense, because wrestling appeals to combat-oriented people, and combat is what they seek.

But drilling also can extend a wrestler's longevity in the sport, according to Smith. "For longevity, drilling is very important," said Smith. "If you want to stay in the sport for many years, then you have to stay healthy. Constant sparring and live goes can beat your body up pretty bad.

"After the world championships, I would drill for three months, with very little sparring. That's when I got better, and I also stayed injury free."

The Adam takedown machine provides an excellent form of drilling. Developed in the 1960s, the machine has become a staple in high school and college wrestling rooms across the country. Shaped like a medium-sized wrestler and made to be extremely durable, it allows wrestlers to shoot hundreds of takedowns per day, for as long as the athlete can hold up. Tom Brands even bought a personal model for training at home.

"I used it so much, pounding on it, that it just quit working one day," said Brands with a sly grin. "I used to beat on it for hours on end, day after day."

That type of devotion to drilling set John Smith and Tom Brands apart from the field and enabled them to become part of wrestling's most elite club—those who have won NCAA, world, and Olympic titles. After the 2004 Olympics, this exclusive group had only nine members.

But not all top wrestlers have been devotees of the drilling method.

"Dave Schultz didn't drill much," said Greg Strobel, former national teams coach at USA Wrestling. "Jordanov (eight-time world champion from Yugoslavia) hardly drilled at all. They would work on techniques, play with things and see how good they worked, during scrimmages. To them, wrestling is live combat.

"The Brands brothers knew how to drill and did it with each other. Zeke Jones (world champion in 1991) could drill really well, but Sammie Henson (world champion in 1998) would much rather go live.

"I coached a guy named Jim Baumgartner at Oregon State who couldn't drill to save his life. But boy, could he wrestle. He made me a believer that not everyone needs to drill. John Van Doren at Lehigh (University) was the same way. They were both All-Americans, but they just couldn't drill effectively; what they could do was *wrestle!*"

Drilling becomes a habit, something that you accept as part of the daily routine of being a wrestler. You do the same techniques over and over and over. Drilling is a philosophy of exercise, and living, that goes back thousands of years, all the way to ancient Greece.

"We are what we repeatedly do. Excellence, then, is not an act but a habit," said Aristotle around 300 B.C.

What would Aristotle, one of the most exalted thinkers of all time, know about wrestling? He was the student of Plato, who was an accomplished wrestler in his youth. And Aristotle was the mentor of Alexander the Great, the finest military expert of all time and a warrior who tremendously appreciated the skill of wrestling and insisted that his top soldiers be trained in that discipline. Obviously, like John Smith, he believed in the art of drilling!

SHADOW WRESTLING

Shadow boxing has long been a basic element of boxing. For decades, the world's best professional boxers would face a wall and throw imaginary punches, rolling their upper bodies in rhythm and moving against a wall. Shadow boxing goes all the way back to the 1920s and the days of such legendary champions as Jack Dempsey, Gene Tunney, and Harry Greb. Smith made consistent use of the technique through much of his career, both as a student at Oklahoma State University and as a world champion.

"I did a lot of shadow wrestling in Gallagher-Iba Hall, late at night," said Smith. "When I changed my style of wrestling and began moving my feet more and more, using more motion—that's when shadow wrestling became very important in my training. The good thing is you didn't have to try and find a workout partner at that time of night. You'd just go into the room and shadow wrestle for as long as you wanted."

Shadow wrestling helped take him to the highest level of the sport, said the six-time world champion: "It was that extra movement that made the difference for John Smith, and made me a complete wrestler!"

After the 1989 world championships, Dan Gable made a telling observation about Smith's style. "He moves so much that it's like trying to take down air," said Gable. "And it's almost impossible to take down air."

Ken Chertow, a 1988 Olympian and one of the nation's most successful camp operators, is also a strong advocate of the largely ignored art. "Shadow wrestling is a great way to develop your skills, speed and conditioning," he said. "I was a boxing fan during elemen-

The wrestler in the top position is practicing head control. Holding a foe's head to the mat strictly limits his ability to move effectively.

tary school, watching legends Sugar Ray Leonard and Muhammad Ali on television. I learned that shadow boxing plays an integral role in the training of every boxer.

"When I started wrestling in middle school, I quickly incorporated shadow drilling into my training program. I was slow and chubby so my shadow drilling was not very fluent, but I steadily improved every day. I would stay after practice and rehearse the moves that I knew until I felt like I could do them reasonably well. I had a mat in my house so I would also shadow drill my moves in the evenings after doing my homework and strength training.

"Shadow drilling teaches you to control your body. Let's face it, until you have self control, how can you execute a move on a partner, especially if he's fighting back?

"Shadow drilling is not just for beginners. It remained a significant part of my training regimen throughout my high school, college and international career. It can play an important role in the success of wrestlers at any skill level" (Chertow 2004, 3).

VISUALIZATION

Many world-class athletes have used visualization in their preparation. As a young boy in Waterloo, Iowa, Dan Gable discovered that the power of visualization could help him develop his future goals and faith in himself. In his backyard, Gable used to grip a baseball bat and swing at imaginary pitches for hours on end, pretending that he was Mickey Mantle or Roger Maris, the two greatest home run hitters of the era. In his basement, he shot takedown after takedown against imaginary foes, dreaming of being a state wrestling champion for West Waterloo High School.

"I won the state title a thousand times in my basement before I ever won it for real," said Gable. "Visualization was very important for me as I was growing and maturing as a wrestler."

But he also used visualization in another completely different manner, one that enabled him to keep working out even after he was nearly spent.

"When I'd get tired and want to stop, I'd wonder what my next opponent was doing," said Gable. "I wondered if he was still working out. I tried to visualize him. When I could see him working out, I'd start pushing myself. When I could see him in the shower, I'd push myself harder."

Visualization was also a huge part of the Brands formula for success. Tom and Terry would talk late into the night about their hopes, dreams, and plans.

"The results were predetermined," said Tom. "I could see them, very vividly, in color. It's not cloudy at all. It multiplies, over and over and over. The same results—winning."

"It all comes back to willing yourself into winning," he said. "You go from level to level by brainwashing yourself into it. Some people say brainwashing is a negative term but it's not to me. It's a positive way of thinking what you have to think in order to win.

"From my point of view, it's very important to talk about the Olympics and world championships at every level, even early on. You go to so many kids' tournaments and people are talking about some kid who is 82-0 or something, but it's useless unless they have a vision to do something with it beyond just winning kids' tournaments. These tournaments are just a stepping-stone for climbing the highest mountain."

John Smith agrees that talking about postcollege opportunities is an important aspect of wrestling for those who dare to dream big. "It's part of our program to talk about the Olympics and world championships, that's for sure," said Smith. "We had three members of our program in the 2004 Olympics, on the freestyle team, and we're very proud of that. Guys like Eric Guerrero, Jamill Kelly and Daniel Cormier can fulfill their dreams right here in Stillwater. As a coach, I feel very fortunate to be playing some kind of a role in that, for them."

"We often hear athletes speak of success in their field as being 90 percent mental," wrote Matt Furey in his combat conditioning Web site. "From my vast experience at the championship level in sports as varied as swimming and wrestling, and from my experience of being a world champion martial artist, I know for a fact that success is mostly mental.

"But the key thing to understand is that physical practice does play a role in being successful. I can tell you that the proverbial blood, sweat and tears are part of the 'preparation' that goes into getting ready for a contest. Failing to prepare is preparing to fail.

"One of the amazing things I learned though about success in sports like wrestling and the style of kung fu I practiced is this: When I combined the physical activity of training with the success imagery I learned from Dr. Maxwell Maltz, my results improved almost instantly. Funny thing is I felt like I was doing less work, not more. The titles and trophies that used to go to the other guy were suddenly showing up in my hands—not my opponents'.

"And the only change I ever made in how I trained was in how I pictured myself as I trained. Instead of mindlessly doing the physical training, I combined the physical with the mental. The results were nothing short of spectacular."

In the little book *The Handbook of Inner Sports*, author James Zabriskie makes the case that sport is really a dance with the gods, that sport is humankind's way of expressing oneself in the universal scheme. He also recognizes the value of visualization and of developing the goal in one's mind before setting out to achieve it.

"We are what our heads tell us we are," he wrote. "One is one's thinking. And whatever we think we believe" (Zabriskie 1976, 56).

Visualization, then, is a way of reinforcing one's belief over and over. It is drilling the mind to believe what one wants it to believe. When Gable was in the backyard working against imaginary pitchers for hours on end, week after week, summer after summer, he was developing his own mind into believing that he could become a superstar. He could be a Mickey Mantle, even if he had to change sports to do it.

He encouraged his athletes to use the same principle and to visualize themselves scoring the winning moves and climbing the victory stand.

"Visualization was a big factor in the success of both Terry and me," said Tom Brands. "We would talk about what it would feel like to be a world and Olympic champion. I would daydream about it during the day, and dream about it at night. I always visualized us up on the victory stand, even when we could barely carry our socks. Visualization is a huge part of winning."

In a calendar from 1980, Arnold Schwarzenegger said he developed "a method of inspiration" early in his career through the process of visualization: "I discovered that the most effective motivator for growth and change was being able to visualize my goals, and to see myself exactly as I wished to be. In the gym, next to the bathroom mirror in my apartment, and even in my car, I taped up photos and statements to keep me constantly aware of what I needed to do in order to reach my goals. I used this method to become a champion bodybuilder and I use it now in training, as well as furthering my career in acting, in running the production company that promotes the Mr. Olympia contest, and in my business and real estate pursuits."

Wade Schalles, listed in the *Guinness Book of World Records* as the wrestler with the most pins (659) in a career, also used visualization techniques with tremendous success. "My junior year in high school, I didn't even make it to the state tournament," said Schalles. "But before my senior year, I visualized myself standing on the winner's platform a thousand times, at least. I made it to state and faced a three-time state champion in the finals. But I had not only visualized myself on the winning stand, but I visualized myself pinning my foe in the finals."

Schalles did score his pin and wound up the season as the undefeated state champion, for Hollidaysburg Area High School, in Pennsylvania. He went on to win two NCAA championships for Clarion University and claim the world university title. He won national titles not only in collegiate wrestling but also in freestyle, Greco-Roman, judo, and sombo. But he is best known for his incredible pinning records. At the famous Tbilisi Tournament in Russia, he pinned six international stars in a row, including two world champions!

And it all started with his visualization techniques, which he used all through his career. "You can never get someplace physically until you've been there mentally," he said. But he quickly added a few words of caution: "That certainly doesn't mean you're going to be sure and get to the Olympic finals, no matter how many times you've dreamed it. The visualization is just the ticket that puts you on the train. There are many other ingredients that will figure in."

SUMMARY

Nearly all coaches and athletes concede that preparation is the turning point in an athlete's performance. Dedication and commitment, the will to win, desire, and discipline are all essential building blocks for success. Then the athlete moves into the area of preparation, when he or she actually sets out on the path to victory. Weight training, running, video study, and diet are important elements of preparation.

Special areas that can make a huge difference are the art of drilling, shadow wrestling, visualization, and, finally, the art of commitment. John Smith said that both drilling and shadow wrestling were key elements in his winning two Olympic championships and four world titles. Tom and Terry Brands used visualization techniques to propel themselves to world and Olympic medals. All great wrestlers realize that they must assemble many different elements to become champions, and they know that commitment is the fuel that propels them forward, year after year after year.

13

The Spirit for Competition

"Competition in its best form is a test of self. It has nothing to do with medals. The winner is the person who gets the most out of themselves," said a man named Al Oerter.

What does Al Oerter know about competition? Four times he entered the Olympic Games in the discus throw, and he was never the favorite to win the championship. Yet on all four occasions—in 1956, 1960, 1964, and 1968—he came home with the gold medal. His story is one of remarkable success at the highest level.

Another way to define competition is through the competitor's intensity. Intense people love to compete, and they want to compete against the best in the world. They can't wait to get on the mat with stars from other countries to see how they measure up. The intensity bubbles up inside them and begins to overflow as they ready themselves mentally for the supreme task.

"The point is that world-class athletes—Gable being exhibit A—want to prove themselves against the best," wrote Douglas Looney in *Sports Illustrated*. "Whenever the subject of Dan Gable comes up in conversation, the word *intensity* is never far behind. And while the word has been cheapened by overuse and abuse, Gable is its epitome. By God, he deserves 'intense' as a descriptive. It's his. He earned it the old-fashioned way: he worked for it" (Looney 1984, 499).

"You've got to look for tough competition," said Greta Waitz, who won the New York Marathon nine times. "You've got to want to beat the best."

COMPETITIVE INTENSITY

At the highest levels, such as the New York Marathon and the Olympic Games, intensity is one of the key elements of competition. Without intensity, the competitive spirit wilts.

When you know that you are ready to compete, you want to test yourself. One way is to go against records. Another is to go against other humans. Another, as Al Oerter has explained, is to go against yourself. But the path is always the same; it is to reach far down inside yourself, to discover what you are truly capable of. Some of those best lessons come in moments of desperation.

Greg Strobel experienced a desperate moment in the finals of the NCAA championships of 1973, when he was a junior going for his first NCAA title. Strobel ran onto the mat to battle for the 190-pound title. He was facing a pinning machine named John Johnson. A powerful and gutsy senior from Northern Illinois University, Johnson had earned a spot in the final with four consecutive pins. He would march straight into his foe, slap on a double underhook, tighten it, and then throw his foe to the mat in a beautiful, high-arching supply, one of the most awesome maneuvers in wrestling.

Strobel had placed fourth in the NCAAs as an Oregon State University sophomore the year before and was unbeaten when he faced Johnson. He knew all about the supply, yet he somehow got caught in the move near the end of the first period and was thrown straight to his back. It was an electrifying moment for the huge crowd and for Strobel. Arching desperately and summoning every ounce of competitive spirit in him, he fought desperately to avoid being pinned.

"I knew I was close to the edge of the mat and so I gave everything I had to scoot out of bounds," he said in 2004. "Johnson had pinned everyone else and I knew what I was in for, but when I was bridging I felt surprisingly calm and relaxed. I just knew I had to get out of bounds.

"As soon as I got off my back and we went back to the center, I had no doubt that I would beat him. I had this inner confidence. I had experienced being down before. I was behind 9-0 against Russ Johnson in the first 30 seconds the year before and still won, 13-11. Having had experiences with comebacks, this situation didn't bother me. I also knew if he was going to beat me, it was going to be the toughest match of his life.

"At the end of the match, he couldn't get off his stomach, he was so tired. I knew that conditioning was in my favor in all my matches and that I could go all out all the way."

Strobel was a focused and intense competitor who never surrendered at any moment of any match. He took that quality into a long coaching career. As national teams director at USA Wrestling for nearly a decade, he helped mold some of America's finest wrestlers and saw firsthand the competitive nature of those who would aspire to be world champions. He used that tremendous experience to become one of the nation's top collegiate coaches. In 1995 he took over as the head man of the Lehigh University wrestling program and quickly directed the Mountain Hawks back into national prominence.

UNFLINCHING DETERMINATION

One of the highlights of his coaching career came in the finals of the 177-pound class at the NCAA championships of 2002. There, he sent senior Rob Rohn onto the mat against favored Josh Lambrecht of the University of Oklahoma.

"Rohn did an unbelievable job just getting to the finals," said Strobel. "He was seeded eighth and only had two pins all season long. Rohn said he had three goals: to relax, have fun, and be the national champion.

"Rohn wrestled like a man possessed. He was losing to Jessman Smith of Iowa in the semifinals, and then went to the cement mixer (a seldom-used pinning move). I yelled, 'What are you doing that for? You don't have to go for the home run yet, just go for the single.' It's a risky move and I didn't think he should go to it at that point. But he did . . . and he got it. He pinned Smith."

Suddenly, Rohn was in the finals. He had torn a rotator cuff during the eastern championships and had not lifted for several weeks because he lacked strength in his right arm. In the finals, Lambrecht trapped Rohn's arm tight and was tilting him all over.

"Lambrecht must have thought, 'This guy is a wimp, he was getting turned so easily,'" said Strobel. "Going into the last period and trailing 14-2, I still thought Rohn had a chance. And then he hit the cement mixer again, and he hit it really well, taking Lambrecht right to his back. There was about a minute and 20 seconds left and Lambrecht was bridging and fighting with all he had.

"When it got down to 30 seconds, I remember thinking, 'You gotta be kidding me. We're going to have this guy on his back for over a minute and still not get the pin.' And then he tightened up and got the pin with just 13 seconds left.

"It was really cool," said Strobel. "Rohn always felt, 'Just let me have my move and I can pull this thing out.'

"It has to be one of the biggest comebacks ever. He was down 12 points at one point. But Rohn never gave up on himself," said Strobel, perhaps remembering his own NCAA experience three decades earlier. "He is really very mentally tough. That was the key."

Mental toughness was also the key for other wrestlers who have achieved remarkable successes through the years. Strobel is a disciple of the school of mental toughness.

"Baumgartner was extremely mentally tough," said Strobel. "Bruce was brutally strong and when he stayed on his game plan, he was truly unstoppable. Bruce went from 1982 through 1997 without losing to an American and he earned 13 world or Olympic medals. He would just refuse to lose; he was that mentally tough. Many times I saw him come up with huge moves at the last minute to pull out a win, like when he won the bronze medal in the 1996 Olympics.

"Although Bruce was beaten for the fourth time by Andrey Shumlin (of Russia) in the quarterfinals (by a 6-1 score), he recovered and battled back for the bronze," wrote Strobel in *W.I.N. Magazine*. "The rematch with Shumlin was the most visible display of mental toughness of the Games.

"Down 1-0 with little time remaining, the theme from *Rocky* playing over the PA system, Bruce shot a single. Shumlin countered, knocking Bruce to his knees. It looked like it was over. Then, with strength hidden deep inside from years of training, Bruce pulled the leg in. Shumlin countered again, throwing Bruce's head to the outside, but Bruce finished with the takedown for the 1-1 tie and the referee's decision."

The 1996 Olympics was a milestone for Baumgartner. He won his 13th world or Olympic medal, the most of any athlete in the world, and carried the American flag in the opening ceremonies. He was invited to escort President Clinton around the Olympic village before the Games started, and he then received a congratulatory phone call from a top performer in another field of entertainment, Garth Brooks.

"As a competitor, other than winning, the most gratifying feeling is knowing that in the face of battle, you didn't flinch," wrote Steve Knight, a national powerlifting champion. "Win or lose, you rose to the occasion and competed, and when the final whistle blew, you were able to truthfully say to yourself, 'I didn't choke. I gave it all I had'" (Knight 2003).

Not flinching in the face of battle is the essence of competition. It means striding onto the mat with head held high, eager to test oneself against the foe, no matter how good that foe may be. In the 2000 Olympics, most wrestling fans around the world felt that Brandon Slay had little chance to leave Sydney with a medal. After all, he was placed in the same pool as Bouvaisa Saitiev of Russia, widely acknowledged as one of the finest wrestlers in the entire world. Saitiev had won the gold medal in the 1996 Olympics and two world titles. He was a superb technician, blessed with lightning reflexes and a natural feel for the mat.

Saitiev and another great Russian, Greco-Roman star Alexander Karelin, were considered the nearest thing to unbeatable that one could find in the 2000 Olympics.

In the second round of the 167.5-pound class, Slay was face to face with Saitiev. A devout Christian with an intense confidence in himself and his training methods, both physically and mentally, Slay was ready to compete. He struck early for a 3-0 lead, but the Russian tied the score at 3-3 near the end of the match. Then, with everything on the line, Slay struck hard and fast with a power double-leg takedown.

When the match ended, America had a new wrestling hero: Brandon Slay had scored a 4-3 decision and was on his way to the finals. Saitiev was on his way to the sidelines.

Brandon Slay did not flinch when faced with tremendous odds. Instead, he relied on his training, his passion, and his mental toughness!

Another wrestler who had supreme mental toughness was the late Dave Schultz, 1983 world champion and 1984 Olympic champion, and one of the most respected wrestlers in American history.

"When Dave Schultz was really focused, he was unbelievable," said Strobel. "He once pinned nine straight men at the freestyle

Dave Schultz, 1984 Olympic champion at 163 pounds, executes a leg lace turn on a foe during the Olympic competition in Los Angeles.

nationals, including Olympians and two three-time national champions. I once saw him pin Kevin Jackson (who went on to become a world and Olympic champion) in about a minute and a half.

"There were times when I worked out with Dave that I felt he could hurt me at any time, very badly. That's a scary feeling."

Mike Sheets was a tremendously intense wrestler, earning two NCAA championships at Oklahoma State in the 1980s. Sheets was a ferocious leg rider who pinned many of his foes by stretching them unmercifully and forcing them to surrender. He gave no quarter on the wrestling mat and asked none. He was Mr. Intensity from start to finish.

"When I knew I was going to be working out with Mike Sheets in practice, I knew there would be no stopping, at any time," said Strobel. "It was total intensity—you had better have your shoes tied, because there were no time-outs, at any time. Mike was there to wrestle, and you had better be, as well."

ATTITUDE FOR SUCCESS

Ed and Lou Banach were as competitive as any collegiate wrestlers of the past 50 years. They exploded on the national wrestling scene during the Iowa–Iowa State meet of 1980. With 10,000 fans in the stands, the Cyclones were on the verge of a tremendous victory. They held a 17-7 edge over the Hawkeyes with just three matches remaining. At 177 pounds, Iowa State had Dave Allen, who was third in the NCAA the year before, going against freshman Ed Banach, a relative unknown. At 190, the Cyclones had unbeaten and top-ranked John Forshee going against Lou Banach, also relatively unknown. And at heavyweight, the Cyclones would put Mike Mann, normally a 190-pounder, against Dean Phinney of Iowa, a massive warrior weighing around 270.

One win in the final three would be enough to lock up the win for the Cyclones of Coach Harold Nichols.

"We were down by 10 points and I knew I had to pull a rabbit out of the hat," explained Ed two decades later. Coach Gable walked up to me in the middle of the 167-pound match and said, 'What are you going to do?'

"I smiled and said, 'I'm going to pin Allen, that's what I'm going to do.' I was fired up, I was ready to go. Pinning was all I thought about. I was going to pin Dave Allen. To me, it was inconceivable that Iowa State could beat Iowa. It didn't even enter my mind that we could lose so I knew that I would go out and score a pin. I just knew it!"

Banach overpowered the Cyclone All-American and scored a dramatic pin, bringing the score to 17-13 and giving notice to the wrestling world that this Hawkeye freshman was going to be a factor in the national scene. His twin brother took the mat and fell behind quickly. A master rider, Forshee controlled most of the match—until the final seconds. They battled to their feet, locked in a bear hug. Lou overpowered his foe straight to his back and scored another dramatic pin.

Suddenly, the Hawkeyes were on top, 19-17, because of pins by two of the most competitive wrestlers in American history. When Phinney posted a decision over Mann, the Hawkeyes had pulled off a stunning 23-17 triumph!

Both Banachs went on to win multiple NCAA championships, with Ed becoming the all-time pin leader in Hawkeye history, with 73 in 141 victories. Both also won gold medals at the 1984 Olympics in Los Angeles. The number one element to their success, said Ed, was their determination and dedication—in short, their attitude!

"Years later, when I was assistant coach at Iowa State and was recruiting, I always looked for attitude first and foremost," said Ed

Banach. "Bruce Kinseth had the attitude, the intensity; there was no stopping him. He would outwork anyone to reach his goals.

"If you have the attitude, then I can teach you all the rest—how to lift weights, how to diet, how to drill and improve technique. But first of all, you have to have the attitude. That's where it all starts.

"There used to a be a drawing of three China men on the wall at the Iowa dressing room. They were called Coulda Ben, Shoulda Ben and Woulda Ben. They were excuses for not winning. It was a good lesson for all of us going past that drawing. I didn't want to be one of those guys."

John Ralston, former head football coach at Stanford University and later the head coach of the Denver Broncos of the NFL, said that the key to athletic success is attitude, that sort of mental outlook expressed by Ed Banach.

"The great ones set a standard for themselves to be the best at what they're doing," said Ralston. "That's attitude. You never worry about outside pressure. The pressure of satisfying yourself by being number one is the only one that counts" (Ferguson 1990, 224).

Intensity can become the trademark of a coach as well as an athlete. One of the most intense athletes at the 1996 Olympics in Atlanta was Tom Brands. And one of the most intense observers was his college coach, Dan Gable. Although he was not an official coach in Atlanta, Gable was still the man Brands looked to for motivation and intensity.

When Brands was just minutes away from his key match with Sergey Smal of Belarus, Gable was pacing the floor of the arena, almost beside himself with pent-up intensity. He stopped anyone he knew, jabbing a finger in his or her direction.

"This is it! This is the match that will determine who wins the gold," exclaimed Gable repeatedly. "Brands has to take it to Smal, he has to overpower him and dominate him!"

That's exactly what Brands did, posting a 5-0 victory that put him into the driver's seat for the gold. When Brands leaped down off the platform at the end of the match, his eyes were blazing and his teeth were clenched so tight that one feared he would break them off at the root. He ran past Gable, slapped his hand, and then disappeared into the press area for interviews.

Gable stalked by a wall, still talking. A crowd gathered around him to listen to his assessment of the match and simply to observe the sport's most intriguing figure up close. Suddenly, with nearly

50 people gathered around him, Gable sagged backward into the wall and slid down, in a half faint.

"Gable passed out!" yelled several people as they looked for someone who knew CPR. But several minutes later, Gable was on his feet again, smiling sheepishly.

"I get myself so worked up and focused sometimes that I go overboard," Gable said softly. "I guess I'm too intense for my own good. But when I see someone I care about like Tom Brands in such a key situation, well. . . ."

Arousal is an effective means of preparing oneself for competition, but taking it to the extreme can be dangerous. Gable wasn't in a competitive mode when he was in Atlanta cheering for Brands, so had nothing to lose in that regard. But an athlete who works himself into a fever pitch of the same magnitude could suffer considerably.

"You have to be careful that you don't get beyond your arousal curve," said John Anderson, PhD, a sport psychologist who works with Olympic athletes (Clarkson 1999, 31).

SUMMARY

Intensity and focus are the core of competition. People may believe that they are good competitors, but if they do not have the focus and intensity to carry them through the tough spots that they will eventually face, they will usually come up short. The greatest wrestlers are athletes of supreme focus and intensity. The best example of the success of the two forces working together was the University of Iowa wrestling program for the two decades when Dan Gable was head coach, from 1977 through 1997.

Intensity comes out of focus. Athletes can best learn how to focus by being around other focused athletes and coaches and by studying the careers of the most successful athletes of the past. To compete at the highest levels of the national and international scene, wrestlers must learn how to focus and how to channel their intensity.

14

The Roles of Underdog and Favorite

Most athletes will come up against long odds at some point in their careers. But few will ever face odds as overwhelming as Nick Ackerman did when he began his senior season at Simpson College, a Division III school located in Indianola, Iowa. As a youngster growing up in tiny Colfax, Iowa, Nick contracted spinal meningitis. To save his life, doctors decided to amputate both legs below the knee. For the next seven years, Nick had to have an annual operation that trimmed off parts of the legs as they grew back.

Nick began wrestling in junior high school and discovered that he loved the sport. As a senior at Colfax High School, he gained a certain degree of fame by placing in the Iowa state high school meet. Still, when he announced that he was attending Simpson College and would continue his wrestling career, few had much hope that he would win much on that level.

His senior season was an unbelievable exercise in drive, determination, and commitment. Battling all odds, he rolled up a 34-4 record as he entered the Division III NCAA championships at Young Arena in Waterloo, Iowa. In his weight class was Augsburg's Nick Slack, the defending champion who was riding a 60-match win streak.

Ackerman made it to the finals, scoring three victories and earning a bye. Then, in front of a sellout crowd of 3,000 roaring fans, he won the 174-pound championship with a stunning 13-11 victory over Slack. As the final seconds ticked off, the crowd began to roar in a thunderous, emotional ovation that lasted over two minutes.

"There wasn't a dry eye in the house," said Bryan Van Kley, publisher of *W.I.N. Magazine*. "It was one of the most emotional moments I have ever seen in wrestling."

Three weeks later, Nick was shocked when he learned that he was sharing the Dan Hodge Trophy with Cael Sanderson of Iowa State. The Hodge Trophy, often referred to as the Heisman Trophy of wrestling, is given each season to the top collegiate wrestler in the country. Sanderson won the trophy in 2000, shared it with Ackerman in 2001, and won his third straight in 2002. The International Wrestling Institute and Museum in Newton, Iowa, and *W.I.N. Magazine* cosponsor the trophy.

"It created a lot of national attention for Nick and Simpson," said Simpson coach Ron Peterson of the trophy. "It was a wonderful honor for Nick. We have a duplicate of the trophy in our display case in the field house at Simpson."

Two months later, Nick was invited by the Cauliflower Alley Club (CAC), a group of former professional wrestlers, boxers, and movie people, to attend its national event, held each summer in Las Vegas. The group, with over 2,000 members, paid the travel expenses for Nick and his mother.

At the awards banquet on the final night of the three-day convention, Dan Hodge and I, acting as the executive director of the International Wrestling Institute and Museum, called Nick on stage to present him the Hodge Trophy (again) in front of the crowd. Then Karl Lauer, vice president of the CAC, issued a challenge to the 600 attendees that night.

"This is the most amazing and heart-warming story I have ever heard in wrestling," said Lauer. "To see what Nick has accomplished, and to see the kind of wonderful young man he is, makes me very proud to be here tonight. I just found out he has about a $10,000 college bill remaining. I think this club should do all it can here tonight to try and take care of that college bill for Nick and his mother."

Old and battered ex-wrestlers and pugilists, many in their 70s, made their way to the stage to drop money and checks in a cardboard box. While Nick and his mother watched in awe, the box began to fill up. When the night was over, some $9,000 had been collected!

The key to Ackerman's incredible journey centers on his mental attitude, pressed upon him by his mother, his coaches and, most important, by himself.

"I've always seen myself just like everyone else," said Nick after winning the Hodge Trophy. "That is just the way I was raised. I sometimes ask what the big deal is. But my mom always reminds me that I'm helping people whether I see myself as different or not."

Peterson, Ackerman's college coach, said he was determined at the outset of Nick's career to treat him the same as everyone else, because he knew that was what Nick wanted and needed to excel at the levels he wanted to reach.

"Ever since he's come into the room he hasn't expected us to treat him any different than any other kid," said Peterson. "We made him run sprints on his knees. We made him do extra pull-ups, all the types of things it takes to be a champion. We yelled at him to keep moving just like everyone else. He never asked for any special treatment . . . even though he is very special.

"It was very, very heartwarming to see him succeed at such a level, and then to win the Hodge Trophy. Simpson is privileged to have Nick Ackerman associated with our school. He is the classic example of a Division III athlete who wrestles for the pure love of the sport. Ever since Nick won the national title, I have been talking to Division III coaches all over the nation. They tell me that Nick winning the title was the most emotional thing they have ever seen in the sport of wrestling."

Ackerman's older brother, Nathan, had earned All-American honors in basketball for Simpson two years earlier. Peterson was quick to point to the work ethic and attitude of the entire family as the reason for their successes.

"I think it is a prime example of people being able to accomplish anything, no matter what the circumstances," said the coach. "The great thing about America is if you set your goals you can accomplish anything. It doesn't matter what the limitations are. You are only limited by your own mind. Nick didn't believe anybody could beat him. He's told us since day one that he could be a national champion and he did it."

Van Kley summed it up succinctly in his story in *W.I.N. Magazine* (2001): "Nick Ackerman has taught us all what the word 'believe' really means."

BATTLING AGAINST THE ODDS

Stories like Nick Ackerman's are hard to match in the world of sport, but many other wrestlers have had to overcome obstacles to achieve at high levels. Many deaf students and blind students have found new self-respect and new self-worth in the sport of wrestling.

Randy Lewis and Kevin Dresser both won NCAA championships despite being born without a pectoralis muscle. Fred Fozzard suffered from polio as a youth and had a withered arm. Yet that arm was terribly strong, and Fred was a three-time All-American at Oklahoma State University, winning the NCAA 177-pound championship in 1967. Two years later, Fozzard became one of the first two Americans ever to win a gold medal in the world championships, winning in the 180.5-pound class.

"Fred was somewhat like Randy Lewis in that he was born with a small physical defect," said J Robinson, who roomed with Fozzard at Oklahoma State and helped coach Lewis at Iowa. "But

Randy Lewis, 1984 Olympic champion at 136 pounds who overcame being born without a pectoralis muscle, works on a foe during the Olympic Games in Los Angeles.

their bodies overcompensated. Fred's arm was a bit withered and he didn't have tendons in his fingers but his arm became an asset when people tried to hang onto it but couldn't. It was very strong. He had really great hips, too. He learned to develop his skills in a different way. He became a national and world champion, so he wasn't too handicapped."

"It was difficult to think of him as handicapped when he was beating everyone he faced, not just beating them but dominating them," said Jim Duschen, a former Big Eight champion who wrestled Fozzard twice, coming away with a one-point win and a tie. "I had heard about his great strength and balance, and I went in as the underdog. I guess I matched up well with him. It was a matter of staying in good position and not going after him, wrestling a strategic match. Fred was capable of tossing anyone.

"He was able to compensate for whatever limitations he had in his right arm, but he was a phenomenal athlete and great competitor."

REVERSING AN UNDERDOG SITUATION

But one story may be even more remarkable than those already told. It's hard to conceive of, but it is true.

Kyle Maynard may be the most amazing wrestler in history, dating all the way back to Milo in the ancient Olympics. The young man was born with a rare disorder called congenital amputation, leaving him with severely undeveloped arms and legs.

"Both of Kyle's arms end just above the elbows and his legs end well before his knees, with small feet turned backwards for balance," wrote Van Kley in *W.I.N. Magazine*. "When he's not using a motorized wheel chair, Kyle gets around on all fours. He refuses to use prosthetics because he does not want the mentality of actually having a handicap. The 18-year-old from Atlanta has learned to adapt to nearly every situation he's been presented with in life."

Kyle shocked fans at the NHSCA High School Senior Nationals of 2004, held in Cleveland, Ohio. He entered the tourney with a 35-16 record and gave a good account of himself in his matches. Kyle faces an opponent down on all fours, with his half arms and half legs solidly on the mat. He then scoots around, looking for a position from which to attack.

His wrestling career began in sixth grade. His father, Scott, and his coach, Cliff Ramos, tucked their own arms inside their shirts to mimic Kyle's situation and try to figure out what moves might work for him. In the high school wrestling room, Kyle was expected to do the same workout routine as everyone else. He didn't want to do it any other way.

Although he didn't wrestle beyond high school, Kyle continued his education at the University of Georgia. An excellent student, his plans were to start his own business and some day coach wrestling.

"I've been privileged to have witnessed some incredible accomplishments in wrestling and other sports," wrote Van Kley in a column. "But nothing, and I mean nothing, even comes close to what I saw" when Kyle Maynard scored a victory at the tournament. "But it's not just the fact that Kyle wrestles with these extreme circumstances (basically, no arms or legs) that makes his story one of a kind. It is everything else about him. It's the way he confidently carries himself. It's his positive attitude on life and his situation. It's his fun-loving personality that draws people to him."

Already an accomplished speaker, Kyle was one of the keynote speakers at the coaches banquet before the start of the high school nationals, impressing everyone with his poise and articulate delivery. Other opportunities are waiting for him as well. ESPN voted him its ESPY Award as the most courageous athlete in America in 2004, giving his story a national platform. A few months later, he was a guest on the Larry King national TV talk show.

The Washington, D.C., speakers' bureau is interested in him, and a screenplay has been written about his amazing life story.

"God did make Kyle for a reason," said his coach. "God has sent a blessing to a wrestling team and to Suwanee, Georgia, in the form of a two-and-a-half foot giant of a person. I think he's the most amazing athlete who ever lived."

As for Kyle, he gives immense credit to two different sources of strength: wrestling and Jesus. "The sport, as far as character goes, it is foundational for any human being," he said in his speech to the wrestling coaches. "You have to learn failure on a basis where you can only blame yourself. It makes the rest of your life a lot easier.

"My salvation through Jesus has been my crutch through those times when things have been tough," he added. "All of us need to focus on the fortunes and blessings of God. My religion and wrestling are the two most important things in the world to me."

Kyle Maynard's courage and positive outlook on life has inspired hundreds of people already and could reach millions if the movie ever comes to fruition. He has battled odds that are so overwhelming that anything the rest of us face pales by comparison. He has proven to the world that the value of the sport of wrestling extends far beyond the boundaries of a wrestling mat.

"Wrestling is a sport with very few limitations," said one national sportswriter. "Big or small, weak or strong, man or woman, blind . . . deaf . . . physically impaired . . . all those athletes have found a home in wrestling."

SUMMARY

The sport of wrestling has seen hundreds of powerful stories in which athletes have overcome terrific odds. The examples range all the way from the Olympic Games in Los Angeles, where Jeff Blatnick kneeled in prayer after winning a gold medal and overcoming cancer, to a high school gym in Georgia where a young man with virtually no arms and legs has taught himself to be a competitor and a winner.

Wrestling teaches people how to get off their backs, and life puts people on their backs time and again. Wrestling teaches values that help us succeed in life; it teaches us the importance of discipline, determination, goal setting, and hard work. Dan Gable says that after wrestling, everything else in life is easy. That is the true value of the sport. Wrestling teaches everyone how to overcome the odds.

15

The Will to Win

Vince Lombardi is probably the most respected professional football coach of all time. He came out of nowhere in the 1960s to blaze a path across the NFL firmament that has never been surpassed, and likely never will be. Lombardi is an almost mythical character in the realm of super coaches. But it wasn't always that way. Like all other athletes and coaches, Lombardi had to pay his dues before being given the opportunity show his genius in the area of coaching men.

Afraid that he would never get a chance to be a head coach in the NFL because he was too old, Lombardi finally received his opportunity from the Green Bay Packers in 1959. The Packers had not enjoyed many winning seasons before Lombardi's arrival. But it did not take Lombardi long to show what he had to offer.

Almost immediately, the Green Bay Packers became the talk of the NFL because of their amazing turnaround from doormat to title contender. With Lombardi at the helm, the Packers won so often that they became part of professional sport legend.

What was the key to Lombardi's incredible success?

"Over the years, we have waived players or traded players or not kept players, not because of a lack of ability but because of the lack of something else we would like to see in them," he said. "This lack is not courage or intelligence. I don't place much emphasis on intelligence; I don't think many of the coaches do. I don't think you have to."

So what is it this "something" that Lombardi was looking for? It was the same quality that Gable was looking for at the University of Iowa. It was the foundation on which Gable and Lombardi built their success.

"I think winning is the result of mental toughness," said Lombardi in the same story. "I think mental toughness is many things, and it is very difficult to explain what it is. First, I think mental toughness is humility; I think that it takes humility to realize that greatness is really simplicity. Mental toughness is made up too of the spartan qualities of sacrifice and self-denial. Mental toughness is loyalty. You cannot win consistently without it, and as you win each man grows because of it" (Riger 1980, 53).

Lombardi broke down mental toughness this way:

1. Humility
2. Sacrifice
3. Self-denial
4. Loyalty

Motivating oneself is the key to success in any chore or task, and that is especially true in sport. We have all known (and even seen) examples of young athletes blessed with tremendous genetic skills. They were able to outrun, outmaneuver, and overpower all the others in their age group. Yet as the years slipped by and they entered their late teens, many of them faded and gave way to athletes who were more motivated. Many top athletes simply lose interest in paying the price required to stay at the top of the heap.

Good coaches want to know where motivation comes from so that they can tap into motivational areas to help athletes reach their highest potential. Why do many top athletes lose interest? Why do many mediocre athletes keep working and toiling despite limited early success and eventually become superstars?

BUILDING ON FAILURE

Michael Jordan used the pain of being cut from a basketball team early in life to spur himself into action. He motivated himself to become, in time, the greatest basketball player of his era, possibly of all time.

"When I got cut from the varsity team as a sophomore in high school, I learned something," he said. "I knew I never wanted to feel that bad again. I never wanted to have that taste in my mouth, that hurt in my stomach. So I set a goal of becoming a starter on the varsity. When I worked on my game, that's what I thought about" (Jordan 1998, 3).

That approach worked for Michael Jordan, but it doesn't work for everybody. Sometimes, a devastating experience such as being cut from a team can send a person into a mental tailspin from which it can be almost impossible to recover. Others simply never receive motivation to excel from a coach or parent, and they drift through the early formative years without any athletic aspirations or goals. Later, when they become motivated, it is too late. Timing can be important. In today's world of high-tech sports, some form of training must begin at a relatively young age.

"I always thought I had the potential to be a top athlete but I never really cared about it as a young boy, not even in high school," said one man late in his life. In his 20s and 30s, he had earned a reputation as a very strong man with a high level of drive and determination, as evidenced in his business and personal life. He loved wrestling and loved to work out, in various ways. He attended numerous NCAA tournaments and was friends with some of the best wrestlers the country has ever produced. Yet, he was often perplexed by his lack of motivation as a young man.

"Somehow, it just never mattered to me, until it was too late to actually do much about it," he admitted. "Looking back, I think I was handicapped by the fact that I had no immediate role models, and my parents expressed no interest in athletics whatsoever. I wasn't motivated at that age towards sports and so I just went about other pursuits."

TAKING PRIDE

Clearly, motivation plays a huge role in the success of any athlete. And just as clearly, there are many ways to motivate an athlete. One of the most powerful methods focuses on the athlete's desire to prove himself or herself in some meaningful way.

Bob Mathias is one of the most remarkable athletes in history. As a mere lad of 17 he made the United States Olympic team in the grueling decathlon event, beating experienced athletes many years older than himself, including the heavy premeet favorite, Irving Mondschein, a veteran athlete in his mid-20s. This raw, relatively untutored young athlete went to London in 1948 and defeated the best decathletes in the entire world.

In his biography, Mathias tells of finding much of his motivation in the remarks of an insensitive coach. "My feelings are not easily hurt but there was one time just before the competition began that I really got upset," he said. "I was just beginning to feel comfortable with all these great athletes when I heard that the Olympic decathlon coach told the press that I showed a great deal of promise for 1952 (the next Olympics, four years later) but he didn't think that I could repeat a win over Mondschein. It was bad enough that I was lonesome and homesick and feeling like a kid among adults. I didn't need some insensitive coach implying to the press there wasn't much sense in my being there.

"To make matters worse, it made me wonder if maybe he was right. Maybe I had no business in being there. But after a while, I was able to put the comment aside. 'The hell with you, Mac,' I thought. 'You just watch'" (Mathias and Mendes 2001, 43, 44).

Mathias led the competition over the last five events and rolled up 7,139 points for the gold medal. Mondschein finished with 6,715 points, in eighth place. Young Bob Mathias had not only won the event in astonishing form but also managed to make the coach swallow his words. He had, consciously or otherwise, found a powerful motivational tool and put it to good use.

Although he swore that he would never go through another decathlon because of the intense pain and mental pressure, four years later he won the Olympic gold medal again, breaking the record set by Glenn Morris in 1936. He went on to become a football standout at Stanford and played in the Rose Bowl. He starred in four movies, including *The Bob Mathias Story*, and served four terms as a United States congressman from California.

INDIVIDUALIZED MOTIVATION

"Motivation comes from within each individual," said Mike Ditka, an All-Pro football player and Super Bowl coach of the Chicago Bears. "It's a personal thing. It's pride, guts, desire, whatever you want to call it; some people have it in their bellies, and some don't."

"I knew early on that I wanted to be an Olympic champion, and I avoided things that would hurt me or burn me out on the sport," said John Smith. "I kept myself motivated by always looking ahead and working to improve."

As mentioned in chapter 12, Dan Gable used a unique form of visualization to motivate himself when he was still active as a competitor. "When I'd get tired and want to stop, I'd wonder what my next opponent was doing," said Gable. "I wondered if he was still working out. I tried to visualize him. When I could see him working out, I'd start pushing myself. When I could see him in the shower, I'd push myself harder."

For others, it's fear, which can manifest itself in various ways—the fear of looking inept, the fear of letting others down, the fear of simply not measuring up to the task at hand.

"Fear of failure is what fuels me, keeps me on edge and sharp. I'm not as good when I'm comfortable," said Alex Rodriguez, one of baseball's brightest stars for over a decade.

Mark Schultz was one of the greatest wrestlers in American history. At the University of Oklahoma, he won three NCAA titles, defeating superb wrestlers from Iowa in the finals each year. He won the 180.5-pound class at the Los Angeles Olympics in 1984, competing with such intensity that he snapped the arm of his first-round foe, the heavily favored wrestler from Turkey. Schultz followed up his 1984 gold medal by winning world titles in both 1985 and 1987.

Yet he wasn't particularly interested in wrestling as a young man. He was a superb gymnast and saw a bright future in that sport. His motivation came from a front-yard brawl with his older brother, Dave, also one of the finest wrestlers in U.S. history.

Mark had also been studying a martial art called tang soo do. When they tangled, Mark found that his superior physical strength was easily nullified by Dave's wrestling technique and skills. He wound up taking more punishment than he dealt out and quickly decided that he wanted to learn to wrestle so that he could better defend himself, not just against his brother but also against others who might challenge him.

"Thinking I was ready to show my brother, Dave, how superior I had become from my four months of training, I got in a fight with him on the front lawn of our house in Ashland, Oregon," said Mark. "I took a swing. He ducked and shot in for a takedown. He got the mount and punched my face into bloody submission. I was humiliated and slept in the car that night. The next day I quit tang soo do and went out for the wrestling team" (Furey 1999, 9).

Sometimes the spark to win comes from sources that go far deeper than mere athletics. According to the 2005 hit movie *Cinderella Man*, heavyweight boxer James Braddock (portrayed by Russell Crowe) was motivated by one of the most basic of all desires—to feed his children. Problems with fragile hands had ruined Braddock's once-promising career and he was forced to work on the docks and beg for money.

Braddock even wound up on relief during the Great Depression of the 1930s. Given a second chance to fight, he was desperate to feed his near-starving family. When he won three bouts in a row and was awarded a title shot, the press asked him why he was fighting. "To buy milk," he responded. Fueled primarily by the motivation to take care of his family, he then proceeded to win the world championship by beating Max Baer in one of the biggest upsets in boxing history!

Dan Hodge used wrestling as a way out of his painful home life. Because of a strange set of circumstances, his parents abandoned him as a young boy, and Hodge grew up with a grandparent who liked to smack him around. He learned how to defend himself through wrestling and then discovered that he was capable of pinning anyone, at about any time. He won three NCAA championships for the University of Oklahoma, and twice was named the outstanding wrestler of the meet. He is the only amateur wrestler ever to appear on the cover of *Sports Illustrated* (April 1, 1957). Hodge also won a national heavyweight Golden Gloves boxing title and has since become one of the top icons of wrestling. The sport's most important collegiate award, the Dan Hodge Trophy, is presented each year to the top collegiate wrestler in the nation.

"Wrestling has been wonderful to me and I love it," he said. "It's hard to imagine what my life would have been like without it."

Bill Smith's motivation was to win a letter and impress the girls in his 10th grade class at Thomas Jefferson High School in Council Bluffs, Iowa. He wanted to try basketball but heard that the wrestling team had an opening at 103 pounds. "All I had to do was show up, make weight and go on the mat and I'd get a letter," he says today with a sly grin. "That sounded pretty darn good to me. I didn't know I was going to end up spending my whole life with the darn sport." But he did, winning two NCAA titles at Iowa State Teachers College while going undefeated in his collegiate career. In 1952, he journeyed to Helsinki, Finland, and was the only American wrestler to win a gold medal in the Olympics, competing at 160.5 pounds. He entered coaching soon afterward and has led his high school teams to state titles in California and Illinois. He has taken American squads all around the world. He is a member of every hall of fame available to him and is a wrestling legend—all because he wanted to impress the girls as a youngster back in Council Bluffs.

Lee Kemp's motivation was to forget the pain of being cut from the basketball team in ninth grade. He recalled feeling sorry for himself as he walked past the wrestling practice room and heard shouts and laughter. He looked in and was hooked. "They seemed to be having a good time in there," he said decades later. "I wanted to be a part of something like that, so I decided to go out for wrestling."

Before he was through, he had won three NCAA titles for the University of Wisconsin and three world championships. President Carter's decision to boycott the 1980 Olympics cost Kemp his shot at an Olympic gold medal, but he has carried the values he learned from the sport with him into the workplace. He is now the owner of a successful Ford car dealership in Forest Lake, Minnesota.

"Wrestling has positively impacted my life in many ways, but perhaps the one singular thing that I gained from wrestling that stands out the most is that wrestling provided me the opportunity to learn mental toughness!" said Kemp. "A person's mental toughness is what allows them to demand of themselves anything and everything necessary to achieve the desired goal, or basically speaking—people who are mentally tough get the job done!"

DISCIPLINE AND DESIRE

Kurt Angle found motivation in the loss of his father, a man he greatly admired and wanted to do something special for. "My father's accidental death on a construction site changed me forever," Angle wrote in his autobiography. "It gave me an inner strength that allowed me to rise above the life of brawling and partying that had destroyed the athletic dreams of my four older brothers in our hometown of Pittsburgh" (Angle 2001, 3).

Angle wanted to win for his father and other family members, and to make them all proud of him. He used that motivation to win two NCAA championships at Clarion University and to capture gold medals in the 1995 world championships and the 1996 Olympic Games, both in Atlanta. But the path he chose wasn't easy, because a huge learning curve intervenes between American folkstyle wrestling and the international freestyle type of wrestling. Kurt took some lumps in the body and ego when he began making trips overseas, and after some discouraging results he almost gave up the sport. He even had a tryout with the Pittsburgh Steelers of the NFL, although he hadn't played football since high school.

Then he decided to go for an Olympic gold medal at 220 pounds in 1996.

"And nobody paid the price like I did for two years leading up to the Olympics," he said. "I'd always trained hard but once I recommitted myself after my Steelers fantasy, I took it to another level. Because the nature of freestyle wrestling forced me to tone down my aggressive style, I decided the only way to beat some of these guys was to wear them down, break their will with better conditioning. So for two years I trained morning, noon and night, just about every day" (Angle 2001, 79).

The concept of fatigue training was what pushed him to the top of the mountain that he was trying to climb. He would push himself to the point of total fatigue—and then really get going! Like many great athletes before him, he learned to block out discomfort and pain, and to focus on the long-term goal.

His morning routine included four-mile runs, a series of sprints, some hill sprints, and then hill sprints while carrying a partner who weighed 185 pounds—over and over and over. He wrapped a bungee cord around him and ran against resistance—"like Rocky Balboa pulling that sled in the movie *Rocky IV*."

That was just the morning half of his daily program. In the afternoon, he wrestled for nearly three hours, sat in a sauna, and studied technique. In the evenings, he lifted weights. But he was building more than physical conditioning—he was building mental confidence. "You can turn a giant into a mouse just by getting him fatigued. That was my whole game plan," he said.

The entire torturous routine, which lasted for nearly two years, had as its centerpiece two elements: his desire and his discipline. He had to have tremendous desire to develop and implement the program, and tremendous discipline to keep coming back to it, day after day, month after month. What Angle subjected himself to in the weight room is hard to comprehend; you simply need to read pages 79 through 89 in his autobiography, *It's True! It's True!* Just reading about Angle's routine will leave you gasping for breath, nearly exhausted. And it will help you understand what the will to win and motivation are all about, and what real discipline means.

"I believe in discipline," said legendary NFL player and coach Forrest Gregg. "You can forgive incompetence. You can forgive lack of ability. But one thing you cannot ever forgive is a lack of discipline" (Ferguson 1990, 3-12).

Tom Landry, who led the Dallas Cowboys into NFL history and into the hearts of the nation by making it America's team, was a huge advocate of discipline. He was a familiar sight for decades, walking slowly along the sidelines of the Cowboys team. Discipline was the key as he led the Cowboys to two Super Bowl victories and a record 20 consecutive winning seasons.

"Setting a goal is not the main thing," said Landry. "It is deciding how you will go about achieving it and staying with that plan. They key is discipline. Without it, there is no morale" (Ferguson 1990, 3-13).

SQUELCHING FEAR AND DOUBT

Fear is also a great motivating factor. Athletes can be afraid of looking bad in front of their friends or large crowds, or of being humiliated. They can fear getting hurt or fear that they have not prepared adequately to show their best.

"I drew my strength from fear," admitted Boris Becker, a three-time winner of tennis's greatest tournament, Wimbledon. "Fear of losing. I don't remember the games I won, only the games I lost."

"Success is doing what it takes in spite of one's fears," said Johnny Rutherford, a three-time winner of the Indianapolis 500 race. The fear that can arise from driving around an oval track at speeds approaching 200 miles per hour is staggering, to be sure. One small error can mean anything from a fiery crash with terrible injuries to instant death. Fear is lurking behind every turn in the track, but racecar drivers are experts at controlling the fear, or at least subduing it to the point where it is almost nonexistent. Otherwise, they would not be able to compete effectively.

Although self-doubt isn't as dangerous as fear can be, it can certainly affect an athlete's performance in a negative way. Like fear, self-doubt has to be controlled before it controls the athlete.

"A true champion knows how to overcome doubts and manage those doubts and turn them into motivation," said Misty Hyman, an Olympic swimming champion.

Pressure, external and internal, is another factor that athletes have to deal with in a positive way. If they don't, pressure can get the best of them, just as fear and self-doubt can. In 2002 Cael Sanderson of Iowa State University became the only four-time NCAA champion to go through his entire career without a loss.

Cael Sanderson battles Lee Fullhart for a spot on the 2004 Olympic team, proving his will to win and his ability to stand up under pressure.

Sanderson racked up 159 consecutive wins, was named the outstanding wrestler at the NCAA championships four times, and won the Dan Hodge Trophy, which goes to the top collegiate wrestler in the country, three straight seasons.

During his junior and senior years in college, the pressure began to mount, and perhaps some apprehension, as well. As he approached Dan Gable's all-time record of 117 consecutive wins in college, Sanderson continually faced comparisons between himself and the biggest legend in wrestling. After he passed Gable's mark, the pressure switched to becoming the first undefeated four-time NCAA champion. Pat Smith of Oklahoma State had won his fourth title in 1994 but bowed out with an overall record of 121-5-2. Sanderson was sailing in uncharted water, and some fear must have lurked in the back of his mind—fear of stumbling just once and letting down thousands of fans.

But he managed to keep his composure through it all. "It's a mind-set," said Sanderson. "It comes from the way you look at things. You just can't show up and say, 'I'm going to win the NCAA.' You have to want to sacrifice to achieve it."

STAYING HUNGRY

But with success, the athlete must adjust the motivation, Sanderson said. His primary goal in his freshman year was to earn the championship ring that Iowa State University gave its athletes if they were national champions. After winning a ring in his first season he had to change his motivation. He needed a new means to stay hungry.

One of the greatest bodybuilders of all time agrees with having that mind-set. "I believe in the philosophy of staying hungry," said Arnold Schwarzenegger. "If you have a dream and it becomes a reality, don't stay satisfied too long. Make up a new dream and hunt after that one and turn it into a reality."

"Only the strong survive," said tennis star Jennifer Capriati. She meant the mentally strong, winners like Sanderson, Schwarzenegger, and Navratilova. But there is often more to it than being strong and prepared. Sometimes an athlete feels that his or her entire identity as a person is assessed in terms of how well he or she performs, week after week, year after year.

For decades, sportswriters and fans have pondered what causes super athletes to continue competing far past their prime, when they seem to have all the financial security and adulation that they could possibly need. Why do many great boxers fight way beyond their peak? Why do many professional football players continue to play the game when the physical injuries pile up to the point that they will never be able to lead normal lives?

The answers lie in the recesses of the mind and in the secrets of what motivated them in the first place to try to reach the pinnacle of athletic success. Once they attain such status, some athletes find it extremely difficult to surrender it all and walk away. The same things that motivated people to be supreme winners can still be at work in stopping them from walking away from their successes and starting a new life independent of sport.

SUMMARY

The will to win has to originate somewhere, and athletes have to develop it and cultivate it. Motivation is often the spark that pushes a person to do all the things required to win. Motivation can provide the mental drive that ignites a medal-winning performance. Anger and fear are powerful motivational mechanisms, whereas self-doubt and pressure can thwart motivational drive unless the athlete recognizes and deals with them.

Most athletes are able to lock into some force that propels them forward and helps them achieve their highest goals. The will to win is not a gift at birth; rather, it is a learned behavior that comes from an inner drive known as motivation, whether the source is the desire to please others or a fear of letting someone (including oneself) down. Motivation is the powerful fuel that drives the will to win. Desire and discipline will fine-tune the process. The power of heart is another factor in developing champions, and it can be more powerful than anything we have talked about so far.

16

The Power
of Heart

"When your luck is batting zero, get your chin up off the floor. Mister, you can be a hero, you can open any door. There's nothing to it. . . . But to do it, you've gotta have heart, miles and miles and miles of heart."

Those are the words from a 1950s song called "Heart," words that could be the motto of nearly every wrestler who ever dreamed of going all the way to the top. One thing is certain: skills are extremely important, but no one will become the very best in the world of sport without a huge supply of heart.

In the popular 2003 movie *Seabiscuit*, the horse trainer shows early on that he understands the essence of what makes a great racehorse, or athlete: "It ain't just the speed, it's the heart," he tells the owner of Seabiscuit. "You want one that ain't afraid to compete . . . ain't afraid of a fight." Later, jockey Red Pollard makes the same point when talking to another jockey about Seabiscuit: "It's not in the feet, George . . . it's right here (tapping his heart)."

If a single line divides elite athletes from the rest of the field, it is probably the heart of the athlete involved.

"I'd rather have more heart than talent any day," says Allen Iverson, several-time NBA scoring champion of the Philadelphia 76ers.

Marcel Cerdan, France's sensational middleweight champion of the early 1950s, was a big fan of Rocky Marciano, who retired undefeated in 1956 with a 49-0 record. Marciano built his reputation on his indefatigable persona and his ferocious, unrelenting style of attack.

"He don't know how to fight, but his heart, she's so big, she does not believe in defeat," said Cerdan in his French-tinted speaking style. "He'll fight anybody and he bleed and bleed and bleed but always he come back."

THE DIFFERENCE HEART CAN MAKE

Rulon Gardner and Cael Sanderson are perfect examples of how heart can make the difference in athletics at the highest level.

In the 2000 Olympics in Sydney, Australia, Gardner came face to face with his own desire and his belief in himself. Did he have the inner workings to defeat the unbeatable wrestler, Alexander Karelin of Russia? Karelin had fashioned the most incredible record in wrestling history, dating back to the fabled Milo of Kroton, who wrestled around 350 B.C. and won six Olympic championships.

Karelin exploded on the international scene in 1988 with his gold-medal performance in the 286-pound class in the Seoul Olympics. At age 20, he looked like Arnold Schwarzenegger at his best, with rippling muscle on top of muscle. The Russian star ran through the competition without surrendering a single point, lifting and tossing foes as if they were featherweights instead of 286-pounders. His reverse lift and throw was the most terrifying hold in wrestling. In a television interview seen around the world during the 1992 Olympics, famed announcer Bob Costas listened in awe as Jeff Blatnick described what it felt like to wrestle Karelin. Costas was stunned when the 1984 Olympic gold medal winner told him that it was well known in wrestling circles that some wrestlers would turn to their back and let Karelin pin them rather than fight him and risk being injured in his throw. After Karelin ran off 12 consecutive world or Olympic titles, most wrestling experts considered him unbeatable.

Gardner, on the other hand, came into the 2000 Olympics with little notice. But he did have a game plan, devised by his coaches, Steve Fraser and Dan Chandler. The plan was to tire out the massively muscled Russian, circle to his right, and hope to frustrate him. In a visit to the International Wrestling Institute and Museum in Newton, Iowa, six months before the Olympics, Fraser looked at a large poster photo of Karelin tossing a foe, his face contorted in a menacing sneer.

"Rulon can beat him," said Fraser quietly. "It may be a long shot, but Karelin isn't the same man he used to be. And Rulon is training very, very hard. He is in great shape. We have a great plan."

On the night of September 27, 2000, with a packed arena looking on and dignitaries like Juan Samaranch, president of the International Olympic Committee, and Henry Kissinger, former secretary of state for the United States, in the audience, Gardner executed a perfect game plan. He kept the score tied for the first three-fourths of the match. He then scored a point when Karelin broke a clinch grip for a mere two seconds. With a 1-0 lead, Gardner called on two of his best qualities—conditioning and heart—to bring home the gold medal.

© Empics

In one of the greatest wrestling matches of all time, Russia's Alexander Karelin (left) tangles with America's Rulon Gardner. Karelin had won 12 consecutive World or Olympic titles and had never lost an international match at the time of their meeting in the 2000 Olympics in Sydney. Gardner scored a 1-0 victory in the Greco-Roman battle in the 286-pound class.

"Hard work beats talent when talent doesn't work hard," said Greg Strobel. Is that true of Gardner and Karelin? Yes, to a degree. Karelin was suffering from several maladies, including strained back and hip muscles and lack of interest. Rumors had circulated that he was not going to enter the Games until political forces in Russia pressured him to do so. He did not look as impressive physically as he had in past years, and he had lost a considerable amount of muscularity. In addition, he seemed rather passive as he stood at the edge of the mat before the finals.

No matter what Karelin's condition was, mentally and physically, he was still the overwhelming favorite. To stay even with him would take a monumental effort on Gardner's part, both mentally and physically. As the match developed, it became apparent that Gardner was up to the task. He had trained diligently, and his coaches had worked hard on his mental attitude. The result was one of the greatest upsets in the history of the modern Olympics, dating all the way back to 1896.

Gardner was respectful in the press meeting after the match. "I still think he is the best wrestler in the world," he said of Karelin. "I can't believe I am standing in front of you after beating that guy. I'm numb. This is still a dream for me."

During the next several years, Gardner appeared on numerous television shows and was in constant demand as a motivational speaker. He became one of the sport's biggest celebrities. But he soon faced other obstacles to overcome. In February 2002, while on a snowmobile trip deep in a mountainous area of Wyoming with two friends in bitterly cold weather, the trio became separated. The two friends returned to their origination point hoping that their friend had made it there too, but Gardner was nowhere to be seen.

As the hours ticked away, friends and local authorities became worried about Gardner's welfare. They set out into the growing dark and frigid temperatures to search for him. At last, in the dead of night, they returned without Gardner, prepared to wait out the night before starting out again at dawn.

Gardner spent a long, gut-wrenching night. His snowmobile had fallen into a gully with shallow water, and Gardner had soaked his boots and lower legs while pulling the 650-pound machine into the snow bank. As the temperature plummeted to around 20 degrees below zero, he started to shiver uncontrollably and began to wonder whether he would survive. He was rescued after nearly 17 hours alone, but the ordeal was not over. His feet had suffered severe frostbite, and the middle toe on his right foot was amputated. At one point, doctors felt that he might lose nearly all his toes.

Forced to take a huge amount of time off for recovery, Gardner had to fight extremely hard to get back in condition and to work on his balance, which was in jeopardy after the loss of the toe. In the meantime, Dremiel Byers had won the world title in 2002 and Gardner needed to defeat him even to make the United States world team in 2003. But he did so and qualified for the 2003 world championships, where he placed 10th.

In March 2004 Gardner was involved in a motorcycle accident and was sent flying through the air after hitting a car that pulled out in front of him. He walked away with only cuts and bruises, and credited wrestling for the diving, midair roll that he executed to avoid serious injury.

As if that were not enough, several days later Gardner dislocated his right wrist playing a pickup basketball game at the Olympic Training Center!

The latter injury was still bothering him when he faced Byers in the Greco-Roman nationals. Gardner lost. That loss cost him the top position in the Olympic trials and forced him to work his way up through the ranks at the final trials in Indianapolis. He did so and then met Byers in the last match, defeating him twice to capture the spot for the 2004 Olympics.

In Athens, Gardner earned a bronze medal. After his final match, he left his wrestling shoes on the mat, signaling that he was retiring from the sport that had given him so much status, recognition, and self-satisfaction. He walked away as the most accomplished Greco-Roman wrestler in American history.

Much of what he accomplished in his career he did with a massive display of heart and pride. Rulon Gardner was an excellent example of what a huge heart can accomplish when coupled with the other ingredients discussed in this book.

DEDICATION AND HEART

The same can be said of Cael Sanderson's march to an Olympic gold medal in 2004 in Athens. Few wrestlers have ever faced more pressure than the sensational Iowa State star did. After going 159-0 in college, collecting four NCAA titles, and winning the Dan Hodge

Trophy three times, some expected Cael to win every freestyle event he entered.

But that would not happen, of course. Nearly every college star has to go through a learning curve in freestyle, with the possible exception of John Smith, who won his first world championship while still in college. After his college career was over, Sanderson lost eight matches in freestyle competition. He took third in the 2003 Pan American Games and second in the 2003 world championships. He finished second in a tournament in Russia and was beaten in the 2004 U.S. nationals by Lee Fullhart. Sanderson then lost a match to Fullhart at the trials, although Sanderson won two out of three to make the Olympic team.

His showdown in Indianapolis with Fullhart for the 185-pound spot on the American team was a true test of the heart of both men, and both passed with flying colors. Fullhart, NCAA champion for Iowa in 1997 and a four-time All-American, had defeated Sanderson in the freestyle nationals, and Sanderson had to come up through the minitrials. In the finals, he edged Fullhart 3-1 in the first match and then lost in overtime, 2-2 criteria. With the suspense building in the arena, the two warriors retreated to their sanctuaries to prepare for the biggest match of their lives. There, with everything on the line for Sanderson, including his place in wrestling history, he scored a 4-1 triumph.

The faces of both men bore evidence of their commitment. Sanderson's right ear sported a nasty gash. Blood was streaked across his face and neck as sweat poured off his forehead. Fullhart had a gash over his right eye and on his ear, and his head was wrapped in a large, white strip for the final match.

"He's real physical," said Sanderson after the showdown with his longtime rival. "It's more of a fight than wrestling match against him." But the ex-Cyclone was pleased to be an Olympian at last.

"That last match wasn't real pretty, but it doesn't need to be," said Sanderson. "I was just trying to get on that team. It's crazy to make an Olympic team because you dream about it for years and years, but it seems so far away. It is strange to finally make it after thinking about it for 20 years. But it's pretty neat."

Talk in the wrestling world was that Sanderson might have lost his competitive fire after his incredible final season of college wrestling and all the hoopla that followed. The emotionally draining experience had not let up for three years. He admitted that was the case and said that his loss to Fullhart in the freestyle nationals helped get him motivated once more. "I've gotten a lot more excited about wrestling again," Sanderson said. "I wrestled poorly in the match at nationals."

Heart played a huge role in his matches to make the Olympics and to win the gold medal two months later on the other side of the world. After a 9-1 victory in the first round of the Athens Games, Sanderson had a close 4-2 match and then had to rally from behind and go into overtime to defeat the Iranian wrestler, 6-5. Facing Yoel Romero of Cuba, who owned a 2-0 record against the American star, Sanderson posted a crucial 3-2 win, putting him in the finals against Korea's Eui Je Moon. There, Sanderson earned his gold medal with a 3-1 triumph.

"You can say all you want about talent, but the reason Cael Sanderson is an Olympic champion is he has the heart of a champion," said Bobby Douglas after Sanderson won his final match in Athens.

Douglas had been witness to that display of heart from Sanderson for five years as his head coach at Iowa State University and as his Olympic coach. He has seen the young man from Utah arrive as a freshman and win 159 consecutive matches, most of them with skill but sometimes with just plain grit and heart. He saw him face up to the steadily mounting pressure as the national media zeroed in, and he saw him sit and sign autographs for fans for hours on end. Sometimes, Sanderson was still in an arena three hours after his match, signing for kids. "He never stopped until every single fan had an autograph," said Douglas.

A week after winning his fourth NCAA title, Sanderson agreed to forego a planned fishing trip to participate in the Dan Gable Classic in Cedar Rapids, Iowa. The meet was being called Spirit of the Heartland to honor America's fighting spirit some six months after 9/11. Among those being honored was Lt. Col. Steve Banach, one of the famous Banach brothers, who had served with a ranger unit in Afghanistan searching for Osama bin Laden.

After the meet, Sanderson and his fiancée, Kelly, stayed for three hours as Sanderson signed for fans. They sat in the outer lobby as a cleanup crew worked in the main arena. The other wrestlers and officials had long since gone to a banquet. When one remaining meet official suggested that Sanderson could cut the line off and escape, Sanderson politely declined. "I'll stay until they all get an autograph," he said with a faint smile.

"He's special, that's all there is to it. We knew he was going to be good coming out of high school, but we didn't know he was going to be *this* good," Douglas had said several years earlier as Sanderson was in the midst of his incredible string. "A lot of it has to do with his upbringing at home and his heart."

THE STRENGTH TO CARRY ON

Many boxing experts consider Muhammad Ali the greatest heavyweight champion of all time. They point to the speed of his hands and feet, his sensational reflexes, his height and reach, and his supreme confidence in his own abilities. But they also point to his heart.

Muhammad Ali had a huge heart, visible time and again in the ring. We saw the first evidence of it on March 8, 1971, in what many have called the fight of the century. That battle showcased two undefeated champions in one ring. Ali, coming off an enforced three-year layoff because of his refusal to enter the army during the Vietnam War, had a record of 31-0. Joe Frazier, who rose to prominence when Ali was on the sidelines giving speeches around the nation, was 26-0 and the champion of the boxing establishment.

On that historic night, the two battled ferociously for 15 incredible rounds. In the closing moments of the fight, Frazier caught Ali with a stunning left hook to the jaw. Ali went down hard but got back up almost immediately. Ringsiders gasped in shock as they saw his jaw ballooning to obscene size from the force of the blow. With a minute still to go, Ali stood and fought with tremendous valor despite the incredible pain from the jaw. He finished on his feet, losing for the first time as a professional fighter. The heart he had shown was applauded everywhere.

Two years later, Ken Norton, an extremely muscular power hitter, caught him in the same spot with a left hook. Ali's jaw was broken again. This time, the punch came in the third round, and Ali fought 10 more rounds with searing pain. Again, he finished on his feet.

In the third Ali–Frazier match, held on October 1, 1975, in the heat of Manila, Philippines, the two fighters battled in a fashion seldom seen in the ring. Both were physically and emotionally spent. After the 10th round, many believed that Ali would have to surrender. But he reached down and found the will to go on. In the 14th, in a stunning rally, he hit Frazier with an avalanche of blows. At the end of the round, Frazier's trainer, Yank Durham, threw in the towel. Frazier was virtually blind from eye swelling, and his face was a battered mask. As he stood to face the final round, Ali was told that Frazier's corner had quit and that he had won. Ali sagged to the canvas in stunned disbelief and relief. Later, he said that the fight was the closest thing to dying he could imagine. Ali's physical skills were tremendous, but he also was blessed with a heart of tremendous depth.

"The game is played with heart. You don't have to drink or swear or hit people in the face when they're not looking, but you do have to be tough to win," said Tom Landry, longtime coach of the Dallas Cowboys and a member of the Pro Football Hall of Fame.

So it is with all the truly great champions of sport. And that is certainly the case in the sport of wrestling.

"Gable was a high school athlete of average ability, very average, but with a heart as big as the Iowa outdoors," wrote one national author in describing what makes the Hawkeye coach special.

Matt Furey is one athlete turned coach who understands what heart means as applied to a Gable workout. Two decades after leaving the world of collegiate wrestling, Furey still fondly recalls his training days in the Iowa room and learning from Gable, as witnessed by a letter he wrote to subscribers to his e-mail newsletter about combat wrestling and conditioning.

"Let me take you back to 1983, when I was a wrestler for the national champion University of Iowa team, under the tutelage of the legendary Dan Gable. Due to my work ethic Gable often called and asked if I would train with him. Most of the time we worked technique and wrestling 'live.'

"Most of the workouts were 'repeats' of previous sessions. Nothing new, per se—just working on 'perfecting' the essentials. One afternoon, however, when Gable and I finished sparring (and yes, I got my butt kicked good), we went to the training room so we could use the new Concept II rowing machine.

"Gable volunteered to go first, which was fine by me. As he started he looked at me and said, 'We'll go five minutes each.' Then he started pulling the handle of the rower like a madman. He never looked away from the machine the entire time. He was in a total trance. Gable wasn't using this machine for cardio. No, this was an all-out five-minute sprint.

"Around the four-minute mark I was totally surprised at what I heard. For a split second Gable came out of his trance and yelled, 'I keep slowing up!'

"This obviously bothered him. He was intent on beating the machine the entire five minutes. He didn't like the idea of something getting the better of him. Honestly, it didn't appear to me that he was slowing 'down' (Gable said 'up,' which is ironic in and of itself) at all. Yet, he was.

"When it was my turn to get on the machine, I tried to sprint the whole thing like Gable did. I failed utterly.

"Why do you think it was that Gable was legendary for his conditioning? He could literally wrestle one person after the other for an hour or longer, and each person who alternated on him would have to stop from exhaustion within 5 to 10 minutes. Despite Gable's light weight (155 pounds), he trounced everyone in the room, from lightweight through heavyweight. I submit the following reasons why Gable was so well conditioned:

1. He believed in sprints; in particular, he really liked stadium stair sprints—a close cousin to hill sprints.
2. He was a master of high-repetition bodyweight calisthenics: push-ups, pull-ups, rope climbing and so on.
3. His body was strong and stable from isometric-style training exercises, such as the wall chair I feature in *Combat Conditioning*. After all, who do you think I learned it from?

"The bottom line of all of this is plain and simple: It's not the size of the dog in the fight—it's the size of the fight in the dog." It's the heart of the athlete that makes the difference much of the time.

Even in a workout, Gable wouldn't give up, not even to a machine. It could be called pride, bullheadedness, obsession, or any of a dozen names. But perhaps the best name is heart. Gable has trained his body and his mind never to give up, under any circumstances.

The key question about heart is, can it be taught or is it simply a product of one's genes or environment?

"I'm not sure if it can be taught, and I don't think anyone can say for sure where 'heart' comes from," said Steve Fraser. "But if I had to guess, I would say it is a product of environment and can be cultivated, if there is already a kernel of it present. I have seen athletes develop a sense of heart when I was doubtful that it was there at first."

Fraser feels that the best way to teach heart is to have athletes observe it or read about it. If they can see examples of it—other athletes rising to overcome obstacles and setbacks by sheer force of willpower, drive, and desire—then they can strive to emulate it.

In the final analysis, heart is probably present in nearly all athletes, but it needs to be cultivated before it can bloom. Cultivation is the task of a coach or parent in most instances.

SUMMARY

Heart is what drives many athletes to reach heights that seem impossible. Heart pushes them past all barriers, physical and mental. Heart can make the difference in the performance of a racehorse or an athlete of any size or shape. When the going gets really tough and an athlete needs to reach deep down inside to find the resources to continue, despite pressure, self-doubt, and physical stress—that's when heart comes into play and allows the athlete to finish his or her task and goals.

Such great champions as Rulon Gardner, Cael Sanderson, and the legendary Muhammad Ali showed tremendous heart in their careers. Whether heart can be taught is open to debate, but it can be observed and, perhaps, imitated. This much is certain: Heart is one of the key ingredients in the success of many world-class athletes, especially in combative sports like boxing and wrestling. Another key is the attacking mind-set. We will explore that area in the following chapter.

17

The Attacking Mind-Set

Aggressiveness in athletics is, in most cases, a learned behavior, but in time it can become locked into a player's personality. If an athlete uses aggressiveness to achieve success and trains the mind that way, it will become a part of his or her persona. The Brands boys at the University of Iowa are a perfect example of that, as was Dick Butkus on the football field.

During his three years as an All-American linebacker at the University of Illinois and as a perennial All-Pro with the Chicago Bears, Butkus developed a reputation for an aggressive style of play that has become the standard for measuring all tough players in the NFL.

"The name Butkus has come to be virtually synonymous with pro football violence," wrote Bob Rubin (1973) in his book *Football's Toughest Ten*. Rubin said that most players in the NFL stood in awe of him and that even his teammates didn't know what to think of his aloof manner and vicious play.

"When he doesn't think something's important, he's shy and withdrawn," said Bears Coach Abe Gibron. "But then, the whistle blows and he sort of goes crazy. In my 22 years in the league, I've never seen a player with greater desire. Sometimes we have to literally pull him back in practice. He's a once-in-a-generation player" (Rubin 1973, 27).

That type of mental approach to the sport has its roots in environment, and an athlete can learn it. But it probably has to come at an early age. As a young boy growing up in Rapid City, South Dakota, Randy Lewis received some stern advice from his father,

Larry—advice that he never forgot. The words changed the way he thought about everything, including the sport of wrestling.

"I was about 10, and was wrestling with a boy who was a lot bigger than me," said Randy in 2002. "We were in my living room. He got on top of me and held me down. I couldn't get up. He said, 'If you give up, I'll let you up.' So, I said 'I give up.'

"My dad was watching and he took me aside and told me, 'A Lewis never gives up, under any circumstances. You always battle your way out of a predicament like that.'"

Randy paused while telling the story, a serious look on his face. He went on to say, "And I've never given up since. Never. In every workout and in every match, I've always fought for every takedown, and every point. Sure, I've lost takedowns and matches, but I've never given up."

Anyone who saw Randy Lewis wrestle in high school, in college, or in freestyle competition, all the way up through the world championships and Olympic Games, knows the truth of that statement. He was 89-0 with 83 pins in his last three years in high school, and he went on to win junior national and junior world titles. At the University of Iowa, he was a crowd-pleasing two-time NCAA champion, always going for the pin.

The pinnacle of his career came in 1984 when he won an Olympic gold medal at 136.5 pounds. In the finals he outscored his opponent from Japan, 24-11.

"I would rather lose 16-14 than win 1-0," said Lewis. "Wrestling isn't about stalling and holding back; it's about going out there, man to man, and seeing who can score the most points. That's what it's all about . . . scoring as many points as you can."

Lewis was the perfect example of an athlete with an aggressive mind-set. That mind-set made him a big crowd favorite during his days as a Hawkeyes star.

"I loved to wrestle in front of those huge crowds. That really turned me on," said Lewis, flashing a big grin. "I wanted to go out there and entertain the fans by scoring as many points as I could, and more than the other guy could."

Many of the most successful stars in sport, from Muhammad Ali and Sugar Ray Leonard in boxing to Curt Schilling in major league baseball, expressed the same attitude. "The bigger the game, the better," said Schilling. "I'm an adrenaline junkie. I feed off big crowds and noise."

Wrestlers come in many different personality types. Lewis and Wade Schalles epitomized the colorful style of going for broke. Lee Kemp and Chris Bono liked to control the tempo of the match and keep the score close all the way, staying in control of their opponents and winning with a carefully executed plan.

Some of the greatest champions are by nature combat oriented, so it is no surprise to find them performing at a high level every time they step on a mat. For them, aggressiveness is part of their genetic makeup or their environment acting on them. For others, being aggressive is a learned trait.

"I realized if I was going to achieve anything in life I had to be aggressive," said Michael Jordan. "I had to get out there and go for it. I don't believe you can achieve anything by being passive" (Jordan 1998, 9).

No athletes personified that in the world of wrestling more than the Brands twins, Tom and Terry. "They went all out, all the time, every match," said Lewis, shaking his head in appreciation. "I never saw the Brands boys back off, in practice or in a match. Never! That's impossible to believe for some people, but it's true."

"As I look back on their intensity, I'm amazed by it," said Gable one day while reflecting on his great stars of the past. "The Brands boys gave it their all, all the time, every time. It's amazing to think back on how intense they were, it really is."

At Iowa, Tom and Terry flourished under the austere philosophy. They asked no quarter and they gave none. Tom won three Big Ten titles and three NCAA titles in his four seasons, compiling a record of 158-7-2. Terry was 137-7, with three Big Ten titles and two NCAA titles. Terry also captured two world championships (in 1993 and 1995) and earned a bronze medal in the 2000 Olympics. Tom won one world title (also in 1993) and an Olympic gold medal in 1996.

At a coaches clinic in Newton, Iowa, in the spring of 2004, Tom started his session on aggressive wrestling with the following words: "The no. 1 ingredient in aggressive wrestling is, without a doubt, *attitude*. It's your job as coaches to spell it out for them— sometimes with a pat on the back and sometimes with a kick in the butt.

"When I came into the room, I tried to win the practice . . . *not* the scoreboard. That's a mistake many wrestlers make, trying to win the scoreboard. They get a takedown then shut down, trying to shut the other guy out. My attitude was, 'I'm gonna beat this guy so bad he'll want to quit.' I want to win the entire practice, every minute of it.

"That might sound arrogant, but it's not! If I wrestle that way, I'll get better—and so will the guy I'm practicing with. He has to! What we are teaching is good, hard-nosed, tough and exciting wrestling."

He paused and looked around at the 200 assembled coaches, all hanging on every word he said. "Do you know how good I feel when I wrestle hard for seven minutes and the other guy breaks? We've had lots of wrestlers who made good wrestlers break. Mark Ironside, Doug Schwab, Cliff Moore . . . they've all made great wrestlers break. It's part of what makes Iowa so tough!"

Ironside won two NCAA titles at 134 pounds and in 1998 won the Dan Hodge Trophy as the best collegiate wrestler in the nation that season. Schwab was NCAA champion at 141 pounds in 1999, and Moore won the NCAA title at 141 pounds in 2004. All employed the same style—pressure, pressure, pressure, every second of every match. They were not the most skilled wrestlers, but they were the most unrelenting, cut from the same mold as Terry and Tom Brands, never giving their opponent a second's respite.

That style of wrestling, however, demands a tremendous amount from an athlete, both physically and emotionally. Few athletes can pour that much intensity into a match and keep it up.

"What works for the person you're imitating may not work for you," said Jimmy Connors, one of the greatest tennis players of all time. Connors was known for his fiery approach to the game and his extremely high output of emotional energy. "And it's impossible to play at a feverish emotional peak for long. . . . Your body would use up far too much energy to keep you at that high level" (Clarkson 1999, 24).

Of course, maintaining an emotional peak is much more difficult in a tennis match, which can last several hours, than it is in a wrestling match, which usually lasts six or seven minutes. But wrestling in a tournament, which can take place over three days and involve six or seven matches, can severely tax the emotional system if the mind is not trained for it.

Kim Wood has spent much of his adult life studying what makes athletes tough and exploring the attacking mind-set. The latter is a subject close to his heart. A standout high school football player and wrestler in Barrington, Illinois, Wood earned a football scholarship to the University of Wisconsin. As a Badger, he developed his mind and body into a physical machine. Although a severe knee injury kept him out of pro football, his passion for weight training led to a career. He spent 18 years as strength trainer for the Cincinnati Bengals of the NFL, where he observed aggressive men every Sunday during the fall.

"My passions are combat sports, and football and wrestling are at the top of the list," said Wood, who has studied all forms of wrestling, from high school to college to the pro ranks in the early days, as few others ever have. "I have seen some very, very tough and aggressive men, and Tim Krumrie is at the top of that list."

Another football player he greatly respects is Phil Peterson, the older brother of Olympic champions Ben and John Peterson. Both Ben and John have said that Phil was their early inspiration in athletics, and Wood fully understands why that would be the case. Phil set a tremendous example in wrestling tough.

© Mary Langenfeld

The headlock is one of the most dramatic moves in all of wrestling and is common in all styles. Here the wrestler on top leans back to exert more force on the hold as he works for the pin.

"Phil and I were both fullbacks on the Wisconsin freshman team, in 1963, and then he was moved to the offensive line," said Wood. "He was a tough, tough farm kid, from a small community in Wisconsin. He must have learned some of the toughness from his environment, but he had it in his genes, too.

"I remember in one practice that he hurt his arm real bad and showed it to the trainer. The trainer was from the old school and just kind of scoffed and told Phil he wasn't tough enough. Phil walked back to the huddle and kept playing. I saw when he put his hand down that the arm would bend one way, then the other. He played the entire practice, and afterwards they discovered he had cleanly broken two bones in his arm. The forearm was just flopping around.

"That was an awesome display of mental toughness. To this day, it is one of the most amazing things I ever saw."

Wood said that all the Petersons were cut from the same mold, with a tremendous capacity for hard work and an amazing tolerance for pain. And they had a love of wrestling, tough and hard.

"We used to go into the wrestling room and work out all the time," said Wood. "We would wrestle each other, or the guys on the varsity. We just loved the toughness that wrestling demanded.

"We also learned that it was the aggressive wrestlers who scored the most and won the most. Wrestling is a sport that pulls the aggressiveness out of you."

Another Wisconsin football player who thrived in the wrestling room was Tim Krumrie, who went on to a long and successful career with the Bengals in the NFL. He is, says Wood, a prototype for the mentally tough athlete, at any level.

"He broke his leg in two places during the Super Bowl game with the San Francisco 49ers," said Wood. "It was a terrible break, his foot was flopping, and he kept trying to get up, screaming, 'I gotta get back in the game! I gotta get back in the game!'

"I remember what Paul Brown (legendary head coach of the Cleveland Browns for many years) once said about Krumrie: 'He's a man with a fierce heart,' and that sums it up.

"The thing with Krumrie is that he wrestled in high school and then one year at Wisconsin, when Russ Hellickson was the coach. He went out for wrestling because he liked Hellickson, and because he liked the way the wrestlers trained. Krumrie was one of the few athletes back then at Wisconsin who really lifted weights hard. He focused on football but he liked wrestlers because they were the tough guys."

The key to the aggressiveness of men like Krumrie, says Wood, is their focus on this attitude: "I'm going to do it, and I'm going to do it *now!*"

"Here's the thing," said Wood, choosing his words carefully. "Other people can coach you and make you tougher, but the key is you saying, 'I'm going to do it for myself.' Some guys just know how to kick into that special gear, and these are the really tough guys, the ones who are ready to perform right *now* . . . and at all other times.

"You have to have the body, of course. The physical training is essential. You can't be Yosemite Sam and go out and win. But, in competitive combat sports, you have to be a little bit of a killer, like Krumrie. Can it be taught? I'm not sure. It can be coached. It can be uncovered."

That is certainly the key with the aggressive attitude needed in wrestling.

THE WARRIOR MENTALITY

The warrior approach to wrestling is one that exists in the minds of many athletes who choose the sport. Mark Schultz and Tom Brands are two of the prime examples, but there are many others, including all those who moved into the area of mixed martial arts. Dan Severn was a sensational high school and college wrestler long before he shook up the mixed martial arts world by winning the Ultimate Fighting Championship (UFC) in 1996.

As a teenager in Michigan, Severn won three high school state titles, the junior nationals, and, in 1977, the junior world championships. As a pure freshman at Arizona State, he was undefeated in his first 30 matches and had pinned many of the All-Americans of the previous year, including the defending NCAA champion.

Severn was knocked out of the NCAA tournament that year by a devastating knee injury that hampered his entire college career. He was a two-time All-American at Arizona State and in 2004 still held the school pin record. He was working as an assistant coach at Michigan State University when he first heard about the UFC and entered the event more or less to test himself and his wrestling skills against other forms of combative sport.

Severn soon found that he could compete at that level, and he eventually became the biggest star of the UFC, using his wrestling skills to win match after match. His victories helped catapult wrestling into a new status in the world of martial arts and self-defense. Within a few years, the most successful UFC athletes all had strong wrestling backgrounds.

Following Severn and ex-college wrestler Don Frye into the mixed martial arts world were former NCAA champions Mark Coleman, Kevin Randleman, Mark Kerr, and Mike Van Arsdale, as well as world-level wrestlers like Randy Couture, Matt Lindland, Matt Hughes, and Tom Erikson. Even Olympic champions Mark Schultz, Kevin Jackson, and Ken Monday tried it.

"It's hard to explain what it feels like the first time you walk down the aisle and into the ring," said Severn. "There's a mixture of fear and excitement. You say to yourself, 'What am I doing here?' But then the warrior mentality kicks in and you give it all you've got.

"At that point, you really don't have any choice," he said with a chuckle. "You have to defend yourself. But I basically just relied on my 20 years of wrestling training and took people down and controlled them. Wrestling was the key to my success, obviously."

Of course, a wrestling background was what it was all about for the former wrestlers. They were trying to make a statement about their sport and how easily it could be applied to the arena of self-defense. But the warrior angle was important as well. Many wrestlers are attracted to the sport by its combative nature and consider themselves modern-day warriors.

"When an athlete looks at himself or herself as a modern-day warrior, the powerful and ancient defense arousal systems can kick in," wrote Clarkson (1999, 55).

Science is also behind the mixed martial arts approach. In his book *Flow*, Mihaly Csikszentmihalyi writes that the experience of performing in such a tremendously competitive and sometimes violent sport can even be joyous to the athlete who is locked into it mentally.

"The warrior strives to reach the point where he can act with lightning speed against opponents without having to think or reason about the best defensive or offensive moves to make. Those who can perform it well claim that fighting becomes a joyous artistic performance during which the everyday experience of duality between mind and body is transformed into a harmonious one-pointedness of mind. Here again, it seems appropriate to think of the martial arts as a specific form of flow" (Csikszentmihalyi 1990, 106).

If an athlete does indeed experience flow, he or she has progressed beyond the physicality of the sport and may be competing on a higher plane of awareness. As we will see in the following paragraphs, an athlete need not be violent or even angry by nature to be successful in the mixed martial arts arena.

THE GENTLE APPROACH

Some athletes who opt for the sport of wrestling do not seem to be ideally suited for it from a mental perspective. Yet they can do very well. They are mild mannered off the mat and not combative by nature, but when they step onto the mat a change takes place and they are able to become fierce competitors.

In his autobiography, Kurt Angle, Olympic champion turned WWE superstar, writes about how tough and mean his older brothers were. At the same time he maintained that he simply wasn't cut from the same mold: "But no matter how many times I heard it, I had a rough time being a hard ass. It wasn't my nature to be intimidating or macho. In a way, that was a blessing, because where my brothers would let their emotions get out of control, I found as I grew older that I had the ability to stay cool under pressure. In clutch situations, I wouldn't crack. I was able to keep things in perspective because I worried only about performing and winning" (Angle 2001, 30).

Another case in point is Royce Gracie, who caught the attention of the combative sports world when he won two Ultimate Fighting Championships back in the late 1990s. Gracie was a calm and poised martial artist who defeated everyone who stood before him. His style was called Gracie jiu jitsu, and he was a master at applying arm bars, joint locks, and chokeholds, with his arms or his legs.

Although he excelled at a combative sport, he was not as aggressive by nature as were many other warriors in the mixed martial arts. In a column he wrote for *Grappling* magazine, he related that his older brother, Rickson, told him, "In a perfect world you would never be a fighter, Royce. You're too nice to be a fighter."

He responded in this way: "In general . . . I think that Rickson's words are a pretty fair assessment of me. I like the technical challenge of winning a fight more than I like the idea of hurting someone just for the sake of hurting them" (Gracie 2004, 6).

Gracie went on to analyze what the sport is all about and how important it is to remain calm and poised during the intense action: "More often than not, undue emotion in the ring or cage will work against you. In the ring, the truth of the matter is that patience, focus and intelligence are your biggest allies. Your mind needs to be clear and unencumbered with rage in order to be flexible and responsive."

Then he offered advice that could have come from any top college wrestling coach across the nation: "The key to developing this type of attitude and mentality is how you practice every day. Be technical on the mat instead of just being wildly aggressive."

For the most part, wrestlers compete the same way that they train. That is the key message that wrestlers learned in the wrestling room at the University of Iowa during the Gable era.

SUMMARY

How you train is the key to how you will compete, say most of the world's greatest athletes, from Michael Jordan to Tom Brands. Intense, hard-driving practices will help mold you into an intensive, hard-driven athlete, in most cases. The attacking mind-set is within the genetic makeup of each person, and the environment triggers it, usually when the person selects the sport that will become his or her primary outlet.

But there are exceptions to the rule. Some warriors are gentle, not aggressive. The approach that suits the intensity and combative nature of Tom Brands is not what a more laid-back Royce Gracie needs or will respond to. Some athletes will flourish in a technical environment and be able to summon a more competitive attitude when they begin the real competition.

Practices need to be rich with opportunities to learn skills and work on techniques, but they also must be flexible to meet the personality characteristics of those who march to a different drummer. But all athletes must be willing to pay the price to be great.

18

The Ultimate Mental Wrestler

"The key to beating really good athletes?" asked Greg Strobel, rhetorically. "Great mental toughness is no. 1. There is so much more to winning at the highest level than just physical ability. You have to be the smartest and the mentally toughest. By smart, I mean street smarts, knowing how to win.

"You can make up for a lot of other inadequacies with great mental toughness. In fact, you can beat guys who are better than you with tactics, conditioning and mental toughness," he said.

That principle holds true in every sport—from wrestling, the most physical of all, to golf, the most esoteric, with an underlying mental edge. "Under pressure, you win with your mind," said Tiger Woods, talking about Jack Nicklaus and expressing his admiration for Nicklaus' mental toughness. "The biggest thing is to have the belief that you can win every tournament going in. A lot of guys don't have that. Nicklaus had it . . ." (Clarkson 1999, 179).

When great athletes compete, almost everyone associated with the highest level of sport agrees that the difference is most often in the mind. The mental attitude, the mental approach, the mental resolve, and the mental toughness are what separate the gold medal winners from the rest of the pack.

Take, for example, the incredible story of Lance Armstrong. Everyone who follows sports recognizes his name immediately as the man who has won the Tour de France six times, an almost impossible feat of endurance and guts. But there is another Lance Armstrong, the man who defeated cancer when the odds were almost 80 percent against him.

In his soul-stirring book *It's Not About the Bike*, Armstrong tells of a conversation he had after surviving surgery, a procedure that easily could have been the end of him. When his friend asks him how he feels—really feels—and Armstrong says, "Great," the friend doubts him. Then Armstrong explains what he means in no uncertain terms.

"'Chris, you don't understand,' I said, starting to cry. "'I'm glad about this. You know what? I like it like this. I like the odds stacked against me; they always have been, and I don't know any other way. . . . it's just one more thing I'm going to overcome. This is the only way I want it'" (Armstrong 2000, 119).

That type of mental toughness is difficult to comprehend. Armstrong has not only faced up to his all-consuming battle with cancer but also has turned his thinking around to the point where he actually welcomes it. Through an intensely savage and personal battle, he has become a new man, willing and eager to show the world what he is made of mentally.

THE THOUSAND-MILE STARE

Matt Furey tells a story to describe what transpires within a person who has become an ultimate mental wrestler. He calls the tale "The Thousand-Mile Stare." The story resulted from Furey's indefatigable study of wrestling as a martial art, a study that has taken him around the world and into sparring sessions with some of the world's most revered martial artists and wrestlers. Furey was NCAA Division II champion for Edinboro University in 1985. He is also a throwback to the days of Farmer Burns and Frank Gotch, world champions in the rugged style known as catch-as-catch-can, which accepts submission moves as part of pure wrestling.

> Back in 1992, well before I went to China and married, I was seeing a lady from central California, who understood the mental focus of a wrestling champion about as well as I understand Aramaic (which is to say, not at all).
>
> One afternoon, while I was busy finishing up a report, she walked around my office looking at different photos on display. I paid no heed, but later that day, she remarked, "That photo of you taken when you won the nationals was strange. You had

this totally emotionless look on your face. I don't understand how you could have a look like that after winning a tournament that important. Don't you feel any emotion?"

The only response I gave her in return was silence. Years later, in 1997, after I won the world title in Beijing, China, in the art of shuai-chiao kung fu, I was given a stack of photos taken of me throughout the event. Some were taken in the hotel, before the tournament began. Some were taken in action, others between rounds—and then there were those taken after I won the title.

Last of all, there were the photos taken of me hours after the tournament. In each and every case, the look on my face was the same as when I won a national collegiate wrestling title in 1985—albeit even more emotionless, if you can imagine.

This look is something I now refer to as the thousand-mile stare. I heard it described as such when doing research on high-level military officers, especially those sent into conflict with the sole intention of assassinating someone of ill repute. In a nutshell, the thousand-mile stare is akin to having such intense mental focus that you are literally in a deep hypnotic trance with eyes wide open. And sometimes this trance is so deep and so strong, that you are still mentally engaged, even after you have finished your duty or achieved your goal.

Nearly eight years ago I recall discussing this look with fellow wrestling writer and historian, Mike Chapman. We talked about the mental aspects of wrestling and how, in the heat of a major battle, some people are defeated as soon as they see the countenance of their opponent. The intent of the eventual victor is so powerful and consuming that the opponent instantly recognizes he will be defeated. In the recesses of his own mind, he privately concedes, even though he still goes through the machinations of "trying" to win.

Dan Gable, who won the world championships in 1971 and Olympic gold medal in 1972, had the thousand-mile stare developed to an art. And so it was Gable's stare that Mike and I discussed that winter afternoon. Mike began by pointing to a photo of Gable on the victory stand, in Munich:

"Matt, do you see that look on Gable's face? Do you see the focus? Well, let me tell you a little story. One week later, when he was back in Ames, Iowa, for a celebration following his victory, he still had the exact same look. It hadn't changed a bit. That's how intense his mental focus was."

I cannot say that my focus was as strong as Gable's. A week after I won the world title I was back to my normal, laughing-and-joking-around self. But if you were to put the photos of Gable and me together and study the expressions we had during tournament time, you would find the look to be virtually the same. That look is the expressionless look of a fully concentrated mind.

Yet, it would be a mistake to assume that this look is void of emotion. Not at all. It is the look of totally channeled, focused, and internalized emotion. It is the look of removing all external appearances of emotion while *all* necessary emotion is specifically directed at a single objective.

Now, just think what you could do in life if you were able to put the thousand-mile stare on whenever you wanted—or needed—to. Many people are under the impression that the thousand-mile stare cannot be taught, but they are wrong. Development of this look doesn't come from the imitation of facial gestures or body language. It begins when you set clearly defined goals that are vividly imagined and deeply concentrated upon.

Like Gable, I knew what my goals were. I held them in mind at all times. I saw myself where I wanted to be—and I trained accordingly. As I trained I thought about my goals. When I ran uphill sprints I pictured myself receiving my gold medal. When training sessions were brutally hard, I channeled the emotion I felt into the mental picture of my goal. When the workout was so brutally hard I felt like giving up or quitting . . . that's when I pictured what I wanted as big as the picture screen at a movie theatre.

And when I did this, the emotion got channeled deeper than ever before. This method of mental focus, I should point out, I first learned from Gable. As a teenage boy I watched a film of him training. In the film, Gable spelled out his formula for all when he said that he "pictured" himself winning a state title as he trained—and he won.

Then he "pictured" himself winning the national title as he trained—and he won. He did the same for the world title and, ultimately, the Olympic gold medal.

I didn't know if this "mental picturing" would cause me to be successful when I first heard it but I was willing to give it a try. In 1985, the year I won a national title at Edinboro, is when I started to get a glimmer of how this mental process worked.

The one thing that helped me a great deal and that I teach to my students today, is the process of writing your goal on a three by five card and carrying it with you to look at throughout the day. As you look at the goal and picture what you want, and do so with intense feeling, miraculous things start to happen. You start to carry an expressionless gaze on your face when you think about those things that you want to have in your life. Almost as if in a dream, you move toward the good things in life.

After college, when I began studying Chinese martial arts, I realized that Gable literally gave away a major part of his mental strategy in that film—and hardly anyone caught it. I'm glad I did. I was 30 when I finally figured out why it worked and how to make it work in all areas of my life, not just wrestling and martial arts.

Yes, what we picture and think about with deep feeling really does seem to cause events and circumstances to line up the way we want them. Once you understand this and apply it, look out world. Make way for the person with the thousand-mile stare.

Courtesy of Matt Furey, author of *Combat Conditioning*. www.mattfurey.com.

Bruce Ogilvie, a man whom some consider the father of modern sports psychology, understands Furey's concept of the thousand-mile stare. "In the moment of truth, the great athletes lose total self-awareness and even lack of consciousness of what's going on,"

A waistlock throw can be spectacular. Here, the bottom wrestler is in the midst of executing such a throw on a foe. Mental strength is needed to pull off moves like this.

he says. "They mentally rehearse their task and even the pressure attached to it. Then they feel comfortable with it when it comes" (Clarkson 1999, 39-40).

REFINING MENTAL TOUGHNESS

"Winning," said Billie Jean King, "comes down to who can execute under pressure. At the highest levels of the game, it comes down to this . . ." (Riger 1980).

Mental toughness is most often the difference between winning and losing at the highest levels. An athlete can't just conjure it up if he or she hasn't trained for years to be mentally tough.

Steve Knight, a world-class power lifter who has studied the mental side of all sports, especially wrestling, places huge importance on the mental side of the sport.

"It is more important to know the strengths of your mind than of your body, especially in wrestling," Knight wrote in *Winning State*.

"I'll take a mental giant over a physical giant any day" (Knight 2003, 69).

As we have already seen, people can build mental toughness in many different ways. Facing fear and overcoming it is one of the best ways. Even at an early age, Tom Brands used a built-in fear of the dark to build his mental toughness.

"I was scared of the dark as a little kid," he said. "So was Terry. We even had to ask to keep lights on at night. It was embarrassing to be afraid of the dark. So finally, when we were left at home alone one night, we shut off all the lights in the house and then walked down to the basement in the total dark, then came back up. We did it over and over. We cured ourselves of being afraid of the dark."

To be the best requires tremendous mental commitment. "You will yourself into it," said Tom Brands.

"You let the mind take over," Tiger Woods agrees. "My mind is my biggest asset," he continued. "I expect to win every tournament I play."

Learning to cope with losing is essential as well. All athletes who aspire to reach the highest levels will lose. Losing is part of the process that builds champions. You need to accept the fact that at some point in a long career you will lose. But then you move on quickly and without looking back.

"Losses infuriated me, but I never questioned my ability," said Brands, with emphasis on the word *never*. "And I've never doubted my ability as a coach. That may sound arrogant, but it's not, because I know I've spent the time and paid the price to prepare myself. Losses will come, but proper preparation allows you to bounce right back, and shake it off.

"In 1995, the world championships were in Atlanta and I did terrible, lousy. Terry won but I finished ninth. I was saying how much I hated Atlanta and Terry said, 'You can't say that. You can't afford to feel that way. You have to come here next year to win the Olympics. Get that thought out of your mind.'

"I didn't do anything different to prepare for the Olympics than I did in 1995," said Tom, "except that I was much more disciplined in all that I did." The result was that Tom won the gold medal without a close contest, giving up just one point in five matches. Clearly, Tom Brands went to another level mentally.

Having that kind of willpower to confront the problem and then correct it helped the Brands twins become world champions. They were, at various times in their careers, the epitome of the ultimate mental wrestler. The have shown tremendous focus and control, discipline and desire, commitment and heart. They were certainly in the zone in many of their important matches. We can even safely assume that they were in flow at various times.

And maybe above all, they were not afraid to look for miracles at certain times in their careers. Dan Gable tells a story about Tom Brands that is almost too stunning to believe. But it is true!

As the story goes, Tom had a badly damaged knee at one point while wrestling at Iowa. The trainer looked at it, and they all decided that he couldn't wrestle for a while. Tom didn't want to accept that. He didn't want to concede the point. He went home and wrapped a copy of the Bible around his knee. He went to bed with the Bible wrapped around the leg. He did some praying. Two days later, the knee was good enough that Tom could wrestle in the upcoming meet.

This story shows just how committed Tom Brands was in his faith, his determination, and his focus. He was probably in the zone for as long a time as any wrestler who has ever competed in the United States. Through use of willpower and drive, Tom Brands is as close to the ultimate mental wrestler as we may have ever seen.

"Focus. Control. Flow. In the zone. Think of any other synonym for mental mastery, and it applies to the level of play that Woods achieved in the Open," wrote Jay Tolson after Tiger Woods demolished the field at the 2000 U.S. Open Golf Tournament. "And while this state of internal calm and power has different names, it boils down to this: When the body is brought to peak condition and the mind is completely focused, even unaware of what it's doing, an individual can achieve the extraordinary" (Tolson 2000, 38).

Throughout this book, we have shown examples of individuals achieving the extraordinary. Cassius Clay overcame immense odds to defeat Sonny Liston in 1964. Evander Holyfield did the same against Mike Tyson in 1996. Rulon Gardner toppled Alexander Karelin in 2000. Rob Rohn rebounded from a 14-2 deficit in the final minute to win the NCAA title in 2002. Randy Couture beat Tito Ortiz in 2003.

We have seen samples of athletes winning national titles with incredible physical handicaps in the stories of Nick Ackerman and Kyle Maynard. We have read about Lance Armstrong's incredibly moving battle with cancer, and of the biggest victory of his life.

We have learned how Arnold Schwarzenegger used his mental drive to become the greatest bodybuilder in the world on his way to becoming one of the richest movie stars and, finally, governor of California. We have read how tennis players and golfers, football players and baseball players, and every kind of athlete imaginable have been able to conquer their own personal worlds.

We have discovered how John Wooden and Dan Gable used mental toughness to help build two of the top dynasties in the history of college athletics, and how Vince Lombardi became a coaching legend for all time.

None of it would have happened unless those athletes and coaches had first learned and then understood the incredible power of the mind and the necessity of harnessing that power to build mental toughness that would carry them to the pinnacle of success.

SUMMARY

The mind can take us to places where we have never been, to places where we never thought we could go. The mind and body interrelate and work together most of the time. Optimum results, in both life and sport, come when the two are in harmony, working together to create results that are beyond the scope of most people's dreams.

Most wrestling coaches list mental toughness as the most important factor in athletic success. It comes through years of training both the body and the mind, and it results from a conscious effort to develop the will to win.

The ultimate mental wrestler is a destination that most people may believe is beyond their reach, yet taking the journey to get there will prove extremely beneficial. An athlete who sets out with the goal of becoming the ultimate mental wrestler may come up short, but if he or she reaches even the halfway point, the rewards in life will be bountiful.

19

The Balance Between Wrestling and Life

Wayne Wells earned a law degree while training for the Olympics. A native of Oklahoma City, Wells was a man destined for greatness almost from the start. He won three Big Eight titles at the University of Oklahoma and was a three-time All-American, placing third, second, and first in his three NCAA tournaments.

Turning to freestyle after graduation, he finished fourth in the 1968 Olympics and second in the 1969 world championships. In 1970, he won the world championships at 163 pounds, even though he was in law school and was an assistant coach for the Sooners. As the 1972 Olympic trials began, he was deeply immersed in his final year of law school. He had to divide his time between grueling workouts sessions, running, weight training, and studying for the bar exams. He made the Olympic team but suffered rib damage, an enlarged spleen, and a knee injury along the way.

But in Munich he was able to focus on the task at hand. He captured a gold medal with six straight victories. Wells then retired from wrestling to focus on family and career, becoming an attorney in his hometown. He was able to keep his commitment to an Olympic goal and reach his educational objectives as well.

Balancing wrestling and life is not easy, especially if one aspires to be a collegiate, world, or Olympic champion. The amount of time required to build the skills and conditioning necessary to reach those levels is astounding. Although success in most sports required only a part-time commitment in the first half of the 20th century, a new philosophy took over in the era of mass media coverage and television. The face of sport changed forever. With greatly increased media attention came much greater incentive to excel. Athletes became willing to pay a much higher price to be the best. The bar went higher and higher. Those willing to work at athletic excellence as though it were a job commonly trained for 40 hours a week.

Wrestling took a quantum leap in the 1970s when the ABC television network and *Sports Illustrated* began describing the gargantuan workload and stunning work ethic of Dan Gable. Frank Gifford summed it up in his book *Gifford on Courage*, which has a full chapter on Gable.

"I think courage has many faces. Dan Gable's single-minded assault on a dream set as a teenager is, to me, heroic. To dedicate one's mind, body and heart to an almost unreachable goal every day of every year from early adolescence through high school, college and two years further requires an extraordinary intensity of purpose and discipline. To push one's body to the limit of endurance and then beyond, to deny oneself normal pleasures while people all around are enjoying those pleasures, to persevere under grueling competition is, to me, a rare facet of courage. Dan Gable's courage" (Gifford 1976, 178).

The Gable story was having an effect all around the country. Young boys who had seen the 1972 Olympics on television were mesmerized. Many would begin wrestling; some would become champions; a few would follow Gable into the Olympic record books.

"Dan's work ethic became the standard, if you wanted to be great in wrestling," said Ed Banach. "I remember sitting at home as a youngster and watching Wayne Wells, Ben Peterson and Dan Gable win gold medals and thinking I wanted to be like them. I knew it was going to demand a very great amount of work from me, because I had listened to what they were saying about Gable. But that did not deter me one bit."

In 1984 Ed Banach became Olympic champion in the 198-pound class, while his brother, Lou, won gold at 220. Gable coached both brothers at the University of Iowa as well as at the Los Angeles Olympics.

Mike Chapman Collection

Known for his intensity as a wrestler, Dan Gable was just as intense as a coach. Here he shouts instructions to one of his University of Iowa wrestlers. Gable led the Hawkeyes to 15 NCAA team titles in his 22 years as head coach.

BEING SINGLE-MINDED

One can pursue excellence in two ways. The first beckons to the totally committed athlete who places wrestling above all else, even shunning long-term relationships to allow the selfishness required to win it all; the second type calls out to the athlete who is extremely organized and is able to segment his life into two areas, one for athletics and one for family or a profession. Discipline and organizational skills are crucial.

To be selfish in athletics is not a negative behavior. By its nature, athletic excellence demands a certain degree of selfishness from its highest performers. Those elite few must be able to block out all distractions and apply a laserlike focus on the goal. Not many can juggle that kind of commitment with outside distractions. But some can.

Chris Evert, one of the finest female tennis players of all time, admits that balancing life and sports excellence is a tough road to walk.

"I hate to say it because I don't think it's the best for developing a person, but the single-mindedness—just concentrating in that one area—that's what it takes to be a champion," said Evert, looking back on an extremely successful career.

Dan Gable and John Smith are just two of the many wrestlers who approached the sport in the manner suggested by Chris Evert. They chose their dreams early and never strayed from the path, making their goals more important than personal relationships and other pleasures at that point in their lives, realizing that they had plenty of time for those pursuits after they had reached their goals. Both Dan and John became dedicated family men, husbands, and fathers, and then became mentors to a new generation of wrestlers. If they were focused and selfish early in their careers, it was from necessity to make their goals become reality. They became giving men after they passed into the second phase of their lives, leaving individual competition behind after creating legacies that would remain for all time.

WRESTLING AS A SPRINGBOARD TO A SUCCESSFUL LIFE

Few wrestlers will become national collegiate champions or Olympians. But the thousands who don't become champions benefit immensely from participation at their chosen level. They take the lessons learned from the sport, apply them to other areas of life, and become winners on an Olympian scale off the mat. They discover that it is possible to love a sport yet find ample time to pursue other interests. Not all who take up wrestling will have the desire to become fanatical about it; they may just want to compete in it for any one of a variety of reasons, and they can reap many rewards.

Dennis Hastert wrestled in high school and college in Illinois, and had considerable success without winning a national title or becoming an All-American. But he learned from the sport and took those lessons into real life. He turned to coaching and in 1976 led his Yorkville team to the Illinois high school state championship. Each summer, he crisscrossed the nation in his effort to continue his wrestling education, attending seminars and camps and interacting with coaches from every state in the country.

Hastert says that he learned valuable lessons in compromise and negotiation while representing Illinois wrestling coaches in several discussions at the Illinois state legislature. He also learned about leadership. Hastert eventually decided to run for the Illinois state legislature and was elected. He put those skills to the most severe test possible when he was elected to the United States Congress in 1986.

Hastert won nine consecutive congressional elections and served as Republican whip to Speaker of the House Newt Gingrich. In 1999 Dennis Hastert received the ultimate vote of confidence when his Republican colleagues voted him to become Speaker of the House, third in line to the presidency of the United States.

Hastert is not alone among top public figures with a strong background in wrestling. On September 13, 2003, some 350 wrestling enthusiasts from around the nation gathered at a special banquet in New York City called Night of the Legends. Among those being honored were Speaker Hastert; Dr. Norman Borlaug, who won the Nobel Peace Prize in 1970 for his work in feeding the hungry; writer John Irving, winner of an Academy Award; and two other kingpins of politics, Secretary of Defense Donald Rumsfeld and Steven Friedman, former CEO of Goldman Sachs and a special economics adviser to President George W. Bush.

"I love wrestling!" shouted Secretary Rumsfeld after being introduced. He told the group about his wrestling background: four years in high school in Illinois, four years in college at Princeton, and four years while serving in the United States Navy. He delighted in telling the crowd how good he felt when he pulled on Iowa wrestling sweats sent to him by Dan Gable, who was in the audience.

Friedman discussed his wrestling career at Cornell University and how much winning the national AAU 160.5-pound freestyle title in 1961 meant to him. He gave credit to the values he learned as a wrestler for helping him throughout his career, as did Irving and Dr. Borlaug.

But few have ever stated the case as well as did Congressman James Leach, in his 14th term, when he was inducted into the Glen Brand Wrestling Hall of Fame of Iowa in 2003, in Newton, Iowa, just a few months after the anniversary of 9/11. On that April day, he made some astute observations in his acceptance speech about the influence of wrestling on his life and its effect on others:

> Wrestling is a pursuit that shares with all sports all elements of competition. What differentiates it is its history, its individual discipline and its "equalitarian" efforts. It does not matter how big or small, rich or poor, black, brown, or white a wrestler is or what state he comes from.

> Wrestling is about rules and judgment calls enforced by a referee. All of which brings to mind images of the past year or past weeks' World Trade Center "cratering" or bombs bursting over Baghdad.

> Wouldn't it be better if man's aggressive instincts could be satisfied on a wrestling mat rather than a killing field? If Osama bin Laden had openly suited up and attempted to take out his angst against America in a wrestling match with Cael Sanderson instead of suggesting that others could reach Nirvana clandestinely using a commercial aircraft to kill innocents?

> Wrestling imbues one with instincts for fairness and a necessity of preparation that is hard work.

> Matches pit individuals of similar size, although dissimilar proportions, strengths, skills, stamina and knowledge . . . knowledge not in the sense of smartness but athletic wisdom which only experience provides. The talented, unschooled athlete can't prevail over the dedicated partner.

> Wrestling is not weightlifting but its participants understand that strength is helpful, very helpful. Wrestling is more technique than muscularity. It is less about using one's strength to block one's opponent and more about harnessing the opponent's strength in such a way that one uses his own momentum to one's advantage.

Wrestling is about nuances. A wrestler must know himself and his limits. He must know about himself and know his opponent; how he matches up stylistically and physically. He must realize the differences which imperfect preparation—physical and mental—play and be prepared for the possibility of a slip and misjudgment or an uncanny move by the opponent.

It is this combination of "knowns" and "unknowns" of minute successes or setbacks which differentiates each match and makes the sport so challenging for participants and so exciting for fans. No matter how successful a wrestler becomes, no matter how accomplished a wrestler becomes, there is an understanding that everyone is vulnerable to either a personal miscue or a skillful move of a competitor.

No activity I know is more of a confidence builder and at the same time more "humility training" than wrestling. It's the challenge of a match that comes more before than during which makes wrestling a great preparer for the difficult decisions of life. The mixture of knowing and unknowing the struggle that we call competition encapsulated in this sport is the American way of life.

And that is why I think all of us here have come to feel that wrestling is a molder of character in each of our lives.

Courtesy of *W.I.N. Magazine*, April 29, 2003.

Ben Peterson and John Peterson are perfect examples of what Congressman Leach was talking about. They are models for those who seek to balance wrestling with life. Although few athletes have ever competed with greater intensity and focus of purpose, the Petersons were always able to step off the mat and return quickly to the work at hand—which was working for Jesus Christ. Always grim and determined on the mat and always in tremendous condition, John and Ben used their wrestling celebrity and travel opportunities to spread the word about their faith. They have taken risks that would make ordinary men shrink in fear, and they have faced the wrath of Soviet officials. Yet they have marched steadily forward, unbowed and unrelenting in their effort to spread the Word of God.

The two boys grew up in a Christian home in tiny Comstock. Their father was a dairy farmer, but when the farm burned down one night, he gave up that career and operated a feed mill. All members of the Peterson family understood the value of hard work, discipline, and commitment. They gave those characteristics great respect, but they honored the Bible above all else.

Phil and Tom, the eldest of the brothers, played football in high school. As mentioned earlier, Phil won a scholarship to the University of Wisconsin, where he was a starter on the Badgers teams. They initially went out for basketball in high school but soon switched to wrestling. And the sport of Jacob soon became prevalent in the Peterson home.

"We all wrestled at home on the living room floor for years," said John with a smile. "That's how Ben and I got into the sport."

John and Ben had high hopes in high school, but both came up short of their ultimate goal of becoming state champions. John didn't even make it to the state tournament as a senior. Ben placed second the next year.

"I had my heart set on being a state champion," said John. "I was devastated when I didn't even get to state."

The pivotal moment in their wrestling careers came when Dr. Harold Nichols, the long-time head coach at Iowa State University, spotted Ben, just a high school senior, at the 1968 Olympic trials. Although Ben didn't win the tournament, Nichols was impressed by the young wrestler's drive and determination. Ben fought hard every inch of the way, asking no quarter and giving none. Afterward, Nichols offered him a partial scholarship to Iowa State, which was one of the top three programs in the nation at the time.

John was in his second year at Stout State College in Wisconsin when Ben arrived on the ISU campus in the fall of 1968. Culture shock hit Ben hard. The Cyclones had a reputation not only for wrestling aggressively but also for playing hard off the mat. Sitting in his dorm room late at night during his freshman year, Ben was often invited to partake in various forms of entertainment. He steadfastly refused. He was at college, he told those who asked, to get an education and to wrestle, not to party.

He wound up as a two-time NCAA champion and three-time All-American, serving as captain of the Cyclones team in his senior year in 1972. Yet when the 1972 Olympic freestyle trials concluded in Anoka, Minnesota, more than a few wrestling experts were shocked by the results at 180.5 pounds and 198 pounds. Those experts were ready to concede that America had little if any chance to place in the top six at those two weights at the 1972 Olympics in Munich, let alone win a medal.

But when it was all over, the entrants in those two classes, John and Ben Peterson, fashioned a combined record of 11 wins and just 1 defeat, with 1 tie. John stood on the awards platform to accept the silver medal at 180.5 pounds, and Ben later stepped to the platform to accept the gold medal at 198 pounds.

In 1976 the two reversed places. John won a gold medal at 180.5 pounds without a close match, while Ben earned the silver medal at 198. In 1980 Ben became one of just four American wrestlers to earn a spot on three Olympic teams, but he was denied a shot at another medal when President Jimmy Carter decided that the United States would boycott the Moscow Games.

Ben also earned gold medals from the 1975 Pan American Games and the 1980 World Cup. John wound up his fabulous career with medals from three world championships and gold medals from three World Cups.

In analyzing the Petersons' remarkable careers, both Bill Farrell, head coach of the 1972 Olympic team, and Dan Gable, their teammate and inspiration for both, quickly point to their work ethic—and to a force outside wrestling.

"What made them so successful? They were extremely hard workers. But I feel it was their strong beliefs that set them apart; faith is a big part of it," said Gable. "They have such a strong basis for life, all revolving around their faith in God. They applied those same principles of strong belief and commitment to everything they did, including the sport of wrestling. It goes from one to the other."

With their competitive days behind them, the Petersons devoted their time to spreading the word about their two passions—the Bible and wrestling. Their Camp of Champs is one of the most popular in the nation year after year, and campers learn as much about the Bible as they do the sport of Jacob.

John has been employed by Athletes in Action since 1977 and travels the world spreading the teachings of Jesus Christ. He has visited the former Soviet Union at least 30 times and becomes excited just talking about his ministry there.

"I can't imagine I'm still involved in wrestling after all these years," said John in 2003, "but it opens doors everywhere. There are places in Russia where wrestling is tops, and it gives me the opportunity to talk about Jesus."

Ben taught and coached at Maranatha Bible College in Watertown, Wisconsin, for many years and continues coaching there today. He gave up teaching in 1998 to concentrate on public speaking and his camps.

Their influence on the sport of wrestling has been immense, both on and off the mat. "I like to think one of the things Ben and I did for wrestling is show that you can stick around for a long time, if you train hard and take care of yourself," said John.

Between them they made five Olympic teams and nearly a dozen world teams. For nearly three decades, they have exerted a positive influence on the entire sport of wrestling and on the lives of thousands of wrestlers around the world.

"I go to their camp every year, because it's good for me," Gable said on a radio talk show in 2002. "Sometimes I may get on the wrong track, or forget what is really important in life, and that's one of the reasons I like to get up to their camp, to get back on track myself."

The Peterson brothers stand tall as two wrestlers who learned to balance wrestling and life, and achieve at an extremely high level in both areas.

SUMMARY

Balancing a nearly obsessive approach to any sport with life in general is not easy. As John Smith, Kurt Angle, and many others have attested, being a world-class athlete requires a person to be willing to make certain tough decisions and set priorities that are selfish in nature. The same is true to a lesser degree at a lower level. Wrestlers aspiring to be youth champions or high school state champions need to discipline themselves by not participating in activities that will hurt their chances for success.

On the other hand, young athletes should have breaks from the routine and have an opportunity to participate in other activities—not just sports, but family and school events outside sports. They will have plenty of time to lead a spartan lifestyle down the road if they choose that path.

Achieving balance is extremely important for a variety of athletic and scholastic reasons. Balance also provides a break from the intense pressure of athletic competition.

20

The Enduring Lessons of Wrestling

Learning how to be mentally tough in sports certainly provides benefits in all aspects of life. "There is no question that the mental toughness developed by world-class athletes has pulled them through trials off the playing field as well as on," wrote Jay Tolson in article titled "Into the Zone" (2000, 44).

One of the key lessons is to take responsibility for (a) determining what you want to be, (b) educating yourself so that you begin learning how to get there, and then (c) starting on the journey. Accepting the fact that whatever you want out of life is largely up to you may be the single most important element of being mentally tough. Many choose to take an easier path that is less demanding in terms of self-introspection and demand.

Lou Thesz was the last of the great champions of the professional wrestling ring known as shooters, men who could really wrestle. Although he was a professional wrestler and engaged in predetermined matches, Lou was the real deal, a man who could really compete when the need arose. He was also a hooker, which meant he knew devastating submission holds. No less an authority than Dick Hutton, a three-time NCAA heavyweight champion at Oklahoma State University (and four-time finalist) who became a world professional champion himself, said that Thesz was the best man he ever met, in any type of wrestling.

Lou engaged in over 6,000 matches in his long life, and was NWA world heavyweight champion for a total of 13 years, longer than any other man. He loved amateur wrestling and could talk for hours about all aspects of the sport. A wise and articulate man who traveled the world and had friends in all areas of show business, he also had a favorite saying about life: "If it is to be, then it is up to me!"

That's one of life's most important lessons—that if you want to accomplish something, then you are the primary reason it will or will not happen. To be a hero, to be a winner, you must do more than think, hope, and pray. You must act.

ONE STEP AT A TIME

"The difference between the possible and the impossible lies in the man's determination," said Tommy Lasorda, former manager of the Los Angeles Dodgers.

Tori Murden is one person who would agree with that assessment. "The impossible just takes a little longer. One stroke at a time, one step at a time, the impossible is easy to achieve," said Murden. And why should we listen to her? What qualifies her as someone who knows what the impossible is all about?

The answer is simple, but mind-blowing. In 1999, between September 13 and December 3, Tori Murden became the first woman to row the Atlantic Ocean alone. Yes, that's right—she rowed across the Atlantic Ocean, covering 3,333 miles in her remarkable odyssey. On an earlier attempt, she had rowed 2,653 miles before a hurricane stopped her. And you thought you were setting high goals in your life!

Rowing the Atlantic Ocean is a goal so preposterous that it seems far beyond the potential of any human being. Yet, Tori Murden set out to do it "one stroke at a time."

During her first solo attempt to row the North Atlantic Ocean without support, she spent 85 days alone at sea. Murden set the world record for spending more days alone at sea than any other female rower. She also set the record for the most miles rowed solo by any American—man or woman. Murden rowed 2,653 nautical miles.

In her subsequent attempt, there was no hurricane to stop her and she finished the task in 81 days, 7 hours, and 46 minutes. She was credited with covering 3,333 miles, including some distance that she had to make up when winds blew her a bit off course.

One stroke at a time—what a lesson for life. That approach is how people accomplish just about anything worthwhile. Taking one step at a time is the key to completing any journey, even the longest journey. To be an Olympic wrestling champion, you have to start out one step at a time. You begin by dreaming, then practicing, then committing yourself, then dedicating yourself, then making sacrifices, setting priorities, and dreaming some more. You visualize yourself scoring the winning takedown, over and over and over.

You visualize yourself on the victory stand, with the "Star-Spangled Banner" playing in the background. You visualize the expression on the face of your proud parents, your spouse, your friends, your supporters. You imagine telling the story to your kids, some time far down the road, and then to your grandkids.

One step at a time! It's a lesson for everything in life. To be good at anything—whether it be the role of spouse, parent, friend,

So much value can come from wrestling, and not just in the attainment of physical strength. Wrestlers who perfect mental toughness develop skills for a lifetime.

mentor, or person—it all starts with one step at a time. And nothing is more important than the mental training that you take into such ventures.

"Today, Americans of all stripes are using mental conditioning not just as a means to a better golf swing but also to make them better corporate competitors, more creative artists, and, some argue, better human beings" (Tolson 2000, 38).

VALUES THAT LAST A LIFETIME

The greatest wrestlers in American history have learned what it takes, both mentally and physically, to compete at the highest levels, and to succeed. They have learned not only how to win but also how to balance wrestling with the everyday aspects of life and how to use the lessons of wrestling to succeed in other pursuits. One of the prime examples of that success can be found in the hallowed halls of the United States Congress.

Dennis Hastert first began to appreciate the intrinsic value of wrestling as a young high school student in northern Illinois. He continued his wrestling journey into college and then as coach of a high school team in Yorkville, Illinois. Twenty years after coaching a high school state championship team, he was still being called "Coach," but by a completely different team. He took the lessons that he had learned in a wrestling room and applied them assiduously to his role as a political leader. In 1986 Hastert ran for a seat in the United States Congress and won. In 1999 he was named Speaker of the House.

Today, Speaker Hastert works at the highest levels of leadership. He has always been eager to credit the activity that prepared him for such a prominent position.

"The sport of wrestling is a tremendous builder of the values and characteristics which are needed to succeed in any walk of life," he said in 2000. "Much of what I have managed to achieve in life I owe directly to the years I spent in the wrestling room, as an athlete and a coach. Wrestling is a great educational tool."

Carl Albert, another Speaker of the House of the United States Congress, several decades before Dennis Hastert, also put it in compelling terms: "This is a sport that has turned many boys into men and many men into leaders. And it is a sport in which you can be a giant regardless of how big you are."

Actor Billy Baldwin learned early on the values of wrestling tough. He grew up in a solid middle-class home in Massapequa, New York. His father was a history teacher at the local high school—the same school that produced Ron Kovic, the subject of the book and popular movie *Born on the Fourth of July*, starring Tom Cruise, and another young man destined to become one of the biggest television stars of all time, Jerry Seinfeld. Baldwin wrestled in high school and later at Binghamton University. Even after he and his older brother, Alec, became well-known Hollywood actors, Billy continued to be a staunch supporter of humankind's oldest sport.

"I have a great deal of gratitude for the sport of wrestling for all it's done for me," he said. "I wish that we could measure the type of values that are instilled through the game that transcend to a young man's academic life, in pursuing his career, his relationships with his wife and his children, and every aspect of life. It's the gift that keeps on giving."

John Irving wrestled in high school and at the University of Pittsburgh. The experience affected him so profoundly that several of his books, including the best-selling *The World According to Garp*, have strong wrestling themes. When *Garp* made it to the large screen, Robin Williams played the lead role. In a wrestling scene, Irving made a cameo appearance as the referee.

"I feel more a part of the wrestling community than I feel I belong to the community of arts and letters," he wrote in 1998. "Why? Because wrestling requires even more dedication than writing; because wrestling represents the most difficult and rewarding objective that I have ever dedicated myself to; because wrestling and wrestling coaches are among the most disciplined and self-sacrificing people I have ever known."

The drive and determination that Irving learned in a wrestling room have served him well in the writing world. In 2000 he was the recipient of an Academy Award for his screenplay *The Cider House Rules*.

Lee Kemp started out as a basketball player in Chadron, Ohio, but when he was cut from the team in ninth grade he turned to wrestling. That turn of events served him exceedingly well throughout the years. He was a three-time NCAA champion and four-time NCAA finalist at the University of Wisconsin, and he then won three world championships as a postgraduate. He made the 1980

Olympic freestyle team and was an overwhelming favorite to come home from Moscow with a gold medal in the 163-pound class when President Carter announced that the United States would boycott those games.

Accepting the pain and disappointment that are by-products of wrestling, Kemp quickly moved on with his life. Within a few short years, he was a highly successful businessman and owned his own Ford dealership in Forest Lake, Minnesota.

"Wrestling has positively impacted my life in many ways, but perhaps the one singular thing that I gained from wrestling that stands out the most is—wrestling provided me with the opportunity to learn mental toughness! A person's mental toughness is what allows them to demand of themselves anything and everything necessary to achieve the desired goal, or basically speaking—people that are mentally tough 'Get the job done!'"

"Through wrestling, through the hard work and the sweat, through the victories and the defeats, we learn a great deal about ourselves," said J Robinson, one of the nation's most respected coaches, many years ago. "Wrestling shows you your limits, your weaknesses, your strengths and, ultimately, you grow because of what it shows you."

Hundreds, even thousands, of such stories in the world of business, politics, entertainment, and elsewhere prove that wrestling has served people well through the millennia.

"Winning is great but it's the long road to get there that makes it worthwhile," said Stan Smith.

The sport of wrestling has proved itself a magnificent training ground for those who dream and struggle to become successful in life. Maybe they didn't become champions on the mat, but they became champions in life. Wrestling offers the tools to make one a success in life, as well as on the mat.

"There are no real secrets, no lucky people, but simply those who set high standards and work on the basics: technique, lifting, conditioning and mental toughness, and who try to get the very most out of their God-given talents," wrote Olympic champion Lou Banach. "It is the same message one hears in the adage a friend of mine likes: 'I believe in luck—and the harder I work the luckier I get'" (Banach 1985, 95).

But it's never easy. Great accomplishments don't happen unless someone puts in tons and tons of work. As Thomas Edison, America's greatest inventor, said, "Genius is 1 percent inspiration and 99 percent perspiration." That's a good motto for wrestling, as well.

In the words of Dan Gable, "After you've wrestled, everything else in life is easy!"

EPILOGUE

Wrestling Tough is designed to take the reader inside the world of wrestling so that he or she can learn what it takes to be a winning wrestler. Many qualities are called on to make a person a winner in this demanding sport, and none is more important than mental toughness. Much will be demanded, in many areas.

Although the book is primarily directed toward athletes, it can also help coaches and parents understand what it takes to be a winning wrestler. Support from coaches and parents is important for young athletes in any sport, especially for those in a demanding sport like wrestling. No other scholastic sport requires as much discipline and determination.

Coaches are the leaders of the team, and young athletes look up to them as role models. Those who want to inspire and guide young wrestlers can gain a great deal by reading what the finest coaches and athletes of the past have had to say about leadership.

Leadership is a matter of having people look at you and gain confidence, seeing how you react. If you're in control, they're in control.
Tom Landry, one of the most successful coaches
in the history of the National Football League

Leaders are made. They are not born, and they are made just like anything else is made in this country . . . by hard effort.
Vince Lombardi, who made the Green Bay Packers
the most respected team in all of football for nearly a decade

You must be interested in finding the best way, not in having your own way.
John Wooden, considered the greatest college basketball coach of all time

You can't tell someone to go out and lead. You become a leader by doing. So, if you want to be a leader, go do it.
Chuck Noll, former coach of the Pittsburgh Steelers

To be a leader, you have to make people want to follow you, and nobody wants to follow someone who doesn't know where they are going.

Joe Namath, legendary quarterback of the New York Jets

Be a positive example for your athletes. If you want your athletes to be dedicated and disciplined, then you have to lead the way.

Dan Gable, the greatest wrestling coach in American history

A leader, once convinced [that] a particular course of action is the right one, must have the determination to stick with it and be undaunted when the going gets tough.

Ronald Reagan, 40th president of the United States

Leadership is the ability to get men to do what they don't want to do, and like doing it.

Harry Truman, 33rd president of the United States

A platoon leader doesn't get his platoon to go by getting up and shouting, "I am smarter. I am bigger. I am stronger. I am the leader." He gets men to go along with him because they want to do it for him and they believe in him.

Dwight Eisenhower, 34th president of the United States

As you take to the mats in the days, weeks, and years ahead, remember the adage that appeared near the start of this book, in the chapter on confidence:

If you think you are beaten, you are;

If you think that you dare not, you don't;

If you'd like to win but you think you can't,

It's almost certain you won't.

If you think you'll lose, you've lost;

For out in the world you'll find

Success begins with a fellow's will.

It's all in the state of mind.

If you think you are outclassed, you are;

You've got to think high to rise;

You've got to be sure of yourself before

You can ever win a prize.

Life's battles don't always go

To the stronger or faster man;

But sooner or later the man who wins

Is the man who thinks he can!

BIBLIOGRAPHY

Angle, Kurt. 2001. *It's True! It's True!* New York: Regan Books.

Arangio, Joseph A. 2002. "Grappling With Gable." *Muscle Media,* July.

Armstrong, Lance. 2000. *It's Not About the Bike: My Journey Back to Life.* New York: Putnam.

Arnold Schwarzenegger Calendar 1980. 1979. New York: Simon and Schuster.

Banach, Lou, with Mike Chapman. 1985. *The New Breed: Living Iowa Wrestling.* West Point, NY: Leisure Press.

Baughman, R. Wayne. 1987. *On and Off the Mat.* Colorado Springs: Baughman.

Chapman, Mike. 1981. *From Gotch to Gable: A History of Iowa Wrestling.* Iowa City: University of Iowa.

Chapman, Mike. 1981. *The Toughest Men in Sports.* West Point, NY: Leisure Press.

Chapman, Mike. 2003. *The Sport of Lincoln.* Newton, IA: Culture House Books.

Chertow, Ken. 2004. "Shadow Wrestling." *American Adrenaline*, July.

Clarkson, Michael. 1999. *Competitive Fire.* Champaign, IL: Human Kinetics.

Csikszentmihalyi, Mihaly. 1990. *Flow.* New York: Harper Perennial.

Doren, Kim, and Charlie Jones. 2002. *If Winning Were Easy, Everyone Would Do It.* Kansas City: Andrew McMeel.

Ferguson, Howard E. 1990. *The Edge.* Cleveland, OH: Getting the Edge.

Furey, Matt. 1999. *G.A.I.N.* September-October.

Gable, Dan. 1999. *Coaching Wrestling Successfully.* Champaign, IL: Human Kinetics.

Gifford, Frank. 1976. *Gifford on Courage.* New York: M. Evans.

Gracie, Royce. 2004. "What It Takes to Be a Fighter." *Grappling Magazine*.

Holland, Stephen T. 1983. *Talkin' Dan Gable.* Iowa City: Limerick.

Houdini: Medical Secrets. February 26, 2004. Discovery Health Channel.

Husar, John. 1988. *Chicago Tribune*, September 30, 12.

Jordan, Michael. 1998. *I Can't Accept Not Trying.* San Francisco: Harper.

Kauss, David R. 1980. *Peak Performance.* Englewood Cliffs, NJ: Prentice Hall.

Knight, Steve. 2003. *Winning State.* Portland, OR: Pearl.

Looney, Douglas S. 1984. "The Ultimate Winner." *Sports Illustrated*, special issue (The 1984 Olympics).

Mathias, Bob, and Robert Mendes. 2001. *The Bob Mathias Story.* Champaign, IL: Sports Publishing.

Murdock, William. 2004. *Brisco.* Newton, IA: Culture House Books.

Naber, John, comp. 1999. *Awaken the Olympian Within.* Torrance, CA: Griffin.

Poliakoff, Michael B. 2004. "Ancient Combat Sports." *Archeology Odyssey* July/August, 4.

Preobrazhensky, Sergei. 1981. *Wrestling Is a Man's Game.* Moscow: Progress.

Pumping Iron. 1976. Columbia Pictures.

Riger, Roger. 1980. *The Athlete.* New York: Simon & Schuster.

Rubin, Bob. 1973. *Football's Toughest Ten.* New York: Lancer.

Shields, Mike. 1987. *Never, Never Quit.* Lombard, IL: Great Quotations.

Skehan, Everett M. 1977. *Rocky Marciano: Biography of a First Son.* Boston: Houghton Mifflin.

Spates, Jack. 1999. *Mat Snacks.* Oklahoma City: Oklahoma Gold.

Tolson, Jay. 2000. "Into the Zone." *US News & World Report*, July 3.

Turan, Kenneth. 1989. "The Last Pure Sport." *GQ*, March.

Tutko, Thomas, and Umberto Tosi. 1976. *Sports Psyching.* Los Angeles: J.P. Tracher.

Wojciechowski, Gene. 1992. *Los Angeles Times.*

Wooden, John, with Steve Jamison. 1997. *Wooden: A Lifetime of Observations and Reflections.* Chicago: Contemporary.

Zabriskie, James. 1976. *The Handbook of Inner Sports.* New York: Zebra.

INDEX

Note: The italicized *f* following page numbers refers to figures.

ABOUT
THE AUTHOR

Mike Chapman is the founder and executive director of the International Wrestling Institute and Museum, an organization that markets the sport worldwide. He has written over 700 columns on the sport of wrestling with his work appearing in a dozen national magazines. He is also the author of 16 books, 12 of which are about wrestling. The former director of communications for USA Wrestling has also attended 35 NCAA wrestling tournaments, two Olympics, and two World championships.

Chapman has been named National Wrestling Writer of the Year four times and was co-winner of the IMPACT of the Year Award by *W.I.N. Magazine* in 1999. In 2002, he received the Lifetime Achievement Award in wrestling from the Cauliflower Alley Club. He is also the founder of *W.I.N. Magazine* and originated both the W.I.N. Memorabilia Show, now in its 17th year, and the Dan Hodge Trophy. Chapman and his wife, Beverly, reside in Newton, Iowa.